CAMBRIDGE LIBRARY COLLECTION

Books of enduring scholarly value

Travel and Exploration

The history of travel writing dates back to the Bible, Caesar, the Vikings and the Crusaders, and its many themes include war, trade, science and recreation. Explorers from Columbus to Cook charted lands not previously visited by Western travellers, and were followed by merchants, missionaries, and colonists, who wrote accounts of their experiences. The development of steam power in the nineteenth century provided opportunities for increasing numbers of 'ordinary' people to travel further, more economically, and more safely, and resulted in great enthusiasm for travel writing among the reading public. Works included in this series range from first-hand descriptions of previously unrecorded places, to literary accounts of the strange habits of foreigners, to examples of the burgeoning numbers of guidebooks produced to satisfy the needs of a new kind of traveller - the tourist.

Narrative of a Voyage to the Polar Sea during 1875-6

The British Vice-Admiral and Arctic explorer Sir George Nares (1831–1915) received several honours for his contributions to science, including a fellowship of the Royal Society. He attended the Royal Naval School, New Cross, before joining the service in 1845. After a varied early career and the successful *Challenger* scientific expedition in the Atlantic, he took command of the British Arctic expedition of 1875–6 that hoped to reach the North Pole. Nares' popular two-volume account of the journey was published in 1878. Volume 1 describes the journey north, and covers the discovery of the channel later called Nares Strait, and the remarkable dog-sled expedition of second-in-command, Albert Markham, that set a new record for the farthest distance north achieved. Nares' official report of the expedition and Markham's account of the journey, *The Great Frozen Sea*, are also available from the Cambridge Library Collection.

Cambridge University Press has long been a pioneer in the reissuing of out-of-print titles from its own backlist, producing digital reprints of books that are still sought after by scholars and students but could not be reprinted economically using traditional technology. The Cambridge Library Collection extends this activity to a wider range of books which are still of importance to researchers and professionals, either for the source material they contain, or as landmarks in the history of their academic discipline.

Drawing from the world-renowned collections in the Cambridge University Library, and guided by the advice of experts in each subject area, Cambridge University Press is using state-of-the-art scanning machines in its own Printing House to capture the content of each book selected for inclusion. The files are processed to give a consistently clear, crisp image, and the books finished to the high quality standard for which the Press is recognised around the world. The latest print-on-demand technology ensures that the books will remain available indefinitely, and that orders for single or multiple copies can quickly be supplied.

The Cambridge Library Collection brings back to life books of enduring scholarly value (including out-of-copyright works originally issued by other publishers) across a wide range of disciplines in the humanities and social sciences and in science and technology.

Narrative of a Voyage to the Polar Sea during 1875-6

VOLUME 1

GEORGE NARES

CAMBRIDGE UNIVERSITY PRESS

Cambridge, New York, Melbourne, Madrid, Cape Town,
Singapore, São Paolo, Delhi, Tokyo, Mexico City

Published in the United States of America by Cambridge University Press, New York

www.cambridge.org
Information on this title: www.cambridge.org/9781108041553

This edition first published 1878
This digitally printed version 2012

ISBN 978-1-108-04155-3 Paperback

A VOYAGE

TO

THE POLAR SEA

VOL. I.

LONDON : PRINTED BY
SPOTTISWOODE AND CO., NEW-STREET SQUARE
AND PARLIAMENT STREET

Permanent Woodbury Print.

ELOEBERG BEACH. SPRING.

NARRATIVE

OF

A VOYAGE TO THE POLAR SEA

DURING 1875-6

IN

H.M. SHIPS 'ALERT' AND 'DISCOVERY'

BY

CAPT. SIR G. S. NARES, R.N., K.C.B., F.R.S.

COMMANDER OF THE EXPEDITION

WITH NOTES on the NATURAL HISTORY

EDITED BY

H. W. FEILDEN, F.G.S., C.M.Z.S., F.R.G.S.

NATURALIST TO THE EXPEDITION

IN TWO VOLUMES

VOL. I.

LONDON

SAMPSON LOW, MARSTON, SEARLE, & RIVINGTON

CROWN BUILDINGS, 188 FLEET STREET

1878

THESE VOLUMES ARE INSCRIBED

IN MEMORY OF THE LATE

RIGHT HON. GEORGE WARD HUNT, M.P.

UNDER WHOSE ADMINISTRATION AS FIRST LORD
OF THE ADMIRALTY

THE ARCTIC EXPEDITION OF 1875

WAS PLANNED AND CARRIED INTO EXECUTION, AND WHOSE
GENEROUS AND CONSISTENT ENCOURAGEMENT AND
SUPPORT WILL EVER BE REMEMBERED
WITH GRATITUDE AND RESPECT

BY

THE AUTHOR.

PREFACE.

In the following narrative I have endeavoured to give a plain and faithful account of the voyage of H.M. ships 'Alert' and 'Discovery' to and from the Polar Sea; together with the results of the explorations which were made along its shores, and over the ice in the direction of the North Pole, by means of sledging.

I have written for the information of future Arctic explorers; and also under a feeling of duty to the many, both in this country and abroad, whose earnest good wishes and kind sympathies were with us during our absence.

As the expectations which were entertained regarding our reaching the North Pole were not realized, I must, in justice to the gallant men whom I commanded, express my firm conviction that it was due solely to the fact that the North Pole is unattainable by the Smith Sound route.

The Illustrations in the present work are either reproductions of photographs taken by Mr. F. Mitchell, Paymaster of H.M.S. 'Discovery,' and Mr. George

White, Assistant Engineer of H.M.S. ' Alert,' or from sketches taken on the spot by Dr. Edward Moss, M.D., Surgeon of H.M.S. ' Alert,' Lieutenant G. Le C. Egerton, and Mr. Mitchell.

The Natural History collections made by the two naturalists who were attached to the Expedition were, on the recommendation of the President and Council of the Royal Society, submitted to specialists, who have most kindly and generously drawn up full reports on the various groups. Many of these papers have already been published in the proceedings of various learned societies. In the Appendices to this work, my friend Captain Feilden, the naturalist attached to the ' Alert,' in addition to supplying original papers, has arranged in an abridged form these valuable contributions to Natural History.

Throughout the narrative the compass bearings refer to the true meridian ; and the temperature observations are expressed in degrees of Fahrenheit.

G. S. NARES.

SURBITON : *April*, 1878.

LIST

OFFICERS AND MEN.

—◆—

H.M.S. 'ALERT.'

OFFICERS.

Captain George S. Nares.
Commander Albert H. Markham.
Captain H. W. Feilden, R.A., naturalist.
Senior Lieutenant Pelham Aldrich.
Lieutenant A. A. C. Parr.
Lieutenant G. A. Giffard.
Lieutenant W. H. May.
Fleet-Surgeon Thomas Colan, M.D.
Surgeon E. L. Moss, M.D.
Rev. W. H. Pullen, chaplain.
Sub-Lieut. George Le C. Egerton.
James Wootton, engineer.
George White, engineer.

MEN.

George I. Burroughs, ship's steward.
Joseph Good, chief boatswain's mate.
John N. Radmore, chief carpenter's mate.
Vincent Dominics, ship's cook.
John Thores, ice quartermaster.
James Berrie, ice quartermaster.
David Deuchars, ice quartermaster.
Edwin Lawrence, gunner's mate.
James Doidge, captain foretop.

Daniel W. Harley, captain foretop.
Thomas Stuckberry, captain maintop.
Thomas Rawlins, captain forecastle.
Thomas Jolliffe, captain maintop.
Spero Capato, captain's steward.
George Kemish, wardroom steward.
John Hawkins, cooper.
John Simmons, 2nd captain maintop.
Adam Ayles, 2nd captain foretop.
Henry Mann, shipwright.
James Self, able seaman.
William Maskell, able seaman.
William P. Woolley, able seaman.
George Cranston, able seaman.
Reuben Francombe, able seaman.
John Pearson, able seaman.
William Ferbrache, able seaman.
Alfred R. Pearce, able seaman.
David Mitchell, able seaman.
Robert D. Symonds, able seaman.
Thomas H. Simpson, able seaman.
William Malley, able seaman.
George Winstone, able seaman.
William Lorimer, able seaman.
James Frederick Cane, armourer.
Robert Joiner, leading stoker.
John Shirley, stoker.
Thomas Stubbs, stoker.
William I. Gore, stoker.

William Hunt, wardroom cook.
N. C. Petersen, Eskimo interpreter.
Frederick, Greenlander

MARINES.

William Wood, colour sergeant.

William Ellard, private.
John Hollins, private.
Thomas Smith, private.
George Porter, gunner.
Elias Hill, gunner.
Thomas Oakley, gunner.

H.M.S. 'DISCOVERY.'

OFFICERS.

Captain Henry F. Stephenson.
Senior Lieut. Lewis A. Beaumont.
Lieutenant Robert H. Archer.
Lieutenant Wyatt Rawson.
Lieutenant Reginald B. Fulford.
Staff-Surgeon Belgrave Ninnis, M.D.
Surgeon Richard W. Coppinger, M.D.
Charles E. Hodgson, chaplain.
Chichester Hart, B.A., naturalist.
Sub-Lieutenant C. I. M. Conybeare.
Daniel Cartmel, engineer.
Matthew R. Miller, engineer.
Thomas Mitchell, assistant-pay-master.

MEN.

George R. Sarah, ship's steward.
George W. Emmerson, chief boat-swain's mate.
E. C. Eddy, chief captain's mate.
Alexander Gray, ice quartermaster.
William Dougall, ice quartermaster.
Edward Taws, ice quartermaster.
George Bryant, captain maintop.
Frank Chatel, captain forecastle.
David Stewart, captain foretop.
Thomas Simmons, captain forecastle.
George Bunyan, ropemaker.
William Ward, armourer.
James Shepherd, cooper.
John E. Smith, sailmaker.

Jonah Gear, wardroom steward.
George Stone, 2nd captain foretop.
James Cooper, 2nd captain maintop.
Henry W. Edwards, able seaman.
Benjamin Wyatt, able seaman.
Daniel Girard, able seaman.
Michael Regan, able seaman.
Thomas Chalkley, able seaman.
John Hodges, able seaman.
James Thornback, able seaman.
Alfred Hindle, able seaman.
Peter Craig, able seaman.
George Leggatt, able seaman.
Robert W. Hitchcock, able seaman.
John S. Saggers, able seaman.
James J. Hand, able seaman.
Charles Paul, able seaman.
Henry Windser, carpenter's crew.
James Phillips, wardroom cook.
Jeremiah Rourke, leading stoker.
Frank Jones, stoker.
Samuel Bulley, stoker.
William R. Sweet, stoker.
Hans Heindrich, Greenlander.

MARINES.

William C. Wellington, sergeant.
Wilson Dobing, gunner.
John Cropp, gunner.
Elijah Rayner, gunner.
William Waller, private.
Thomas Darke, private.
John Murray, private.
Henry Petty, private.

SAILING ORDERS.

ADMIRALTY, 25th *May*, 1875.

SIR,—Her Majesty's Government having determined that an expedition of Arctic exploration and discovery should be undertaken, My Lords Commissioners of the Admiralty have been pleased to select you for the command of the said expedition, the scope and primary object of which should be to attain the highest northern latitude, and, if possible, to reach the North Pole, and from winter quarters to explore the adjacent coasts within the reach of travelling parties, the limits of ship navigation being confined within about the meridians of 20° and 90° west longitude.

2. Her Majesty's ships 'Alert' and 'Discovery' having been specially fitted out for this service, I am commanded by their Lordships to signify their direction to you, so soon as the said vessels shall be in all respects equipped and ready, to take the 'Discovery' under your orders, and put to sea with both vessels, calling at Queenstown to complete with coal, or sending in the 'Valorous' (which will accompany the expedition to Disco), for that purpose if more convenient, proceeding thence to Disco, in Davis Strait, and northwards by way of Baffin's Bay and Smith's Sound, to carry out the special service of discovery and exploration with which you have been entrusted.

3. Her Majesty's ship 'Valorous' will receive on board extra coal and stores, &c., for the expedition, and will be available for towing when requisite. Captain Loftus Jones has been directed to consider himself under your orders temporarily, and after transhipping stores, &c. at Disco, he is to return to Devonport in the Valorous' in final execution of his orders.

4. The 'Alert' and 'Discovery' after leaving Disco should proceed to the settlements of Proven and Upernivik for dogs,

Eskimo drivers, &c., and then pass up to Smith Sound in the prosecution of the enterprise, and it will be a question for you to consider whether you would leave a depôt of provisions and a boat at the Carey Islands on passing.

5. Both shores in the vicinity of Capes Isabella and Alexander should be examined in order to select a suitable position for the depôt or relief ship which will, in the event of the expedition remaining in the Arctic regions, be despatched in 1877 ; but as such a position cannot be absolutely determined on beforehand, and it is necessary to decide where information will be found by any ship which may be subsequently sent out from England, Lyttelton Island, in the opinion of competent authorities, meets all the requirements of a fixed point of rendezvous. Here a conspicuous cairn should be erected ; one record placed in the cairn, another laid beside it on the north side, and a third buried twenty feet due north of it. These records should contain proceedings of the voyage and such information as may be necessary for the commander of the ship to be despatched in 1877.

6. The ships should then proceed up Smith Sound with all speed, so long as its navigation is not seriously obstructed by ice, a careful scrutiny being made of its shores for places of security for the ships, stopping only to erect cairns on such conspicuous points as may be conveniently landed on. Similar information should be placed at these cairns, and after the same method as described for the cairn on Lyttelton Island. It is, moreover, necessary to be borne in mind that these records of the progress of the expedition and of any change of plans you may have found necessary to make, form an important feature in these instructions.

7. It is desirable that these cairns should not be more than sixty miles apart. By way of illustration, may be named Capes Frazer, Back, and Beechey on the western shore, and Capes Jackson and Bryan on the eastern shore; to these prominent headlands the attention of any searching party would naturally be directed. A small depôt of provisions and a boat might also be advantageously left at one or more of these points, to serve either for exploring parties or to aid in the event of an abandonment of the ships. Timely endeavours should be made to secure anchorage suitable for winter quarters, and every precaution during that rigorous season, which your former experience, as well as that of other Arctic voyagers, may suggest, is to be taken, for the health

and comfort of the officers and crew. Ample supplies have accordingly been furnished to the expedition ; and you have been furnished with a memorandum from the Director-General of the Medical Department of the Navy on the subject.

8. The general design of the expedition should be, that while both ships would share as far as possible in the objects of discovery and exploration, one must be so placed that she would not only serve for the crew of the other to fall back upon, but also, that the united crews could, without doubt, escape from her to the relief ship at the entrance of Smith Sound, by means of their sledges and boats over the ice. Consequently, the second ship must not be carried northward of the 82nd parallel ; such a position would secure this most important object, and also afford every prospect of exploration into very high latitudes.

9. The eastern or the western shore may be selected for her winter quarters according to circumstances ; the advantages of the former are, that animal life has been found to exist there through-out the winter, and that the ship would be favourably placed for exploring the northern coast of Greenland, or adjacent land, in the spring of 1876 : on the other hand, if the land is found to be more continuous on the western side, it may afford a counter-balancing advantage in the greater facility and security of com-munication between the ships, and their co-operation in subsequent operations ; this point must, therefore, be left to your judgment to decide ; if you should select the western shore, then you should be careful in passing, or subsequently, to place a record on the eastern side of the probable or absolute position of the second ship ; and in the absence of any conspicuous cairn, a ship or party visiting the bay wintered in by the ' Polaris,' in about 81° 35' north, would naturally seek the position of Hall's grave, where, and at twenty feet due north of it, records would be expected to be found.

10. The captain of the second ship, wherever placed, would follow such instructions as he will have received on parting com-pany, or subsequently, from yourself.

11. It should be a matter for consideration, whether, before parting, you would leave a depôt of some six months' of the ' Alert's ' provisions with your consort, so as to be available for your own crew should they have to retreat, but time and circum-stances must govern your decision on this point.

12. Having assured yourself of the safety of your consort, and increased your own crew by such portion of her crew as you may deem necessary to enable you to accomplish a sledging attempt to reach the Pole (this being the main feature of the expedition), and also the exploration of your share of the coast-line extending northwards, you should, as leader of the expedition, then push on northward, and explore by ship as much of the unknown area as the season and the state of the ice would permit. But it is not contemplated that the two ships should winter at a greater distance apart than about 200 miles ; and if you advance with your ship beyond that point in 1875, you should use every endeavour to return within the 200 miles' distance ;—or the case may arise, in which it may be even wise to rejoin your consort and unite the forces of both ships for exploration in the spring and summer of 1876.

13. Should the advance ship, after leaving her consort, carry continuous, or nearly continuous land up to a high northern latitude, you should avail yourself of opportunities to land small depôts of provisions at intervals, with cairns and records as already described ; and also to deposit at the most northern station, a depôt of provisions and a boat, for your spring travelling parties.

14. Your own crew having been increased as above referred to, by such portions of the crew of your consort as you may deem necessary, it is expected that you will have at least six strong sledge parties, and four dog sledges, with which to commence further exploration in early spring. All these parties should be employed in the first instance to push out the North Pole party (which should be provided with at least one boat), and upon return from this work, some weeks later, the parties for the exploration of the coast-lines should be sent out.

15. It must not, however, be lost sight of that, in the absence of continuous land, sledge travelling has never yet been found practicable over any considerable extent of unenclosed frozen sea, although conditions may be found to exist which would enable parties to travel for limited distances by sledge and boat operations combined, and for this purpose the best boats and sledges that can be devised have been supplied.

16. You will be careful to furnish ample instructions to the captain of the ' Discovery,' especially in regard to the explorations to be undertaken by him during the spring and summer of 1876,

should the ships winter apart; and in this event, the first consideration should be, in the autumn of 1875 or early spring of 1876, to ascertain their respective positions; this, unless under very unfavourable conditions, would be probably accomplished by dog parties, without interfering much with the objects of exploration. In connection with this subject, you should bear in mind the necessity of giving such instructions as would govern his proceedings in the event of this proving to be a final separation.

17. It has already been mentioned that the limits of ship navigation should be confined within about the meridians of 20° and 90° west longitude; but even within these limits, the possible contingency of a final separation might arise from some sudden and unforeseen movement of ice from which one or both of the ships could not be extricated; resulting, it may be, in the advanced ship being carried by the southerly drift passing the eastern shores of Greenland supposing Greenland to be an island.

18. It will be impossible therefore to give any positive or detailed instructions for your guidance after quitting your consort, further than that you should use your best endeavours to rejoin her in the navigable season of 1876, and in company with her return to England, provided the spring exploration has been reasonably successful. But in the event of another season being absolutely required to complete a reasonable amount of exploration, still it will be a matter for careful consideration, whether it would not be advisable that the advanced ship should fall back towards her consort from any advanced position she may have wintered at; and, should it still remain doubtful whether a final retreat could be effected, the second ship might not be moved southward to such a position as would secure it.

19. In 1877 you are at full liberty to abandon your ship as early as convenient, if, in your opinion, the explorations of the preceding year have been final, or, if from your experience of the navigable seasons of 1875 and 1876, in your judgment, her escape in 1877 would be doubtful; you should in this case so time this abandonment as to reach the relief ship at the entrance of Smith Sound not later than the first week in September 1877.

20. In the event of your remaining out in the hope of extricating your own, or it may be both ships, during the summer of 1877, you should consider the propriety of reducing your own or both crews, sending away all that can be spared to the relief ship

at Lyttelton Island.   In this case one or both ships would remain
out for the winter of 1877, if unable to extricate themselves in the
summer of that year, a contingency which is hardly possible.

21. You must, however, bear in mind, that it is not desirable,
under any circumstances, that a single ship should be left to
winter in the Arctic regions.   If one ship remains up Smith
Sound, a second ship should remain at the rendezvous at its
entrance.

22. In the summer of 1877, a relief or depôt ship will be despatched to Smith's Sound, and she will be directed, in the first
instance, to repair to Lyttelton Island, and then to follow such
instructions as you may have deposited in the cairn there.   The
instructions you will leave for this ship, so far as they need be
decided on at present, are, that she is to be found at the rendezvous,
specified in the records at the cairn, not later than the last week
in August 1877.   She will be equipped and fitted for wintering in
the Polar Seas, and, in the event of there being no tidings of the
expedition nor instructions to the contrary, in the records to be
found at the rendezvous you will have named, she will be ordered
to pass one winter at that rendezvous, returning to England in the
latest part of the navigable season of 1878.

23. If, under the circumstances alluded to in paragraph 20,
the retreating parties should arrive at Lyttelton Island in 1878,
and find no relief ship there, or no intelligence of her, it will be
taken for granted that some unforeseen accident has prevented her
reaching Lyttelton Island, and in that case the retreating parties
must rely on their own resources for reaching Upernivik, looking
out, of course, for the whalers on their fishing grounds, between the
months of May and August.   The expedition will, in any case,
on its return, revisit the cairn on Lyttelton Island, and leave
records.

24. Should the season of 1875 be so unfavourable as to
prevent the expedition from penetrating beyond the 79th parallel,
it is left to your discretion to decide whether the ships shall winter
there, or return to England and renew the attempt the following
year.

25. Although the expedition intrusted to your charge is one of
exploration and discovery, it must be kept in view that detailed
surveys are unnecessary.   The requirements of hydrography and
geography will be provided for if the prominent features and

general outline of the shores are sketched in as faithfully as circumstances will admit; and to ensure their recognition by future explorers. In the determination of the astronomical position of the principal points, no doubts should be permitted to exist as to the fidelity of the results that may be arrived at, so as to ensure confidence and respect.

26. Further, as the object of the expedition is for the advancement of science and natural knowledge, the memoranda furnished by the Royal and Royal Geographical Societies of London, at the request of their Lordships, are supplied for your guidance. The most approved instruments have been furnished to you for the purpose of pursuing research in the several branches of physical science, and as certain of your officers have been specially instructed in the modes of observing, you will take care to give them every fair opportunity of adding their contributions thereto.

27. You will also receive assistance from the two gentlemen who have been appointed as naturalists to the expedition; and every reasonable facility should be given for the collection and preservation of such specimens of the animal, vegetable, and mineral kingdoms as can be conveniently stowed on board the ships. These specimens are to be considered the property of Her Majesty's Government, and to be at their disposal.

28. In case of any irreparable accident happening to one of the ships, the officers and crew of the disabled vessel are to be removed to the other, and such arrangements are to be made as appear to you to be the most expedient and conducive to the objects of the expedition.

29. In the event of the 'Alert' being the ship disabled, my Lords hereby authorise you to take command of the 'Discovery,' and in the event of any fatal accident happening to yourself, Captain Stephenson is hereby authorised to take command of the 'Alert,' placing the officer next in seniority in command of the 'Discovery.' Also, in the event of your own inability, by sickness or otherwise at any period of this service, to continue to carry these instructions into execution, you are to transfer them to the officer the next in seniority to you employed in the expedition, who is hereby required by their Lordships to execute them in the best manner practicable for the attainment of the objects in view.

30. Every available opportunity is to be taken to communicate your proceedings to me for their Lordships' information.

31. On your arrival in England, you are forthwith to repair to the Admiralty, to lay before their Lordships a full account of your proceedings; having previously received from the officers and all other persons in the expedition the journals or memoranda they may have kept, and the charts, drawings, and observations which they may have made. Such of these journals and documents as may be of an unofficial character will be returned to the writers when no longer required for the public requirements of the expedition.

32. In conclusion, my Lords desire me to state, that having full confidence in your judgment and discretion, and being aware that you are already familiar with Arctic service, they do not deem it necessary to furnish you with more definite instructions than are embraced in the foregoing. With the ample means at your command, you are at liberty to vary the detail according to circumstances, but the main points herein laid down for your guidance should be kept in view, all other objects being subordinate to them.

I am, Sir,

Your obedient servant

(signed)   ROBERT HALL.

Captain GEORGE S. NARES, R.N.,
    H.M.S. 'Alert,' at Portsmouth.

CONTENTS

OF

THE FIRST VOLUME.

———◆◆———

CHAPTER I.

CHAPTER II.

CHAPTER III.

a 2

CHAPTER IV.

CHAPTER V.

CHAPTER VI.

CHAPTER VII.

CHAPTER VIII.

CHAPTER IX.

CHAPTER X.

CHAPTER XI.

CHAPTER XII.

CHAPTER XIII.

CHAPTER XIV.

LIST OF ILLUSTRATIONS

IN

THE FIRST VOLUME.

MAP.

INTRODUCTION.

Iᴛ has been frequently said that Arctic discovery is
the heritage of our nation; it was bequeathed some
three centuries since by Davis, Hudson, Baffin, and
other illustrious seamen whose names and deeds will
ever retain an honoured place in their country's
history. It was not, however, until early in the
present century that the legacy was accepted by the
Government. The termination of a long war was not
deemed an unfitting time to renew the encouragement
of that spirit of enterprise and adventure which had
been transmitted from the earliest maritime period,
and had ever been a characteristic of the seafaring
profession.

It is doubtful, however, whether that long series of
brilliant achievements in the frozen North which called
forth so much daring, so much fortitude, so much
endurance, would have adorned the annals of the
British Navy but for the untiring energy and perseverance of one man—himself an ardent admirer of
the deeds and sufferings of those *ancient Arctic worthies*
which his pen has so ably chronicled; it need scarcely
be said that this individual was the late Sir John
Barrow, whose singular determination of character,

coupled with the influential position he occupied in the naval administration of the country, enabled him to carry out his favourite enterprise, the renewal of Arctic discovery. Hence between the years 1817 and 1845 an almost unbroken series of efforts were made by this country to penetrate the frozen regions within the Arctic or Antarctic circles. Connected with these attempts the names of Parry, Franklin, and Richardson, Back, John and James Ross, Beechey and others scarcely less eminent, have become famous; and a band of officers and seamen have been trained and educated in a school, the stern necessities of which have been instrumental in forming and fostering those qualities of fortitude and habits of self-reliance and self-denial which are certain to tell with effect at some period or other of a seaman's career, and which no maritime nation can afford to hold lightly.

To enter into the briefest relation of the earlier expeditions of the present century would be to repeat what has already been frequently said; nor is it necessary, further than to remark that, with the exception of Parry's attempt to reach the Pole in 1827, and James Ross's expedition to the Antarctic regions in 1840 and following years, chiefly in the interests of the science of terrestrial magnetism, they may nearly all be said to have centred in the solution of the all-absorbing problem — the discovery of a North-west passage.

The last of these expeditions was the ill-fated one under Franklin, which left these shores in the month of May 1845 never to return. Just thirty years had elapsed when in the same month in 1875 Polar research was resumed by the despatch of the 'Alert' and 'Discovery' on the voyage which is narrated in the following pages by its distinguished commander.

The expedition under Franklin was in reality the last which was sent forth by this country in the pursuit of Arctic discovery. Those which subsequently followed, seven in number and consisting of no less than twenty-four vessels, twenty of which were equipped by the Government, and which by ship and sledge traversed the Arctic seas for over ten years, were sent exclusively in search of the ' Erebus ' and ' Terror,' and their geographical discoveries were purely incidental to that search.

Notwithstanding all that has been written concerning this unfortunate expedition, it has so direct a bearing on the one which has lately returned from an attempt to reach the Pole, that it is imperative briefly to recall its main features, and to follow for a time the footsteps of those who so long and so unsuccessfully persevered in their attempts to lift the veil which shrouded all connected with it in the deepest mystery.

Franklin and his companions, like many who preceded them, went forth to accomplish the North-west passage, that is to sail north-west from the Atlantic to the Pacific Ocean ; and with the knowledge—or perhaps it would be more correct to say the ignorance— which then existed as to the difficulties by which the task was surrounded, there seemed a fair probability that their mission would have been successful. At any rate there were none who doubted that the way they would go would be open to their safe return. They had two stout ships, the best ever despatched on such service. These vessels were furnished with steam power, though to a limited extent, and their *personnel* comprised the flower of the naval service.

It is probable that few, if any, at this time believed that practical results useful to navigation or commerce would accrue were the passage accomplished; still problems of scientific interest, which were less understood then than now, would be solved, and success could not but redound to the national honour and renown.

Looking back with our present knowledge it may well seem unaccountable that the idea of succour becoming necessary never entered into the minds of Franklin, or the most experienced of his contemporaries, and that no single precaution for relief was ever contemplated before the expedition sailed. We now, indeed, know that if it had been arranged that in the summer of 1847 an expedition should proceed to some appointed rendezvous in Barrow Strait, there to remain until the autumn of 1848, it is certain that most if not all the surviving crew would have been rescued; we know this now because we know where the ships were abandoned, and that the spot was within reach of such succour; but had they penetrated a hundred miles further westward it would have taken them out of such reach; all attempts however at rescue, at whatever time undertaken, would have been in vain, unless prearranged with Franklin. This is the fatal mistake which experience has taught us, and which can never be repeated; but had it been recognised as a necessity to send a second expedition one or two years after the departure of the first, to secure its safety, would the 'Erebus' and 'Terror,' it may be asked, have sailed at all? Would not the question have arisen, 'Is expedition to follow expedition while a ship remains absent?' and there could probably have been but one reply. Much has been written by theorists, after the event, to prove that the long and fruitless search was made in the wrong direction, and that where Franklin was ordered to go, there he should have been sought. This is specious enough, but what are the facts? Instructions to the leaders of such expeditions can be considered only as advice to be followed under certain assumed conditions ; but in the uncertainties of Arctic navigation, circumstances are almost certain to occur which may render it impossible to act upon instructions, however ably conceived. Franklin was indeed ordered to go to the south-west in the direction of Cape Walker, but none knew what was beyond that cape. If baffled there he was to try the Wellington Channel, only sixty miles to the eastward, which had been seen and pronounced a promising channel by Parry, and which being nearer the open sea is probably always free from ice before the more sheltered inlets to the westward. In all probability the south-west was tried and found closed ; it is certain, as we know now, that he did ascend the Wellington Channel to 77° N., and finding the outlet westward sealed, returned, wintered at Beechey Island, and later on in the year 1846 succeeded in penetrating to the S.W. beyond Cape Walker ; but a ship's keel leaves no track behind, and no scrap of paper was ever found, or probably ever left, to indicate the course taken by the 'Erebus' and 'Terror,' until the fatal one discovered by M'Clintock's parties on King William's Land, which recorded the abandonment of the ships and thus revealed the sad story that all must probably have perished ten years before.

The only clue ever found by the searching ships previous to this—the three graves on Beechey Island at the entrance to Wellington Channel—a significant clue indeed—probably led those who followed, in a direction at once in the track of the lost expedition, and at the same time hopelessly astray. Be this as it may, it must be confessed, and perhaps with humiliation,.that the united wisdom and judgment of the most experienced Arctic navigators, and the energy and perseverance of the most able leaders, were alike at fault, so that it was left for the solitary little 'Fox,' equipped by Lady Franklin and her friends, and commanded by M'Clintock, to solve the mystery, which had previously baffled so many able commanders (himself among the number), with means and resources unlimited. His success, however, complete as it was, detracts in no way from the credit of those who went before. Working in the dark, so to say, they did all that undaunted perseverance and devotion could accomplish, in the face of difficulties and hardships which have rarely been equalled.

But to return from a digression which to some may scarcely seem relevant. The special influence exercised on the renewal of Arctic discovery by the lost expedition and those which followed in its search was twofold. The shock which the nation sustained in the tragic fate of the former, and the disappointment experienced by the entire failure of the latter, after ten weary years of effort and an enormous expenditure of money, may be said to have sealed the Northwest passage indefinitely, and thus narrowed the fields of discovery to the one other point of interest—the Pole. Again, the search for the missing ships involved the minute examination of a vast extent of coast-line, which neither ship nor boat could approach, and this task could only be accomplished by the manual labour of dragging heavily laden sledges along the margin of the frozen sea for weeks or months together. The art of sledge-travelling in this manner was initiated, and perhaps brought to the highest state of perfection it is susceptible of, during the progress of this long search. As much as four hundred miles in a direct line on an outward journey had been accomplished by these means, each man dragging between two and three hundred pounds, including his provisions, clothing, and equipment, and being absent from the frozen-in ships frequently from ninety to a hundred days. It was manifest, then, that if such distances could be accomplished in search of men in distress, they could be equally well performed in the pursuit of geographical discovery, and no stronger argument than this could have been used in urging upon the Government the expediency of further explorations. The effort, however, was a long and uphill one, and after the abandonment of the Franklin search, Arctic discovery, so far as this country was concerned, slumbered for over twenty years.

Yet its advocates never lost heart. They cannot be said to have been numerous, but they were enthusiastic and influential ; and perhaps there is no more striking instance of perseverance on record than that with which, year after year, successive presidents of the Royal Geographical Society forced their favourite project on the notice of that popular assembly, until it became almost a point of national honour that it should be carried out. It would be incorrect to say that Arctic enterprise had been strictly a popular sentiment since the loss of the Franklin Expedition ; indeed, in many respects it was the reverse. The public press, with few exceptions, gave no countenance to it ; the leading journals were either avowedly opposed or kept silence ; science held aloof, and was converted almost against its will ; the naval service generally could scarcely view it with favour, for the reason that comparatively but a very inconsiderable number of its members could hope to share in so small an enterprise, while the honours and rewards which in consequence fell to the lot of the favoured few who could, indirectly tended to check the ordinary flow of promotion in a service where advancement is proverbially not too rapid. Yet, against all these and other obstacles, a few enthusiastic men, principally those who had been engaged in former voyages, cordially aided by—or perhaps, more correctly speaking, aiding—ardent and influential geographers such as Murchison and Rawlinson, succeeded in carrying their point. It is probable, however, that without pressure of another character, success might have been long delayed. During our protracted inactivity other nations had not been idle. The United States of America, which had generously joined with us in the search for Franklin, made several bold and more or less successful attempts to reach a high northern latitude, and Hall in this respect had all but won the palm from Parry. Petermann, the eminent German geographer, had been as warm and earnest an advocate of Polar research as some of our own men of science, and had roused the enthusiasm of his countrymen, who with Sweden and Austria also entered the field ; and if, with their limited means, they did not achieve great discoveries, they proved that they were not less enterprising or less endowed with those gifts of perseverance and endurance than our own countrymen. Certainly, from a scientific point of view, they did not accomplish less ; but what was, perhaps, more convincing still, they encountered greater perils and underwent more severe hardships than any expedition from our shores, probably because their means and resources were less ample, and yet they all returned without any fatal disaster.

This alone was a powerful argument, and went far to obliterate the deep impression produced by the disastrous termination to the voyage of Franklin. It was shown that the ' Erebus ' and ' Terror ' went into the unknown and the illimitable, without any misgiving as to their return, and therefore without any attempt at provision for their succour. Indeed it was now apparent that no possible human precautions could have rendered their safety certain, and it was proved, beyond reasonable doubt, that an expedition towards the Pole could be so circumscribed in its area of discovery, and its succour so certainly provided for, that the risk was reduced to a minimum. In short, the public mind was now ripe, and the time had come at last when this country was to resume her foremost place, and put forth her whole strength in the renewal of Arctic discovery.

This decision having been come to, the only difficulty which presented itself was where to find a commander, for experience in similar service was, above all, a necessity in the leader of such an enterprise. A generation had done its work on those who had conducted or held responsible posts in former voyages, and it was not deemed convenient to send a flag officer into the Arctic regions, or the selection would have been less limited. After mature consideration it was decided to recall Captain Nares from the command of the Scientific Expedition then being carried out in H.M.S. ' Challenger,' and to appoint him to the chief command. The loss to that expedition, however ably his place was filled, could not have been otherwise than great, but Captain Nares had gained credit as a very young officer in the last of the Government searching voyages, and the selection of a leader with experience was very properly regarded as the paramount object.

The general plan of operations had been virtually long decided by consent of all competent authorities. The first object was, if possible, to reach the Pole. Many other subordinate and collateral objects there doubtless were, both of a geographical and a purely scientific kind, but the main object was the attainment of the highest possible northern latitude. The subject had been exhaustively discussed by the Royal Geographical Society for years. Differences of opinion among the best informed undoubtedly existed. The physical conformation of the land around the regions of the polar circle almost forbade the hope of any nearer approach to the Pole by ships than had already been attained, unless indeed by the opening between Greenland and Nova Zembla, which to some offered a promise of success.

The latter-day theory of an open Polar Sea rested, however, on no foundation, practical or philosophical. Even if it could have been shown that a somewhat higher mean temperature was theoretically due in that area where the sun is for nearly six consecutive months above the horizon, and for a similar period below it, it would avail nothing; for the dissolution of the winter's ice is not dependent on the influence of the summer's heat alone, otherwise the difficulties of Arctic navigation would disappear, at any rate for some short period during every season. A variety of other elements are equally important.

Chief among them is the action of the winds and tides to break up the decaying floes, but paramount above all others is the necessity for sufficient outlets for the escape of the ice so broken up throughout the vast area of the Polar basin. These outlets we know do not exist; an insignificant point of land, moreover, will act as a wedge, or the prevalence of an unfavourable wind for a few days at the critical period will suffice to decide the question whether such inlets so important as Wellington Channel or Smith Sound will be closed or open during a season. From a ship's mast-head or a mountain-summit the visible horizon is limited by the curvature of the earth, and those who have navigated in these regions will well remember how one short hour has carried them from an apparently open sea to a dead-lock with no streak of water in sight. Water-skies are delusive; an insignificant crack or lane in the ice will produce them, and the only admissible evidence of a Polynia or navigable Polar basin must be the fact that a ship has sailed through it.

The probability of the existence of a navigable Polar Sea was therefore never entertained by those whose duty it became to consider and advise on the subject of renewed explorations; but there did appear strong reasons for believing that a high northern latitude, or even the Pole itself, might be reached by sledging parties. The Americans under Hall had wintered in 81° 38′ N. or within 500 miles of the Pole, and their reports went far to induce the belief that the land trended still away to the north, and so to strengthen the hope of success in this direction. It was under these circumstances that Smith Sound, which had always seemed the route of greatest promise, was finally and unanimously decided upon, and by Smith Sound the 'Alert' and 'Discovery' were ordered to make their way. They sailed under the brightest auspices, and with the nation's earnest wishes and sanguine hopes for their success.

It is not my place to anticipate the narrative of that memorable expedition. All went well until the day when Captain Nares placed his ship on the open shore of the Polar Sea in the latitude of 82° 27', when the picture darkened, and to his experienced eye at least, it must have been apparent that so far as the first great object of the Expedition was concerned, all hope of success was at an end. From the highest eminence attainable no land was visible to the north. Nothing met the eye but a dreary waste of frozen ocean, the ruggedness of which defied all human efforts to penetrate it by ship or sledge. Where the land trended east and west, there alone with any hope lay the path of the explorers with the return of the sun in the coming spring.

Much stress has naturally been laid on the superior equipment of this Expedition, and on the great advantages it possessed over previous ones in being provided with full steam-power; but when we come to analyse these advantages they are more apparent than real. Doubtless no ships could have been more efficiently equipped or better provisioned, yet in this respect there could scarcely have been any appreciable difference between them and the numerous expeditions which had been employed previously in the search for Franklin. In all their arrangements the Government were actuated by the one principle—efficiency and comfort—regardless of expense. Yet we find the travelling parties of the present Expedition attacked by malignant scurvy, which almost prostrated them after one winter in the ice, though happily the mortality exceeded that of no former expedition. If we turn to the records of the condition of the crews of Collinson and M'Clure's ships after three and four winters passed in a much lower latitude, we find an absence of any severe cases of the same disease, and so in other voyages of shorter duration; but where the exposure and labour of the travelling parties was excessive, we find a still more marked exemption; while, on the other hand, we learn from the recovered records of Franklin's fatal expedition, which wintered more than 700 miles to the south, and whose crews were not subject to the labour of sledging until they finally quitted their ships, that before three years had elapsed no less than twenty-four deaths had occurred (nine among them being officers), whether by scurvy or not none can say. These are significant facts, the causes of which have hitherto been past man's finding out.

As regards steam-power, its advantages, up to a certain point, cannot be overrated. Formerly ships were compelled to hold on where they could by the fixed land ice, sometimes for weeks, and where they could not, were drifted to the south, helpless in the moving pack. With steam-power, where a ship can find sufficient room to move in an ice-encumbered sea, she can force her way; hence a distance which in the days of sailing ships required some six or eight weeks to accomplish has been made good with steam in half the number of days, and the harassing labour of warping with hawsers and cutting into dock for continuous days and nights has been entirely spared. This is much; but here the advantage ends. When this partial navigation ceases and the solid floe is reached, however inconsiderable its thickness, steam is of no more avail to penetrate it than it would be to propel a ship through the crust of the earth.

But if the main object of the explorers was not attained, it cannot be said that they were less successful than any of their predecessors. The bold and skilful seamanship which carried the ships to the extreme limit of navigation, and placed the 'Alert' alone in a position in which no ship before had ever passed an Arctic winter, was worthy of the leader, and an earnest of what would have been accomplished had it been in man's power to command success. The subsequent deeds of the officers and crews, under circumstances of trial and suffering which have rarely been equalled, can never be surpassed.

If, indeed, the full accomplishment of the objects sought in such voyages as these were to be taken as the test of success, then should we look in vain for success in the annals of Arctic history. The discovery of a water passage between the two oceans along the coast of America was the result of the most persevering though unsuccessful efforts of officers of the Hudson's Bay Company and the Royal Navy, from the time when Hearne and M'Kenzie traced the two great Arctic rivers to the shores of the frozen ocean, until the last link in the chain of this discovery was furnished by Franklin in the very hour, so to speak, when he gave up his life in the cause. Parry, who was perhaps the most successful of all Arctic voyagers, never passed west of Melville Island from the Atlantic, and the intrepid M'Clure, though thirty years later he reached the winter quarters of the 'Hecla' and 'Griper' from the Pacific with a sledge crew and deposited his record by the side of his great predecessor's under the same stone, yet 70 miles of fixed ice intervened between the

'Investigator' in Mercy Bay, of Bank's Land, and Parry's farthest on Melville Island. Though the North-west passage may be said to have been accomplished jointly by these two distinguished seamen, in this high latitude, as the passage further south was completed by Franklin five years earlier, no ship has ever yet passed from ocean to ocean. The subsequent expeditions in search of Franklin were not able to reach so far west as Parry did from the Atlantic, until a division of Sir Edward Belcher's squadron under Kellett did so in 1852, while Belcher with his own ships penetrated no further than the head of Wellington Channel, which we now know Franklin himself did with the 'Erebus' and 'Terror' in 1845. But for all this it would be ungenerous as well as unjust to pronounce these enterprises failures. Perfect success has never been achieved in these instances, simply because it is not in the power of man to cope with the forces of nature in those stern inhospitable regions. To say that the accomplishment of the North-west passage will never be realised, or that the attempt to reach the North Pole will never be renewed, would be a bold prophecy. Both are objects worthy of the national enterprise of a maritime people, and it would be safer to predict that both will be attempted, and, it may be, eventually accomplished. The former, like the search for Franklin, was abandoned when but one route remained untried, and that route, east of King William's Land, dearly bought experience would seem to point out as the one which offers the best hope of success. The Pole must be sought by ship alone, and by the only track which has not yet been found impossible for steam to penetrate—by the Sea of Spitzbergen.

Doubtless no Arctic expedition can ever depart without a full equipment of sledges, any more than an ordinary ship can sail on a voyage without her proper complement of boats, for the reason that sledges are the only means of locomotion in these regions; but whether it is justifiable to equip another essentially sledging expedition with any lesser objects than these—that is, to trace the barren outline of desolate coasts probably wrapped in eternal ice, and never again to be visited, and this at the cost of so much suffering and so much treasure—is more questionable. Let the nation decide. Geography has little to gain by it, science perhaps less, for whatever science has gained by such voyages—and the gain has been considerable—has been by exploration in the neighbourhood of the ships' winter-quarters, and not through the efforts of extended travelling parties, who have neither the time nor the means to devote to it. There are wide fields for geographical and scientific research in other regions, by which the whole human race would be gainers; and though England, as she is bound to do, does more than any other nation in such work, she is very far in these respects from fulfilling her mission. Hundreds of her national ships plough the ocean in time of peace, their almost sole occupation the training and preparation for war, and in the very nature of things, so far as scientific research is concerned, they leave no deeper mark than the track which the sea obliterates behind them, while the few—too few—grudgingly appropriated from the largest navy in the world place their ineffaceable stamp on works of usefulness which last for ever.

GEORGE HENRY RICHARDS.

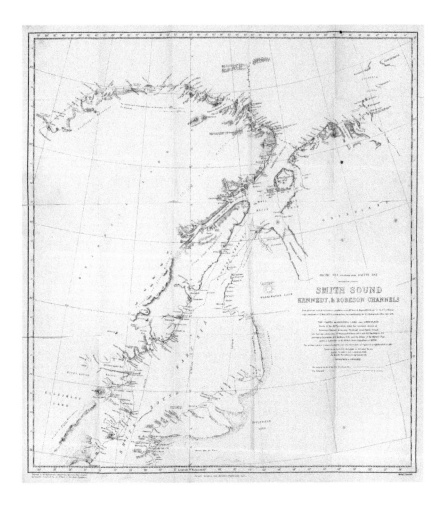

The material originally positioned here is too large for reproduction in this reissue. A PDF can be downloaded from the web address given on page iv of this book, by clicking on 'Resources Available'.

NARRATIVE

OF

A VOYAGE TO THE POLAR SEA

DURING 1875-76.

CHAPTER I.

DEPARTURE FROM PORTSMOUTH — BANTRY BAY — SEA BIRDS — PART
COMPANY WITH 'VALOROUS'—HEAVY GALES—CARRIER PIGEONS—
DEAD WHALE—EAST GREENLAND DRIFT ICE—SIGHT 'VALOROUS'
—SEALS AND WALRUS—DESCRIPTION OF PACK ICE—ANTARCTIC
ICE—A GALE—DISCOLOURATION OF SEA—INACCURACY OF CHARTS
—SIGHT 'DISCOVERY'—DREDGE ON TORSKE BANK—CROSS ARCTIC
CIRCLE—GREENLAND MER-DE-GLACE.

AT 4 P.M. of May the 29th, 1875, H.M. ships 'Alert'
and 'Discovery' cast off from the dockyard wharf,
Portsmouth, and proceeded to sea. Shortly before our
departure I had the honour of receiving the following
telegram, dated Balmoral, from Her Most Gracious
Majesty: 'I earnestly wish you and your gallant
companions every success, and trust that you may
safely accomplish the important duty you have so
bravely undertaken.' This special mark of interest
displayed by the Queen towards the Expedition was
speedily communicated to the officers and crews of the

vessels under my command, and the great honour con-
ferred by Her Majesty was fully appreciated.

The interest taken by the country at large in the
Arctic Expedition culminated in the demonstrations
attending its departure.   No one on board our two
ships can ever forget the farewell given to the discovery
vessels on that occasion.   Closely packed multitudes
occupied each pier and jetty on both sides of the harbour ; Southsea beach as far as the castle was thronged
to the water's edge ; the troops in garrison paraded
on the common, the men-of-war in port manned their
rigging and as we passed greeted us with deafening
cheers, whilst the air rang with the shouts of the spec-
tators on shore and on board the steamers, yachts, and
small craft which crowded the water.

On passing through Spithead, H.M.S. ' Valorous,'
Captain Loftus Francis Jones, joined company ; the fires
were banked and all sail made before a northerly wind,
several yachts accompanying the squadron.   By 8 P.M.
we were south of the Needles, with only one friendly
yacht left, belonging to the Rev. Mr. Conybeare, who as
father of one of the officers of the ' Discovery,' naturally gave us a lingering farewell.   By midnight we were
abreast of the Portland Lights, the three ships running
down Channel, under sail, at the rate of six knots an hour.

The following day, on passing the Eddystone, Admiral the Hon. Sir Henry Keppel, Commander-in-chief
at Plymouth, visited the ships.   In the evening the
' Valorous ' parted company for Queenstown, to complete her coal, and to bring on the latest letters
to Bantry Bay, where the ' Alert ' and ' Discovery '
arrived on June 1.

Leaving Bantry Bay the following day, the 'Valorous,' which had left Queenstown the previous afternoon, joined company. After communicating with her, and receiving our farewell letters and telegrams, sail was made to a fair wind from off the land. The ships running quickly to the westward were abreast of the Bull, Cow and Calf Rocks by 4 P.M. Before dark, owing to the mist, land was lost sight of astern, and the Expedition was fairly started on its mission.

The first four days in the Atlantic were fine, with light airs and calms. Some kittiwakes (*Rissa tridactyla*) followed us thus far from land, and a few shearwaters (*Puffinus anglorum*) were observed passing the ship. After crossing the 54th parallel of north latitude, we first met with the fulmar (*Procellaria glacialis*), and this bird accompanied us on our voyage until we entered the ice of Smith Sound.

The Atlantic swell proved to be anything but in agreement with the period of the heavily laden 'Alert.' Rolling as she did twenty and thirty degrees each way, it was rather annoying than otherwise to those on board of her to observe that the 'Valorous' and 'Discovery' were comparatively quiet; their time, however, was to come. The 'Valorous,' although she set every possible bit of canvas, and disconnected her paddles from the engines to permit them to revolve, could not keep up under sail alone with the Arctic ships; I accordingly gave her permission to part company and to rendezvous at Godhavn, in North Greenland, early in July.

On the morning of the 9th we experienced a freshening wind from the northward and rejoiced at last in

a double-reefed topsail breeze sufficiently strong to keep
the ships steady and prevent them from rolling to windward. During the previous week I had been striving
to get to the northward, in the hope of experiencing the
easterly winds prevailing in about latitude 58° N., but
we were not fated to enjoy any of them.

Next day, the barometer having fallen previously,
the wind shifted to the north-westward and forced us
to stand to the southward; it also increased considerably, the seas breaking on board the deeply laden
vessels to such an extent that the hatchways were
obliged to be battened down. By the afternoon of the
12th, the gale had evidently blown itself out, and the
sea going down enabled the hatchways to be opened
and the mess deck dried up; but as we were congratulating ourselves on the prospect of finer weather the
barometer again commenced to fall and the wind to
freshen from the south-west.

For several hours the ships were run to the northward in the hope of getting on the northern side of the
path of the vortex of the new gale; but the wind quickly
increased and forced sail to be shortened, until there
was nothing set but a close-reefed main topsail and
fore-staysail; the 'Discovery' staggering along in her
endeavour to keep station with a reefed foresail in
addition. A great number of storm petrels (*Procellaria
pelagica*) followed in the wake of the ships, with
fulmars, and a few of the large shearwaters (*Puffinus
major*). In the early part of the night the barometer
fell very rapidly, and as it was evident that we were
nearing the centre of the cyclone the 'Alert' was hove
to. At midnight the barometer registered 28·80, the

wind blowing furiously, and the 'Discovery' out of sight. Expecting a change the ship was wore, but not without a heavy sea breaking in over the stern, fortunately without damage. While lying-to on the starboard tack the ship rolled very heavily, large quantities of water coming in alternately over either gunwale; at last a sea broke into a whale-boat hanging at the waist davits outside the ship; the weight of the water tearing out one of the bolts by which she was secured; the boat was left suspended perpendicularly by the after fall alone, and by the time that she was again secured had become so badly damaged as to be beyond repair.

By the following morning the barometer had risen slightly, but the heavy sea and strong gale continued until late in the day. Sail was made as soon as the violence of the wind permitted, in order if possible to steady the ship; but it proved a total failure, she continued to roll to windward in spite of all we could do to prevent it. The 'Discovery' was nowhere in sight, and as her boats were even more exposed than those of the 'Alert,' we were naturally somewhat anxious as to how she had got through the gale. Many thoughts were also directed towards the live sheep on board of the 'Valorous,' and doubts were expressed as to whether their lives could have been saved.

On the 15th we experienced a calm, but owing to the heavy sea the ship rolled worse than ever. There was, however, one agreeable advantage in the Arctic ships, for owing to their very great solidity, the incessant creaking of each ladder and bulkhead usual in ordinary ships was completely prevented, and but for the constant falling of chairs, books &c., we should have enjoyed perfect silence. On the 18th a single storm petrel was seen in lat. 57° 26′ N., the most northern point at which this species was observed by us. After three days of fairly good weather the barometer again began to fall, and on the 19th and 20th we had to put up with our third gale from the westward in as many weeks. The hatchways being necessarily battened down, it was very dark, wet, and uncomfortable below, to say nothing of the closeness of the atmosphere. By this time our small stock of poultry had succumbed to the weather, and drowned fowls were said to figure prominently on the wardroom table. On the 21st, although the barometer was still low, we made good way on our course, and for the next three days experienced light winds and calms. Taking advantage of the fine weather, one of a pair of homing pigeons was granted its liberty, in the hope that, as the mate was sitting on eggs, it would remain in attendance; but after one or two circles round the ship it deserted us and flew off to the southward to find, in all probability, a watery grave. The story is told that a pair of carrier pigeons, despatched by Sir John Ross from the Arctic regions, returned to their home in Scotland. This error has been perpetuated in more than one popular work on Arctic discovery; it is almost needless to say that the tale is not worthy of serious consideration.

On the 25th we passed Cape Farewell at a distance of about 100 miles, and sighted a homeward bound vessel returning to Scotland with a cargo of cryolite from the mine at Evigtok. Nearing the land many birds collected around the ship, kittiwakes reappeared, fulmars and great shearwaters were numerous, and also a darker and somewhat smaller species (*Puffinus griseus*). The next day a large dead whale (*Balœna mysticetus*) was seen, floating on its back.

On the 27th, as we approached the cold ice-bearing current which sweeps round Cape Farewell towards the north, we experienced a thick fog, the temperature of the air being from 42° to 36°, and the water 40°.

A fresh northerly wind springing up gave me a good opportunity to stand in towards the land to ascertain the distance of the outer edge of the ice-stream from the shore. As the wind freshened the fog cleared off, and we fell in with the ice in lat. 59° 33′ N., long. 49° 0′ W., the pack being apparently close and unnavigable. The difference in the temperature of the water may be taken as a certain guide to denote the neighbourhood of the ice-stream.

Ten miles outside of the ice-stream the temperature of the sea-water was as follows :—

Surface	40°·5
5 fathoms	40°
15 ,, ...	38°·5
22 ,, ...	38°

At the edge of the ice the surface water was 39°, and amongst the floes themselves it was 38°. Near the land it is stated by Graah to be never warmer than 34°, the cold water therefore hugs the shore line of South Greenland.

The temperature of the sea ranging from 34° to 38°, being from four to eight degrees above the melting point of salt-water ice, the floes in its neighbourhood melt with great rapidity. As the ever-decaying pack drifts to the northward, the breadth of the stream narrows considerably until at a distance of 180 miles to the northward of Cape Desolation, there is little or none of the East Greenland drift ice left unmelted.

Next day the wind prevented our using steam except at a large expenditure of coal, so I beat to the northward close along the edge of the ice-stream in order to take advantage of the northerly running current. We experienced a current of about sixteen miles a day in our favour, but I think now that had I stood out farther from the land into the warmer water we should have found a stronger current. A few small icebergs were seen occasionally.

During the morning the 'Valorous' was sighted. She informed us by signal that 'all was well,' and, much to the relief of many, that the sheep had not suffered by their rough voyage across the Atlantic. In the afternoon the wind dying away, we steamed to the northward close along the edge of the ice. During the night we experienced a thick fog.

On the morning of the 29th, when passing at about forty miles distant from Cape Desolation, off which the ice naturally accumulates, I found that we had run deeper into the ice-stream than I had intended, and was forced to haul out from five to ten miles farther away from the land. The temperature of the sea surface ranged from 32° amongst the ice to 37° in the more open spaces, the temperature of the air being also much affected by the neighbourhood of the pack, and varying from 37° to 34°. A few seals and a single walrus were observed asleep on the ice.

Having entered deeply into the pack we had a good opportunity of judging of its nature. It was totally different to Baffin's Bay ice, inasmuch as each piece had a smooth flat top without any sharp hummocks of pressed-up ice. I remarked in my journal: 'The pack consists of very old floe-ice, floating frequently from eight to ten feet, and occasionally twelve feet, above the water. Each piece is deeply scored horizontally at the water line, leaving long tongue-pieces projecting below the surface which form a very large base; thus this ice, floating high out of water, has probably one quarter of its thickness exposed. This estimate would make it from thirty to forty feet in total thickness. I am much astonished at its unusual massiveness; if all the ice on the East Greenland coast is of a like nature we may cease to wonder at the misfortune which overtook the " Hansa " belonging to the German Expedition of 1869–70.'

We are now able to clear up all doubt respecting the birthplace, age, and thickness of this ice. It is the last remains of the heavy floes formed originally in the Polar Sea, which attain upwards of 100 feet in thickness. These, drifting south through the main outlet between Greenland and Spitsbergen, are carried by the current along the East Greenland coast round Cape Farewell; gradually melting as they reach the warm Atlantic water of Davis Strait, the ice has all decayed before reaching Godhaab Fiord in lat. 64° N.

As this pack closely resembles that met with in the Antarctic Ocean, we may conclude that a large proportion of the ice-floes formed there have attained as considerable an age and thickness before they drift into warmer latitudes as those encountered by us in the Polar Sea.

During the morning we experienced a dense fog, which prevented our seeing clearly the most open channels through the pack. At 10 A.M., after struggling through a very thick part, which nearly obliged us to retrace our course for a short distance to the southward, we suddenly entered perfectly clear water at a temperature of 38°; the line of demarcation between the pack-ice and clear water being very decided, proving that had we kept farther from the land we should have met with less impediment in the shape of ice. As we left the pack the thick fog-bank cleared off, rolling away before a northerly wind, which shortly afterwards increased to such an extent that we were forced to lie-to during the following night with a close-reefed main topsail and trysails. The current running to the northward against the wind produced a very short and high sea breaking heavily, and causing the ship to roll quicker and deeper than she had in the Atlantic. Many seas broke on board, endangering the boats, and compelling us to batten down the hatchways.

This northerly gale, occurring with a falling barometer, was peculiar. As we ran out of the pack in the forenoon the barometer was stationary at 29·50, the weather calm, with a very decided golden-coloured hazy appearance to the northward, and a clear sky overhead; this lasted for about half-an-hour, and was then replaced by an arch of clouds which quickly rose and spread themselves over the sky. At sunset, 10·30 P.M., by which time the barometer had fallen to 29·10, the western clouds were remarkably red and windy-looking from near the horizon to 20° in altitude ; the gale was then at its height, blowing with a force of seven.

On the morning of the 30th the barometer rose quickly ; the gale dying out by noon was succeeded by calm and beautiful weather, which enabled us to proceed to the northward under low steam. When fifty miles off the coast north of Frederikshaab, the edge of the pack obliged us to haul out a little farther from the land, and during the following night, when a little south of Fiskenœs, we could not get nearer the shore than fifty miles. Since we had been in the neighbourhood of Cape Farewell, and near the ice the water had changed its colour to a dark olive green, occasioned by the presence of innumerable diatoms ; in the break of the sea during the gale the crest of the waves showed a dingy yellowish green colour.

The 1st of July was a magnificent day, the barometer high and steady. At 9 A.M., when we were in latitude 63° 5′ N., at about forty-five miles' distance from land, we appeared to have passed all the shore ice, but there may have been some small unimportant streams close in by the land ; at noon by good observations we were on the west edge of the Torske Bank, off the Grœde Fiord of Fiskernœs, thirty-eight miles distant from the land. Expecting to find shallow water we tried for soundings, but did not reach bottom with 130 fathoms of line out, the minimum temperature of the water above that depth being 33°·5 ; at 4 P.M we again failed to reach the bottom with the same quantity of line out ; it is therefore evident that this bank is wrongly placed on

GODHAAB DISTRICT.

the chart. In fact the whole of the coast-line, although probably relatively correct, is very roughly delineated, and the charts must not be too fully relied on.

Late in the evening the 'Discovery' was sighted, and on the two ships closing and comparing notes, we were much relieved to find that she had not suffered more than ourselves. The two vessels had never been more than fifty miles apart, and had experienced very similar weather. In consequence of navigating farther in-shore than we did, she had found herself in the heavy pack-ice during the gale of June 29, and had passed anything but a pleasant night; but fortunately the pack was drifting to leeward nearly as fast as the ship, and so she escaped any real damage.

Next day we obtained soundings in thirty fathoms on the Torske Bank in latitude 65° N. In the hope of obtaining some fish the ships were stopped. The 'Discovery' succeeded in catching eight large halibut weighing from 20 to 25 lbs. each; the 'Alert' was not so successful, failing to get on board those hauled up to the water's edge owing to the want of a boat. The dredge was also lowered, and on its recovery was found more than half full of rounded stones and pebbles, chiefly granites, gneiss, quartz, and, more sparingly, basalts. The swabs attached to the dredge were bristling with sea-urchins and star-fish, and its living contents showed that there is great abundance of animal life in this part of the ocean.

During the night of the 4th the Arctic circle was crossed; the sun at midnight being less than a degree below the northern horizon, the evening and morning twilights blended into each other. From this date to September 3, when we had arrived at the position which proved to be our winter quarters, and the sun set to the northward again, we experienced perpetual day.

During the remainder of the passage to Disco we experienced remarkably fine weather with occasional northerly winds. When sufficiently calm the two ships steamed slowly to the northward at about ten miles' distance from the land, sail being used whenever the wind was strong enough to enable us to make headway. The dark-coloured lowlands were observed to be generally bare of snow, with here and there a snow-filled ravine, but at an altitude of some 600 or 800 feet there was much unmelted snow still left on the hill sides. In the upper lands the glacier-filled valleys bridged the whole into a fairly level white surface, above which the higher mountain tops occasionally broke through the clouds, at so great an altitude as to render their outline scarcely distinguishable.

Only a few stray icebergs were sighted until we had passed Knight Island in latitude 67° N.; but on approaching Disco Bay, the most southern large birthplace of icebergs on the west Greenland shore, a great number were met with; the northerly running current evidently wedges them away from the Greenland coast south of Holsteinborg.

CHAPTER II.

ON our arrival on July 6 at the Danish settlement
of Lievely, situated on the south-western side of the
Island of Disco, we found the 'Valorous' at anchor in
the outer bay. She had arrived two days previously
after experiencing very similar weather to that which
we had encountered. On rounding Cape Desolation
she had to thread her way through ice-streams, and in
so doing slightly damaged the floats of her paddles ; a
more distant offing would I think lead a vessel north
without any danger from the ice. We were received
at Lievely with a salute from the small battery in front
of the inspector's house, a courtesy which I could only
return by dipping our ensign.

At Disco I was much pleased to meet Herr In-
spektor Krarup Smith, the governor of North Greenland. Nothing could be kinder or more courteous
than his reception of the Expedition, and his anxiety
that all our requirements should be provided for. In

order to personally attend to our wants he had most considerately put off his periodical tour of inspection to the outlying settlements until after our visit.   He informed us that the previous winter had been a mild one, followed by a backward spring.

At this date a considerable quantity of snow was still unmelted on the hill-sides and in the ravines, whilst, bordering the shore, the snow-drift was still visible.   By the time of our departure from Disco, July 15, the snow had all melted from the sides of the hills and but little was left along the beach : the tints of the fast-growing vegetation bordering each side of the mountain rivulets with a rich fringe of bright green moss deepened day by day, or appeared to do so as we became more accustomed and so more reconciled to its scantiness.   Many patches of snow left unmelted in the hollows were tinted red from the presence of *Protococcus nivalis*.   Leaving England in summer, and arriving at an Arctic port in the month of July, it is difficult to realise that one has overtaken the season, that the thaw has only lately commenced, and that summer will not be at its height for a week or two. On the 10th Mr. Krarup Smith was anxious to quarry coal, in readiness for Captain Allen Young, who had asked me to order a supply for the use of the ' Pandora,' but the snow was still lying thick, and the ground was so hard with frost near the coal seams, that they could not be worked before the 17th.

Whilst on shore, on July 7, with Captain Feilden, we found a snow-bunting's nest with six eggs in it.   The flowers by that date were fast bursting into bloom ; the white-blossomed *Cassiopeia tetragona* gave quite a heathy look to the fells, *Azalea procumbens*, the arctic poppy, the bright yellow *Pedicularis* and several saxifrages were common; and in sheltered clefts of the basalt ridges ferns were unfolding their bright green fronds.

The settlement of Lively is built on an ice-worn islet of syenite, which is separated at high tide from the island of Disco by a narrow boat-channel; the high cliffs of that island protect it in a great measure from the winds occurring in Davis Strait, and its climate is considerably milder than that of any of the other trading ports in North Greenland. Situated in a high northern latitude and yet free from the presence of the main pack, it is the most convenient and suitable of the North Greenland ports for the transhipment of stores. The neighbouring sea is encumbered with a large number of icebergs which are discharged from the Jacobshavn and other glaciers on the east side of the bay, but no drift-ice need be dreaded after the end of May, and as the sea is not frozen over until late in December communication can be maintained, if necessary, for at least six months in the year. Small icebergs, entering through the western channel with the flood tide, drift about the outer harbour, but those of sufficient size to endanger a ship become stranded at the edge of the shallow water before reaching the inner anchorage.

In the course of conversation with Mr. Krarup Smith, he mentioned that during the previous summer an Eskimo passing in his kayak under the cliffs of Ovifak, had descried two pieces of stone under water, close to the spot where Professor Nordenskiöld discovered the so-called meteoric iron-stones, which were removed in

1871 by the Swedish Expedition under Von Otter. The Greenlander was of opinion that the masses he detected were precisely similar to those taken away by the Swedes. I decided to have the place examined, and on the 9th, Captain Feilden with Lieutenant Aldrich and a boat's crew, accompanied by the Greenlander who gave the information, started for Ovifak. Landing with considerable difficulty at the spot indicated, a careful search was instituted, but owing to the roughness of the sea, or to the removal of the stones themselves by the action of the waves, the search proved unsuccessful so far as these particular masses were concerned. Subsequently, we procured some lumps of iron from the same locality. It appears that the metallic iron of Ovifak is distributed throughout a particular basalt, in small grains as well as in masses, whilst particles of the basalt are freely dispersed throughout the lumps of iron, thus pointing to the telluric origin of the mineral.

On Sunday the 11th, the opportunity was taken of holding a sacrament service in the chapel on shore, when most of the officers and a number of the crews of the three ships attended.

While we were near the Greenland coast, farther to the southward, the temperature of the water was never above 40°, but in Disco Bay we found it considerably higher, ranging to 49° in the more open parts of the sea near the southern shores. With the temperature of the air occasionally up to 50°, and the water at least 10° above the melting point of fresh-water ice, the numerous icebergs were melting very rapidly. Large masses constantly broke asunder and, falling into the sea, caused great commotion. The balance of the ice-bergs being consequently altered, they rolled backwards and forwards until equilibrium was restored and they settled down to a new line of flotation or a position of poise on the ground. In the latter case, the grooving effect produced on the bottom by these enormous masses of ice oscillating to and fro must be very great. Large quantities of sea-weed (*Laminaria*) rising to the surface, show what havoc is caused by the grounding and overturning of these ice-islands, and the many dead fish, chiefly *Cottus*, cast up on the beach of Disco Island, owe their destruction no doubt to the same agency.

The supply of fresh water having run short and there being several small berg-pieces studding the harbour, one was towed alongside the ' Alert ' and broken up, the pieces being transferred to one of the water-tanks. This proved a mistake ; the cold air in the tank converted it into a perfect ice-box, and it was found necessary to pour hot water into the tank in order to melt the ice.

A number of sealskin over-boots were obtained, which were afterwards found most comfortable for wearing in a cabin with a cold draught near the floor, but owing to some misunderstanding regarding my wishes, the supply of sealskin soles for the travelling mocassins was not so plentiful as I afterwards desired. It is scarcely possible to lay in too large a stock of this invaluable material, which is far more durable than ordinary leather ; but a large expedition, such as ours, should not expect to obtain a sufficient quantity of seal-skins at the Greenland settlements unless they have been ordered beforehand.

Eider ducks of two species (*Somateria spectabilis*, and *S. mollissima*) were very common around Disco Island. The natives brought a considerable number to our ships, and we found them such good eating that a larger supply would have been deemed acceptable. It has been stated that eider ducks are uneatable on account of their fishy taste, but we did not find that to be the case. The fish obtained from the Greenlanders, chiefly rock-cod, and a species of salmon-trout, were good but not plentiful. Our crews being fully employed we were unable to use our own nets, or probably we should have obtained a large supply, the neighbouring fisheries being very rich.

The light canvas Berthon boats, available for one or two persons, proved of great service. A few of the officers became rather expert in the use of the kayak, but not without one very narrow escape. When a kayak is overturned it becomes an air-float acting in the most undesirable manner by preventing the immersed man from coming to the surface; in the case referred to, the officer had the presence of mind to disentangle himself from his trousers, and wriggle his body, whilst under water, out of the tight-fitting aperture of the kayak, leaving his nether garments behind.

An endeavour was made to obtain a bearing of the 'Parry Rock,' lying six or seven miles to the southward of the harbour; its existence is undoubted, and situated in the fairway, if unmarked by icebergs aground, is a most dangerous reef.

On the evening of the 15th, after obtaining satisfactory sights for rating our chronometers, and taking on board twenty-four Eskimo dogs, the Expedition started for Ritenbenk, situated at the S.E. end of the Waigat Strait. Mr. Krarup Smith kindly accompanied us, to insure our obtaining the remainder of the dogs we required, and a supply of coal for the 'Valorous,' Captain Loftus Jones having decided to take some on board from the coal mine on the western side of the strait.

The Arctic ships, having on board three years' supplies, were necessarily very deep in the water, and the upper decks were much encumbered with stores of provisions for which room could not be found below. As it was necessary to keep supplies ready for immediate use in case of accident to the ships when navigating through Melville Bay, and Smith Sound, such provisions as the boats could hold were stored ready to hand : in addition, a month's supply for all hands was kept prepared on the deck of each ship, to be landed at suitable places in the event of the crews having to retreat south by boat. These were named respectively the A, and B depôts, and had been prepared in England before the Expedition started. The positions selected for their deposit were one of the Cary Islands in Baffin's Bay, and Cape Frazer in Smith Sound ; the mainland would have been preferable to the first-named place, had it not been necessary to take precautions to hide it from the Eskimo, who inhabit the coast of Greenland between Cape York and Hartstene Bay.

After a calm but very foggy passage along the south shore of Disco Island, threading our way amidst a vast number of icebergs, we arrived at Ritenbenk at 11 A.M. of the 16th, and anchored in seventeen fathoms.   The derivation of the name of this settlement, as I was informed, is somewhat fanciful.   Founded about the year 1755, it received the name of Berkentin after a nobleman of that name, who at the date mentioned presided over Greenlandic affairs in Denmark. The minister by a transposition of the letters of his name converted it into Ritenbenk.

The anchorage being deep and exposed to drifting icebergs cannot be deemed a secure one.   Whilst arrangements were being made for completing our supplies a shooting party started for a neighbouring 'loomery,' on the north-west coast of Arve Prins Island ; they returned in the evening with seventy-five guillemots and razor-bills (*Alca bruennichi* and *Alca torda*).   The loom or guillemot of the Arctic seas differs from its close ally *Alca troile*, found so commonly around the British Isles, in its short stout bill ; on the wing it would be impossible to separate the two species.   We did not observe the razor-bill north of the Waigat.

When at Godhavn, Disco, we remarked how densely each fresh-water pool was inhabited by the larvæ of mosquitoes just on the point of changing their condition to the winged state.   A few days later at Ritenbenk the mosquitoes on shore were intolerable, and when getting under weigh, the weather being calm, these persistent annoyers fairly took possession of the upper deck.

Before parting company with the 'Valorous,' owing to the large percentage of officers in the Expedition, I decided to carry only one paymaster to superintend the victualling of the two ships.   Mr. Edgar Whiddon, belonging to the 'Alert,' was there-

fore ordered to return to England, Mr. G. Le Clerc
Egerton, sub-lieutenant, being appointed to super-
intend the issue of the provisions on board the 'Alert.'
No serious disadvantage arose from this arrangement.

On leaving Ritenbenk there were thirty Eskimo
dogs on the upper deck of the 'Alert' and twenty-five
on board of the 'Discovery,' still further encumber-
ing the narrow gangways left available between the
piled-up provisions. My journal thus alluded to these
animals : ' Being in strange quarters they are baying
in concert, the distracting noise frequently diversified
by a sharp howl as a sailor in forcing his way through
their midst uses the toe of his boot. The packs
collected from different settlements are strangers to
each other. The king-dog of each team is necessarily
tied up, his subordinates of both sexes clustering
around, and crouching at his feet In their anxious
endeavours to protect their followers, the females of
whom are rather given to straying, and if possible to
maintain and extend their rights, these king-dogs are
straining their very utmost at the ropes, snarling and
lifting their upper lips, evidently longing for the time
to arrive when they may fight it out, and decide who
is to be ruler over all. By sheer fighting each has
worked his way up to the position he now holds, the
most determined and enduring animals gaining the
day. A long series of combats will be undertaken
before the supreme head is acknowledged, and hereafter many an attempt at revolution will be fought out
by rising aspirants for power, as the old chiefs become
worn out from age or other causes. It would appear
as if fighting were an enjoyment or natural condition

of their existence. In maintaining discipline amongst the weaker sex, punishment is left entirely in the hands, or rather mouth, of the favourite queen, who, except when jealousy may occasionally warp her judgment, uses her prerogative pretty fairly, whilst it frequently happens that the king-dog himself submits without resentment to a snarl from his queen.

Frederick the Eskimo, who joined us at Lively to take charge of the dogs, has readily settled down to his work; his broad, flat, good-humoured face is certainly not handsome, but his character is most excellent, and above all he is unmarried.'

Early on the morning of the 17th we left Ritenbenk under steam, the ' Discovery ' in tow, bound to the northward through the Waigat Channel; the ' Valorous ' having parted company a few hours previously proceeding to the coal mines on the west side of the Waigat. After clearing the anchorage the two ships made sail before a southerly wind : crossing the entrance of Svarte Vogel Bay, a large ' loomery ' was sighted on its northern shore. The Waigat Channel was found to be much encumbered by icebergs and broken ice, which were streaming out from the neighbourhood of the Tossukatek Glacier through the fiord north of Arve Prins Island, and driving quickly towards the north-west before a breeze of fair strength. From their dirty unwashed appearance the majority of these icebergs were evidently newly broken off from the glacier, and although the temperature of the water was 40° they had not yet decayed sufficiently to alter their balance. They were extremely rugged in outline, and appeared as if formed of a collection of boulder ice refrozen into a solid form, such as would be the case with a glacier forced over a rough steep incline; some were table-topped, as if broken from a smooth-surfaced glacier sloping at a small angle to the water.

None of these icebergs were more than fifty feet high, but their number was sufficient to render great care necessary in choosing a passage between them. Not expecting to experience such close sailing the boats had been left hanging to the davits outboard, and were occasionally endangered when passing through the narrow water-channels.

When abreast of Atanekerdluk five kayaks, and an omiak containing women and children, were met; they paddled alongside, keeping pace with the ships, and we had the satisfaction of being able to supply them with biscuit, no doubt a very welcome addition to their usual meat and fish diet.

Thinking that the 'Valorous' with her projecting paddles would not be able to force a passage through such ice as we encountered, all hopes of meeting her again were given up, but during the afternoon she was sighted lying quietly at anchor off the coaling station, having found, as we afterwards learnt, a channel much clearer of ice near the land. Wishing to put on board our last letters, we hauled to the wind and beat to windward for her anchorage, but a very thick fog setting in as the wind moderated, the separation of the 'Alert' and 'Discovery' was feared; hence we were forced to abandon our intention of communicating, and proceeded to the northward. By midnight, when we had run through the most ice-encumbered part of the channel, the wind died away, but as the fog continued very thick, it became necessary either to get up steam or secure the ships to an iceberg to prevent them drifting into danger. I adopted the latter course.

When a vessel is under steam nothing is simpler than for a seaman to descend by a rope ladder from the bowsprit end on to the ice below, keeping well away from its edge, but in landing from a boat care is necessary when scaling the side of a berg. On our drifting near an apparently convenient piece of ice a boat's crew were sent to fix the ice-anchor and hawser. One of the men, in spite of the decayed condition of the ice, managed to crawl up it in safety; but at the first blow from his chisel a large mass broke off, fortunately shooting clear of the boat and crew below. The amount disengaged was sufficient to disturb the equilibrium of the iceberg, which began to rock backwards and forwards; the man, naturally frightened, was obliged to struggle as best he could along its slippery surface, like a squirrel in a circular cage, much to the amusement of his shipmates on the forecastle. The performance, however, involved a certain element of danger, which I should have preferred to avoid.

In the Waigat, like all narrow channels bounded by lofty hills, the winds are very local, and while blowing with force at the entrance seldom prevail throughout the whole length; hence the icebergs driven before the wind accumulate at the locality where the breeze ends. With a strong south-east wind at the southern entrance we found the icebergs collected in great numbers in the middle of the strait, but at the north-west entrance near Hare Island few

were met with. Those seen had melted considerably
since their formation ; floating in water at a temperature
of 40°, deep grooves had been worn horizontally at the
water edge, the many old flotation lines thus marked
showed that they had frequently altered their position
in the sea.

The difference of climate, due to the aspect of the
hill sides, was remarkably well displayed in the Waigat.
The Greenland shore, with its southern frontage, had
on the 18th scarcely a trace of snow left on it ; but the
opposite shore of Disco was still snow-covered, with
its mountain summits capped by a perpetual glacier.
Ice cascades were very conspicuous in the upper parts
of the steep gullies, descending like giant steps from
one upland ridge to the next below ; with enormous
boulders plentifully dispersed throughout the descending streams. The many glacier ice cliffs, with a distinct overhanging snow covering and yet having no
débris lying at the foot, forms a question for interesting
investigation.

On both sides of the strait some of the smaller
torrents appeared to be still frozen, but I think that
must have been due to abnormal and local difference
of temperature, for when passing the mouth of the
Makkak River, which drains the Noursoak Peninsula,
its muddy and discoloured waters extended three or four
miles out to sea, showing that it was running strongly,
and depositing a large amount of alluvial matter.

A fine breeze from the S.W., with misty weather,
carried us quickly to the north, and on the morning of
the 19th, when abreast of Svarten Huk (Black Cape),
the mist partially cleared off, bringing Skale and

Kingatak Islands into view, and enabled us to ascertain our position with sufficient accuracy to steer in towards Proven; but the headlands along the coast are all so much alike in form and colour that in misty weather, with only one in sight, a stranger would be puzzled to ascertain his whereabouts.

After passing between Kingatak and Tukingarsuk the south-westerly wind died away, and a strong tidal current obliged us to get up steam. Taking the 'Discovery' in tow, the harbour was entered about an hour before midnight, when we were received by the few inhabitants, who clustered upon the slopes about the settlement, in their many coloured picturesque clothing. Following the chart, it would appear practicable to enter the anchorage direct from the southward, but a sunken reef blocks the channel and obliges vessels to pass round on the western side of the outer island and to enter by the northern channel. The water being very deep, except on one ledge close to the shore near the settlement, a pilot is necessary to point out the anchorage, which after all is very rocky and untrustworthy holding ground. During the night a southerly wind, force five to six, causing squalls off the high land, made me rather anxious, but the anchors held on, the cables, however, grinding a good deal against the rocky bottom.

The inhabitants of Proven amount to about 106 souls, and were presided over at the time of our visit by Governor Möldrup, who obligingly assisted us in completing our supplies. The island on which the settlement is built is composed of gneiss, but the islands that lie more to the' southward, and the great peninsula of Svarten Huk, are apparently analogous in their formation to Disco Island and the Noursoak Peninsula. A line drawn W. and E. through the settlement of Proven and extended inland would roughly define the limit of the granitoid rocks from those of later origin. To the northward along the coast, ice-worn mountains, plentifully sprinkled with enormous erratics, rise in endless succession; southward the flat-topped hills, the horizontal bedding and varied coloured strata, with bands of columnar basalt, show that the land has, from some cause or other, escaped the tremendous degradation that has obliterated every trace of the softer tertiary strata, which in all probability at some former period covered the gneiss hills to the north of Proven. The whole of the island is bestrewed with erratics, many of prodigious size; they are chiefly gneiss, granites, and syenites, but on the very summit of the island a few boulders of basalt were observed. The flora of Proven is by no means as rich as that of Disco, but *Betula nana*, the dwarf birch of the Arctic zone, was common. Snow-buntings were numerous, and by this date the young in a nest were well fledged; several parties of young wheatears (*Saxicola œnanthe*) were flying about the rocks near the shore, their familiar ' chuck chuck ' resounding on all sides.

My chief object in visiting Proven was to endeavour to obtain the services of Hans Heindrich, the Greenlander who had previously accompanied three American expeditions to Smith Sound. On our arrival he was absent in charge of a boat, but having seen the ships approaching, he returned to the settlement with all

speed, and after a short consultation with his wife
agreed to join our Expedition and leave his family
behind.   He proved himself to be an admirable hunter
and an excellent dog-driver.   Hans when a lad of
nineteen joined Dr. Kane's expedition in 1853.   After
rendering invaluable services to his companions during
their two winters' stay at Rensselaer Harbour, Smith
Sound, he married Merkut, the daughter of Shanghu,
one of the 'Arctic Highlanders,' who tended him when
lying sick at Hartstene Bay; he remained behind with
his wife when Dr. Kane abandoned his vessel and
travelled south to Upernivik in boats.   In 1860, after
he had passed five years with the 'Arctic Highlanders,'
Dr. Hayes finding Hans at Cape York, took him and
his wife and child on board his vessel the 'United
States'; on the homeward voyage in 1861 he was
landed with his belongings at Upernivik.   In 1871 he
joined Captain Hall in the 'Polaris,' taking his wife
and three children with him.   He was one of the party
who were separated from the 'Polaris' in a gale of
wind, and drifted during the long winter of 1872–73
from Smith Sound to the southward of Hudson's
Straits; during that time he and Joe another Eskimo
preserved the lives of their companions by their
indefatigable and noble exertions in hunting and
procuring seals.

   Hans having bid farewell to his wife and children,
we left Proven on the evening of the 21st.   The
weather being calm we proceeded to the northward
under low steam with the 'Discovery' in tow; having
a pilot on board we adopted the inner passage, and
threaded our way between the numerous islands that

lie between Proven and Upernivik. The scenery between these two places is superb; magnificent cliffs of gneiss rise sheer from the water's edge to a height of 1,000 to 1,200 feet; the rich colouring of the rocks presented an almost inconceivable richness of hues, and formed a striking contrast to the glaciers and *mer de glace.* Passing a small settlement picturesquely situated in a little bay on the island of Kasorsoak, of which Sanderson's Hope forms the western headland, two men came out from the land to meet us; paddling in their kayaks they dexterously picked up the food thrown to them in parcels buoyed up by empty bottles.

At midnight we were abreast of the noble headland of Sanderson's Hope with its noted 'loomery.' Being desirous of obtaining a supply of birds I stopped the ships for a couple of hours, and sent the boats away; but the result, as compared with the reported successes of prior visitors, was unsatisfactory, only 122 guillemots being brought to bag by the united endeavours of sportsmen from both ships. The razor-bill, which shared the cliffs at Ritenbenk with the guillemot, was not observed here. As the boats approached thousands of birds flew from the cliffs sweeping numbers of eggs off the ledges, which broke as they reached the water; at this date the young were nearly ready for hatching. In spite of the swell one of the party managed to get on to the rocks, and procured several eggs; one was taken from underneath the sitting bird, who remonstrated by pecking at the hand of the spoiler. A thick fog setting in obliged me to recall the boats.

Feeling our way carefully along and trusting entirely to the chart, for our Greenland pilot became at a loss in the fog, we entered Upernivik Harbour, and anchored at five in the morning, before any of the residents knew of our arrival : indeed the fog was so dense that the ships approached within a hundred yards of the settlement before it was sighted. We found two or three small icebergs aground on the bank forming the only shallow water anchorage, where they occupied a considerable part of the available space. This bank from its steepness is in all probability the moraine of an ancient glacier. In the early season before the floe ice has been finally driven off to sea, the anchorage can scarcely be considered a protected one, for floating ice must frequently necessitate a change in the ship's position.

We met at Upernivik Governor Fliescher and ' Sophie ' his wife ; the latter the considerate friend of all English voyagers since the first of the Franklin Search Expeditions. I had the pleasure of presenting her with a thoughtful present of crockery from Sir Leopold M'Clintock.

I am afraid that few of the transient visitors to these North Greenland settlements think of the dreary winters which the Danish inhabitants must necessarily pass. Disco and Ritenbenk are in the same latitude as Igloolik, where Sir Edward Parry wintered between 1821 and 1823, and as King William's Land, where Franklin's ships were lost. Upernivik is very little south of Lancaster Sound, where so many expeditions have passed their winters. With a well found naval expedition newly arrived from southern climes the monotony of a long dark winter, which appears something dreadful and dismal in the anticipation, is considerably relieved by the charm of novelty. The Danish inhabitants, who are obliged to endure a yearly recurring period of equal darkness with only one or two associates, can but contrast the monotony of one winter with the past; life under these circumstances must be hard indeed, and the Danish officials and missionaries who voluntarily undergo it are entitled to our liveliest commiseration.

Since 1721, the year of Egede's settlement at Godhaab in South Greenland, the Danes have consistently endeavoured to improve and ameliorate the condition of the Eskimo inhabitants of Greenland. Their efforts have been crowned with marked success, and the paternal rule of the Danish Government has been conducted with such complete regard for the interests of the Greenlanders, that we find the native population scattered along the coasts of that inhospitable land enjoying the blessings of religion, law, order, and a considerable degree of civilization. This enlightened policy has been carried out by a succession of worthy officials and missionaries, whose self-denying labours reflect the utmost credit on themselves and the country to which they belong.

CHAPTER III.

LEAVE UPERNIVIK—INTRICATE NAVIGATION—'ALERT' AGROUND—THE
'MIDDLE ICE'—MELVILLE BAY—CAPE YORK AND THE 'NORTH WATER'
—NATIVES OF CAPE YORK—BEVERLEY CLIFFS—CARY ISLANDS—
NORTHUMBERLAND AND HAKLUYT ISLANDS—CAPE ALEXANDER.

THE barometer remaining very steady at 30·5 inches, I
hastened to take advantage of the favourable weather.
Having succeeded in obtaining observations for correct-
ing the chronometers, the Expedition left Upernivik
on the evening of the 22nd. A thick fog to seaward
rendered it very unadvisable to attempt a passage in
that direction, but the weather being perfectly clear inshore, with the assistance of an Eskimo pilot we passed
safely through the narrow and intricate channels leading
to Kangitok. The scenery in this passage is exceedingly
picturesque. At first starting it is necessary to pass
through a narrow rocky channel not more than fifty
yards broad, the dark-coloured rocks rising on the
left hand to above the mastheads, though on the right
sufficiently low to disclose the mainland beyond, which
presents a line of grand rampart-like cliffs rising for at
least 1,000 feet abruptly from the water's edge. The
giant portals on either side of the many glacier-cut
fiords which break the continuity of the coast, are
conspicuously marked by corresponding lines of stratification. This narrow channel continued for about

two miles, and then widened into a large ice-encumbered inland sea. To seaward all but the base of the nearest islands was enshrouded in dense fog, but in the direction of the ice-clad mainland of Greenland the atmosphere was singularly clear, and all objects remarkably distinct; although in consequence of the light reflected from the *mer de glace*, the sky-line was ill defined. On the slightly inclined ice-cap, numerous rounded elevations, conspicuously scored with crevasses, denoted the undulations of the buried land below. The coast glaciers were unfortunately hidden from our view by the outlying rocky islets, and these again were fronted by innumerable icebergs so completely reflected in the calm sea as to render it difficult to distinguish the intermediate water-channels. The whole scene was brilliantly lighted by an unclouded midnight sun.

Our Eskimo pilot, who promised to guide us safely past Kangitok, joined us very willingly at Upernivik, his kayak being lifted on board; but as the distance from his home increased he became very uneasy, and had I not forcibly detained his means of conveyance he would certainly have broken his share of the bargain, and left us when amongst a bewildering group of islands during a thick fog. However, after being convinced that might was on our side, he became sufficiently reconciled to his fate to be useful, but never regained complete confidence. So long as we headed inshore we experienced clear weather, but whenever we tried to proceed seaward we met the fog. Arriving near Kangitok, the outlying island of the group, we were forced to wait for the fog to clear, it being occasionally so thick as to hide from our view the 'Discovery,' in tow astern of us. In vain did I look for an anchorage, or a suitably grounded iceberg to which to secure the ships; the first was unobtainable in consequence of the water a ship's length from the shore being a hundred fathoms in depth, and the few icebergs aground were so close to the land as to occasion uncertain eddy currents in their near vicinity. After drifting about in an unknown neighbourhood for six anxiously spent hours, a momentary clearance of the atmosphere took place, and we observed two Eskimo in their kayaks close alongside. Everything was so quiet, and the neighbourhood apparently so destitute of life, that their appearance quite startled us; and it is difficult to imagine the first impressions of the natives at so unexpected a sight as our ships must have presented on suddenly emerging from the fog. After a short consultation through Petersen and the pilot they volunteered to conduct us to an anchorage.

Following the kayaks, at the same time steaming very slowly and sounding carefully, I suddenly felt the ship strike the ground; hailing the 'Discovery,' her officer of the watch, by smart attention to the helm, avoided running into us. Before I could take steps to lighten the ship, the quickly falling tide had fixed her hard and fast on shore. As it was nearly low-water and the fog still thick outside, I allowed the ship to remain quiet where she was, the 'Discovery' still hanging to us by the towing hawser. Advantage was taken of the enforced delay to land the ship's companies. The officers spread themselves over the island, some taking magnetic observations, others with their guns hoping to obtain game; both king and common eider ducks were found and females of both species were shot off their nests. The island is composed of red gneiss; veins of quartz with large garnets in it traverse the rock in a north and south direction.

As the tide rose our stragglers were recalled, and just before noon the ship floated, without having incurred any strain or damage. The fog having cleared considerably, we at once proceeded to sea, discharging our pilot, greatly to his delight and relief. At 4 P.M. we were abreast of the Brown Islands, with a sea perfectly clear of drift-ice. A high and steady barometer denoting that the calm weather which we had lately experienced would probably continue, and finding the ice at a great distance from the Greenland shore, I decided to attempt a passage through the 'Middle Ice' rather than to proceed by the ordinary route round Melville Bay. Accordingly the two ships proceeded at full speed to the westward, racing in company for Cape York, with only about a dozen icebergs in sight. After midnight, having run sixty miles from the Brown Islands on a west by north course true, we sighted the pack, the temperature of the water falling from 36° to 33°, and at 1.30 A.M. we steamed into it. The pack consisted of open sailing ice from one to three and occasionally four feet in thickness; the floes first met with were about two hundred and fifty yards in diameter and very rotten. In order to shorten the passage between the floes, it became necessary to force many of the smaller pieces aside, but beyond the momentary check of speed and the scratching of the ice along the ship's side, little trouble was experienced. Occasionally when a thicker piece than usual refused to succumb to the blow, it would hang evenly balanced across the stem, and being forced ahead in front of the ship, collect other pieces, until at last the accumulation of ice would render it necessary to stop the engines and turn the ship's bow in another direction. When we had run thirty miles through the pack on the same course it gradually became closer and the floes larger, measuring a mile and more in diameter, obliging a discriminating selection of the best leads to be made from the crow's nest. Only one iceberg, and that a small one, was sighted at this part of the passage, but it proved a most valuable mark when steering through the tortuous passages, towards the more open water-spaces.

Looking from the masthead over a boundless extent of ice-covered sea, with no prominent objects to direct a course, it is very easy to run off from the desired direction without being aware of it. A compass in the crow's nest materially assists the look-out man on such occasions.

The lanes of water lying in a north-west and south-east direction, permitted a rapid advance, and by 8 P.M. of the 24th we had run sixty miles through the pack. The ice was never close enough to cause anxiety that we might be caught in it, but still kept me fully employed in choosing the best leads from the crow's nest. The heaviest ice met with was not more than four feet thick, with hummocks rising some six feet above it. After 8 P.M. the channels between the floes became decidedly broader and more numerous, denoting that we had passed through the thickest part of the barrier so I gradually altered course to the north-ward, steering direct for Cape York. After midnight, when we were in latitude 79° 9′ N. and longitude 65° 30′ W., 140 miles to the westward of the Devil's Thumb, the ice was so open that the officer of the watch could see every obstacle from the bridge, and was able to direct the ship without the help of a look-out man in the crow's nest. Officers soon gain ex-perience in these matters; the heavy pieces that ought to be avoided float higher out of the water than the light ice which may be struck with impunity, and are consequently readily distinguished. If, however, a mistake should be made, the shock is sufficient to bring nervous people on deck, and cannot be good for the chronometers.

Throughout the night the temperature of the sea was 31°, and young ice formed on the surface to about the thickness of half-an-inch, showing the partial freshness of the water. Towards morning, before the daily thaw had set in, the opening out of the pack during the calm was rendered apparent by the many water-spaces from which the young ice had been drifted off, like dross from quicksilver, leaving a pure unblemished surface which reflected the hull and rigging of the ships with such distinctness that it was difficult to determine where the object and the reflection met. The sharp crackling sound made by the vessels as they tore their way through the plates of young ice, was rather agreeable than otherwise when contrasted with the dead silence around unbroken even by the hundreds of little auks (*Mergulus alle*), swimming close alongside; these little birds, scattered in large flocks over the water-spaces, refused to move until almost touched by the ships. then they dived in company, propelling themselves under water with great rapidity, all the individuals in a flock coming to the surface again at the same moment. In the ' Middle Ice ' we observed a bear, a walrus, two species of seals (*Phoca grœnlandica*) and (*Phoca hispida*); amongst the birds many fulmars, a few ivory gulls (*Pagophila eburnea*), a single dovekie (*Uria grylle*), some guillemots, and a diver (*Colymbus*). The water was filled with a quantity of diatomaceous brown flocculent matter, which was also incorporated in the floes ; this dark substance, absorbing the sun's rays, exerts a very potent influence during summer in the destruction of Baffin's Bay ice.

At 9.30 A.M. of the 25th we sighted the high land about Cape York, and at 11 o'clock, when forty-five miles directly south of that cape, we were fairly in the ' North Water,' having passed through the ' Middle Ice ' in thirty-four hours. Although we made so successful a voyage through a locality justly dreaded by experienced ice-navigators, the conclusion must not be hastily arrived at that a similar passage can always be commanded. Had a strong breeze set in while we were amongst the ice we should have been beset in the pack and, at the very least, delayed for several days.

By good observations at noon we found that we had been set eleven miles to the west-north-west ; but our frequent change of course, and adopting the most western of any two leads otherwise equally good, may have given rise to some of the difference between the position by log and that by observation.

Hans Heindrich being desirous that his brother-in-law should be allowed to join the Expedition, and thinking it also important that the Eskimo who live between Cape York and Port Foulke should be aware of our presence, I directed Captain Stephenson to proceed to Cape York and endeavour to communicate with the natives. Our consort was speedily hidden from our view behind a vast assemblage of the largest sized bergs, which were thickly crowded together off the cape. Many of them were table-topped and therefore newly launched, most of them were aground. The majority of these icebergs doubtless derived their origin from the great glaciers of Melville Bay, and had been drifted to their present position by the current sweeping towards the north and westward, which continues its course as far at least as Hartstene Bay at the entrance to Smith Sound.

Captain Stephenson found most of the Eskimo, including Hans' brother-in-law, absent from the settlement, which was situated on the eastern side of a bay to the eastward of Cape York. While the ' Discovery ' was secured to the land-ice inside the grounded icebergs, a female narwhal (*Monodon monoceros*), with a well developed tusk, was killed, also a great number of little auks. Seventeen natives, fifteen men and two women, with three dog-sledges, visited the ship. They appeared poorly clad in hooded seal-skin jumpers, and bear-skin trousers cut off at the knees; wearing nothing underneath, they showed a broad margin of body between the two garments. On being given some of the narwhal they ate it in great quantities, tearing the raw flesh asunder with their teeth. Their hair was long and matted, but their splendid row of even white teeth showed to advantage out of the setting formed by the flat mahogany-coloured visage. They were given a supply of lucifer matches, biscuits, knives, &c., which appeared to please them greatly.

In the meantime the 'Alert' proceeded on her way towards the Cary Islands, there to establish a depôt of provisions and deposit a boat for use should we unfortunately be fated to retreat south from Smith Sound,

GROUP OF ARCTIC HIGHLANDERS.

leaving our vessels behind us, as two out of three expeditions which preceded us had been forced to do. Expecting to find a southerly current in the offing, where there were few icebergs, I steamed along the Greenland shores within a couple of miles of the land and inside a long line of immense bergs lying aground parallel to the coast, trusting to the grounded ice to point out any hidden dangers. At this season little snow remained on the Beverley Cliffs, though behind them the inland ice-cap was visible, and down the ravines between the dark walls of rock many glaciers made their way into the sea. Several of these glaciers showed conspicuous medial and lateral moraines, and some of the smaller ones that had not reached the sea, terminal moraines. A few patches of red-coloured snow appeared in sheltered hollows, but it required the aid of a glass to distinguish it. A yellow lichen growing over the cliffs gave a brilliant colouring to some of the rocky slopes. Myriads of little auks were breeding in these cliffs ; they flew from the water to the land with their cheeks puffed

BEVERLEY CLIFFS, 'CRIMSON CLIFFS' OF SIR JOHN ROSS.

out in a most ludicrous manner, from the food contained
in them, which they were carrying to their young.
A few Iceland gulls (*Larus leucopterus*), were seen
perched on the bergs, and this was the most northern
locality where we recognized that species.   Guillemots
were abundant, a large loomery being visible near Cape
Parker Snow.   I had intended to pass inside of Conical
Rock, but as we approached it towards midnight, a
strong northerly wind sprang up and enabled me to
make sail, beating to the northward.   On standing off
the land at 6 A.M. of the 26th, when twenty-four miles
south-west of Conical Rock, the wind died away, and
observing that the current was apparently carrying us
rapidly to the south, I proceeded again under steam.
It was calm all day, with thick fog.   At noon, when
we must have been fifteen miles south-west of Wol-
stenholme Island, the surface temperature rose to 40°.
In the afternoon, not knowing our exact position
with regard to the Cary Islands, and not wishing to
pass them, I stopped, and while waiting for the fog
to clear, got a sounding in three hundred fathoms
with no bottom ; using an ordinary deep-sea thermometer, the warm stratum of water at a temperature of
about 39° was found to extend to a depth of sixty feet;
at a depth of twenty fathoms the temperature was 29°.
Doubtless had a reversible thermometer been used we
should have found an underlying warmer stratum.
The ' Discovery ' sounding in thirty-two fathoms near
the Cary Islands obtained a temperature of 32° at that
depth, but this was probably due to local causes.

Towards evening the fog cleared and we found ourselves fifteen miles south-east of the Cary Islands.   The

' Discovery ' was observed fast approaching us from the direction of Cape York. At midnight we were along-side of the most south-eastern island, and immediately commenced landing a depôt of 3,600 rations. These would have been more convenient if placed on North-umberland Island or on the mainland, but I was much afraid of the Eskimo finding and plundering the depôt. Before leaving Disco I left a notice for Captain Allen Young, or anyone likely to follow our foot-steps, stating that it was my intention to form this station on the western island of the Cary group, where a party from Admiral Austin's expedition in 1857 landed and erected a cairn. But on considering the probably exhausted condition of a party of men re-treating southward from perhaps the northern part of Smith Sound, I decided to alter its destination, and to place it as near as possible to the line of retreat. Ac-cordingly having selected a convenient position on the east end of the south-east island, the provisions and a boat were placed in a crevice of the rocks above the wash of the sea or pressure of ice. Another paper and a few letters were placed in a cairn on the summit of this island, which attains an altitude of about 600 feet. Numerous rounded fragments and pebbles of red sand-stone are strewed over the top of the island, which is composed of a red-coloured gneiss dipping at a very high angle to the west. Eider ducks, with their broods of downy ducklings some four or five days old, were swim-ming about in the salt water. A large colony of bur-gomasters (*Larus glaucus*) were nesting on some bright green ledges of a steep cliff; one of our party, having taken off his coat and shoes, climbed up to the topmost ledges and brought down two nearly full-feathered young ones. Flowering plants were scanty, the most conspicuous being the yellow-blossomed *Potentilla*, *Cochlearia officinalis*, *Papaver nudicaule*, and a *Draba*, also a creeping dwarf willow. Traces of foxes and ptarmigan were observed.

It was high water at the Cary Islands about 5 A.M. of the 27th. The current from midnight until 2 A.M., the first half of the flood-tide, set to the northward, at 3 A.M. it was setting towards the north-east, and from 4 to 6 A.M., when we left, it set to the southward. This agrees with the supposed set of the current the previous night, when we were south-west of Conical Rock, the latter part of the flood-tidal-stream running to the southward instead of setting to the northward. The 'Discovery,' steering one steady course from Cape York, also experienced a current which set the ship to the south and west.

Near the many icebergs stranded on the shallows about the Cary Islands, the temperature of the surface water fell from 40° to 31½°, but immediately we left the ice behind us, steering towards the Greenland coast for Hakluyt Island, it rose again to 38° and 40°, agreeing with the observations of the previous day. Coupled with the native report that the sea near Hakluyt Island is never completely frozen over during the winter, this high temperature is remarkable.

The 27th brought us a continuation of calm clear weather. The two ships, one in tow of the other, passed in the afternoon between Northumberland and Hakluyt Islands. A sounding in mid-channel gave 100 fathoms with rocky bottom. The water was literally black with the multitudes of little auks, and guillemots were numerous; there is an immense breeding station of these birds on the north-east face of Hakluyt Island. The passage between these two islands is very imposing; on either side rise almost perpendicular cliffs of sandstones to a height of not less than 800 feet; near to the sea strata of a bright red sandstone predominate, but higher up the cliffs these alternate with light yellow, the whole series dipping at an angle of 4° or 5° to the south. The summit of Northumberland Island being covered with an ice-cap,

NORTH-WEST POINT, NORTHUMBERLAND ISLAND.

presents a miniature of the Greenland *mer de glace*; many small glaciers descend its flanks, and one of large size occupies its north-west face. The appearance of these descending ice-streams presented a marked contrast to the warm-coloured sandstone cliffs, whilst the effect was enhanced by the bright green vegetation growing on the ledges, fertilized by the presence of innumerable sea-birds.

Passing Inglefield Gulf we noticed the ice stretching from shore to shore east of Cape Acland, completely closing it; but Murchison Sound and Whale Sound were clear. The Prince of Wales Mountains on Ellesmere Land, and the coast range from Cape Faraday to the north were distinctly visible.

To the northward of the Cary Islands, and as far north as Cape Alexander, the icebergs were of the largest size, the majority of them being table-topped. The 'Discovery' measured one rising two hundred and ninety feet above the water-line.

Cape Acland on its north-western face presents an escarpment of bright red rock, probably sandstone, and the cliffs of the mainland as far north as Sontag Bay show similar coloured horizontal stratification. Early in the morning of the 28th we were close to Cape Alexander, and passing Sutherland Island at a distance of about a mile and a half. This island, composed of a rough-grained sandstone, appears to have been worn down by glacier action: I estimated its height at about 300 feet. Cape Alexander is a noble headland presenting a sea face of probably 1,400 feet; it is separated from the main by two enormous glaciers, which, descending on either flank, enter Hartstene Bay on the one side, and on the other submerge directly behind Sutherland Island. The cape is composed at its base of a light yellow sandstone, horizontally stratified, midway a band of dark columnar basalt rests upon this sandstone, and above that point, intercalated beds of basalts and sandstones continue to its summit. This same formation extends along the whole south side of Hartstene Bay.

CHAPTER IV.

WHILE we were steering close under Cape Alexander
a breeze sprang up from the northward and retarded
our progress, but by 7 A.M., of the 28th, we were at
anchor in twelve fathoms on the north side of Hartstene Bay. The anchorage I selected was a bay on
the southern side of Sunrise Point, a very convenient
halting-place, but only fit for use while northerly or
easterly winds prevail. Generally speaking the shore
was bordered by an ice-foot, but this was not quite
continuous ; a number of detached heavy pieces of
ice, the remains of hummocks formed during previous
gales, lay aground in thirty feet of water, pointing
out the shallows, while many rocks, both above and
below water, studded the shore. A stream of some
volume, which drains the valley lying north of Dodge's
Mountains, empties itself into the bay.

The red gneiss, which forms the basement on
which rest the sedimentary strata and basalts of
Foulke Fiord, forms the shore-line from the settlement
of Etah. Northwards at Cape Ohlsen and Life-Boat

Cove, and as far as we could see inland, granitoid and gneissoid rocks prevail.

The total absence of drift-ice between Cape York and Smith Sound, and the fact that a strong northerly wind was bringing no ice down, led me to conclude that the main pack to the northward had not yet broken up, and that we had arrived at Hartstene Bay at the most opportune time, when the ice at the head of Baffin's Bay had drifted south and before the northern ice, which breaks up later in the season, had drifted through Smith Sound. A few days subsequently the sea between Littleton Island and Cape Sabine, which now permitted free progress, was so ice-encumbered as to prevent any vessel crossing the channel.

As a northerly wind prevented our advance except at a large expenditure of coal, I took the opportunity to visit Life-Boat Cove, where a part of the crew of the U.S.S. ' Polaris ' wintered in 1872–73. I was in hopes of finding the pendulum and other instruments which were necessarily abandoned on the retreat of the party, in small boats, to the south.

Leaving the ships at anchor, and accompanied by Commander Markham, we started in a whale-boat. Owing to the strong breeze and the ebb-tide running to the southward we had considerable trouble in rounding Sunrise Point, but after passing Littleton Island the wind fell, and the fog ascending, gradually gave place to a fine bright afternoon. There is so little depth of water in Life-Boat Cove, that the ' Polaris ' must have grounded close to the entrance of the bay. The land being quite free from snow, we had no difficulty in finding the locality where Polaris

House stood.   No part of that structure remained intact, but pieces of wood, cases, empty tins, bits of clothing, worn-out sea-boots, seal-skins, and a hetero-geneous collection of odds and ends, marked the site. The cairn mentioned by Dr. Bessels and Mr. Bryant as the depository of instruments and boxes of books was readily discovered, but contained nothing.   Numerous small *caches* containing seal and walrus-meat were scattered over the small peninsula and near the site of the house.   Apart from each other, and with-out any protection, we found four or five boxes, each covered with heavy stones to prevent the wind moving them, and having the lids secured on by a rope. Besides one thermometer, unfortunately not a self-registering one, they contained scraps of skin-clothing, old mitts, carpenters' tools, files, needles, and many small articles of the greatest use to the Eskimo, but apparently they had not been disturbed since the abandonment of the place.   A few books were found, which were afterwards forwarded to the United States, but no pendulum, transit-instrument, or chronometer. Three skin-boats left on the shore, weighted down with stones, were in fair order.   The smallest one was taken for conveyance to Cape Sabine.

On our return we landed at Littleton Island, and on the S.W. brow erected a cairn, and deposited a notice containing a short account of the movements and prospects of the Expedition up to that time.   There was not a particle of ice in sight from a high station on Littleton Island; but our sportsmen who roamed over the higher grounds on the main land reported that they had distinguished an ice blink to the northward;

which news proved to be correct, for ice was met the next day at a distance of twenty miles from the island.

A great number of eider ducks were nesting on the north shore of the largest island; the ducklings were about a week old, but several nests still contained eggs. With the rising tide the current between the islands set towards the N.E. The time of high and low-water agreed with the observations of Dr. Hayes. In the record left on Littleton Island I stated that it was my intention to cross direct to the west shore of Smith Sound, and to proceed northward along that coast. Anticipating that it might be difficult for a sledge-party to communicate with the island, I added that should the cairn not be visited by a party from the Expedition before June 1876, our despatches would be found on Cape Isabella, and that I hoped to leave records at Cape Sabine, Dobbin Bay, Carl Ritter Bay, and Cape Bellot.

During my absence from the ships, explorations were made in various directions. Captain Stephenson, accompanied by several officers, explored Foulke Fiord to ascertain its suitability as a winter-harbour, and visited the valley at its head, where Dr. Hayes' expedition obtained as many reindeer as they could consume. Our sportsmen were, however, not so fortunate, for after a very arduous walk amongst the valleys at the base of Brother John's Glacier, ascending it and crossing its face to the other side of the valley, only seven reindeer were seen and one secured.

The settlement of Etah was visited, but no natives were there; it consisted of three stone *igloos*, and one hut roofed over with canvas spread on spars.

Many relics from the 'Polaris' were lying about, such as clothes, pieces of books, ice-chisels, fish-hooks, and bottles.   A large amount of seal and walrus-blubber was *cached* in the neighbourhood.   A dog-sledge made entirely of bone, with runners ingeniously constructed of pieces of tusk of the walrus, was found hidden in a cleft of the rock ; it was of course not interfered with. Arrows were found in the Eskimo huts and in the neighbourhood.

The remains of numerous ancient settlements are scattered along the shore between Jensen Point and the village of Etah ; the sites are marked by enormous quantities of bones lying around, which speaks forcibly to the animal wealth of this neighbourhood.   It would be difficult to assign any definite age to these remains, but evidently Port Foulke must have been a favourite and productive station of the natives for a long course of years.   Reindeer and walrus bones were the most prominent in these kitchen-middens.   It was remarked that all the bones of the deer which contained marrow had been split, the *crania* had been broken in through the front of the skull, and sometimes the base had been knocked off, in order to render easy the extraction of the brain.   Remains of seals were very abundant, with bones of foxes and hares, also thousands of the *sterna* of little auks.

The cliffs on both sides of Foulke Fiord present bold escarpments, and are a continuation of the strata which form Cape Alexander.

These formations, which consist of various coloured sandstones abounding in ripple marks and inter-bedded with traps and basalts rest unconformably

on gneissoid rocks, and have a thickness of about a
thousand feet. Unfortunately no fossil organisms
were found, but a piece of coal was picked up not
far from the head of the fiord. Judging from their
appearance, Captain Feilden is of opinion that these
strata may be an extension of the Miocene deposits
of Disco Island and the Noursoak Peninsula.

Hartstene Bay is the best winter-station on the
North Greenland coast; its shores are washed by a
warm current coming from the southward, whilst the
projecting promontories of Cape Hatherton and Cape
Ohlsen deflect the Polar current to the other side of
the sound. Owing to the narrowing of the channel
at the entrance of Smith Sound the velocity of the
tidal currents is greatly augmented, and even in winter
large water-spaces are kept open. The moisture and
warmth imparted to the atmosphere by the uncovered
water moderates the climate in its vicinity to some
extent, and consequently we find in the neighbourhood of Hartstene Bay a land comparatively well
vegetated and a great abundance of animal life. As
Port Foulke can be visited yearly from the southward
in all but very exceptional seasons, it can be recommended as an important base if further explorations by
Smith Sound are hereafter undertaken.

On the morning of the 29th the ships crossed
Smith Sound under sail, with a northerly wind, steering direct for Cape Isabella. The snow-clad coast of
Ellesmere Land was very clearly defined, the black
headlands, separated by glacier-filled valleys, standing
out prominently from the white background. Cape
Sabine, which is formed of a red syenite, differs much in

colour from the headlands north and south of it, and is very conspicuous. I had at first determined to send the ' Discovery ' direct to Cape Sabine, there to establish a station, while the ' Alert ' erected a cairn at Cape Isabella ; but considering it important that all the officers and men in both ships should be acquainted with the exact position of each cairn and depôt of provisions, I kept the two vessels in company. However exact the description of the position of a depôt may be, it is extremely difficult for a traveller during the spring to find a cairn or mark which has been established during the period of the year when the land was wholly or partially free from snow. The choice of a spot on which to build a cairn that can be readily found by a stranger is not so easy a matter as may be supposed. In the present case it was rendered more difficult in consequence of the necessity of guarding against the depredations of the Eskimo, who are said to wander round the shores of Ellesmere Land. To obtain this safety for the provisions destined for our travellers it was necessary to hide them away in clefts of the rock at some distance from the cairn which contained directions for finding the depôt.

As we approached the western shore a snowstorm worked its way over the land from the S.W., and reached us just as we arrived at the cape. In order to take advantage of the fair wind, and the snowstorm preventing those on board the ' Discovery' seeing the position chosen for the cairn, I ordered Captain Stephenson to proceed to Cape Sabine. Commander Markham accompanied by Captain Feilden landed in a small bay on the south side of the extreme point of the cape. After an extremely rough scramble up one of the gullies, a cairn was erected on the outer spur of Cape Isabella, 700 feet above the water-line; a cask for letters and a few cases of preserved meat being hidden away on a lower point, about 300 feet high, magnetic west of the cairn. Cape Isabella is formed of a fine-grained grey granite and a coarse orthoclase granite, the difference in colour between these two rocks being very distinctly shown on the face of the cliffs. While the party was on shore the surf on the rocks prevented the boat remaining at the landing place; on their return at 5 P.M., we proceeded to the northward, the weather continuing misty with snow.

At 4 A.M., of the 30th, having run thirty-eight miles by the patent log, we stopped steaming and waited for the weather to clear. During the night we had passed a quantity of loose pack-ice which obliged us to keep well out from the coast. At 5 A.M., we observed the 'Discovery' close to the land, with five or six miles of heavy pack-ice cutting us off both from her and the shore. Although the land was hidden by fog the atmosphere at sea was clear and the weather calm. Perceiving a likely-looking channel leading to the westward, we steamed towards it, but before reaching the entrance it closed up and prevented our advance. At 9 A.M., an hour before high-water, on the slackening of the flood or north-running tide, the ice opened considerably. Observing that the 'Discovery' was not moving, we bore into the pack, and at 3.30 P.M., succeeded with a little trouble in gaining the land and securing the ships in a convenient harbour formed by a group of rocky islands. These we supposed by our latitude at noon to be near Leconte Island, but on the atmosphere clearing we found that we were inside of Brevoort Island and within two miles of Cape Sabine, which had been placed on the latest chart ten miles too far north. During our eleven hours' run from Cape Isabella, half the time with an ebb and half with a flood-tide, we were set by the current ten miles to the southward.

The ice through which we had passed consisted principally of old heavy floes, ten to twelve feet in thickness and a hundred yards to a quarter of a mile in diameter. Intermixed with these were others of one-season ice, so rotten and honeycombed as to show that they had not recently been subjected to heavy pressure. Scattered amongst the pack-ice were several icebergs, nearly all of which were flat-topped; very few of them had altered their line of flotation since they first separated from their parent glaciers.

Finding no bottom at a depth of twenty fathoms close to the shore, the ships were secured by hawsers to ice-anchors buried in the level ice-foot or ice-ledge lining the shore. The northerly wind kept the ships from swinging broadside against the land, they were thus ready to start at a moment's notice. The upper surface of the ice-foot was twenty to forty feet broad, dependent on the inclination of the land, and level with the high-water rise of spring-tides. At low-water the rocks at the base of its vertical sea-face were bare, leaving a cliff about ten feet high, which when the tide was out could only be ascended through one of the slippery passages cut by the water running down from the land. The harbour, which was named after

Lieutenant Julius Payer, the distinguished and successful Arctic traveller, is a most convenient waiting place
for vessels attempting to proceed northward by Smith
Sound. Brevoort Island, a syenitic rock which attains
an altitude of about 500 feet, shelters it completely
from seaward. Stalknecht Island and a long peninsula about 150 feet high protect it from the southward.
The harbour has three entrances, one from the northward and two from the southward, one of which is
sure to be clear of ice, whenever the outside pack,
driven off shore by a westerly wind, would permit
navigation. The channels being narrow prevent the
entrance of large floes ; but, owing to the great depth of
water, icebergs readily enter and have to be guarded
against.

During the afternoon Captain Stephenson and the
crew of the ' Discovery ' were engaged landing a depôt
of provisions, consisting of 240 rations, for the use of
any sledge-party that might be travelling from the
north towards Littleton Island. This depôt was
placed on the peninsula that forms the southern protection of the harbour. A cairn was built on the
summit of Brevoort Island, in which a record paper
was subsequently placed.

Having established our provision depôt and record,
I felt very desirous of ascertaining how far the water in
the middle of Smith Sound would permit our advance
to the northward. The ice in the offing being fairly
open, I accordingly started with the two ships at
10 P.M., just before high-water. We had far greater
trouble in pushing our way through the pack than
when we passed through it the previous morning, and

during the intervening time the ice-stream had doubled in width. The ships, consequently, did not arrive in the clear water until past 1 A.M., of the 31st. Following the edge of the pack but not entering it, we were led off to the N.E., for about twenty-five miles; it then bent round to the S.E., and effectually cut us off from the east coast of Greenland.

It was now perfectly certain that our struggles with the ice were about to commence, and I had to choose whether to force our way through the pack or to advance along the eastern or western shores of the Sound. A middle passage through the heavy pack drifting to the southward, through an ever-narrowing channel, was quite out of the question, and Dr. Kane had fully proved the impossibility of forcing a passage along the exposed coast-line eastward of Rensselaer Harbour. I therefore decided to proceed to Cape Sabine, and endeavour to force our way along the western shore.

On returning to the western side of the strait, a heavy snowstorm quite obscured the land and prevented my selecting the best water-channels through the pack. While waiting for the weather to clear, the ships were made fast to the lee side of an iceberg, where the faster drifting surface-ice kept a pool of water clear. After passing an hour in this position, partly from the wind shifting and partly by the iceberg turning round, we found ourselves being forced against the side of the berg by the pressure of the pack, and were obliged to make a hurried retreat. Fortunately our ice-anchors slipped out easily, or we should have been entrapped.

The wind having now freshened from the N.E., and the flood-tide preventing the ice drifting to the southward, there was every probability that the pack would close together and endanger our reaching the shore. Accordingly I pushed on through the snow and mist rather blindly, but was rewarded by suddenly finding that we were back at the entrance of Payer Harbour, and before noon, as I thought at the time, we had bidden a long good-bye to the main pack. During the afternoon a strong north-westerly wind and ebb-tide, which carried the ice and icebergs quickly to the southward, completely imprisoned us ; but we had the satisfaction of knowing that a large water-space was forming farther to the north, ready for our use by-and-by.

The north-westerly wind continued throughout August 1, and combined with the ebb-tide brought the ice so fast to the southward that at 9 A.M., there was no longer any water in sight in the middle of the strait from our look-out hill. The only pool left was in the bay immediately south of us, which was kept open by the slight westing in the wind. To the northward, between our position and Bache Island, not a single pool of water was to be seen. For a short time, during the strength of the flood or north-running tide, both the surface-ice and the icebergs were carried to the northward against the wind, which was blowing with a force of 2 to 5 ; but from its having less effect on the deeply immersed icebergs, they were moving slower than the pack.

At 11 A.M., in a heavy squall, the ' Alert's ' ice-anchors slipped out of their beds in the ice-foot, and

obliged us to let go the bower anchor in twenty-one
fathoms, the ship drifting into thirty-five fathoms.
In the evening the weather cleared up and enabled
me to get a few bearings with a theodolite from the
summit of Cape Sabine, some 1,200 feet above the
sea-level. The Victoria and Albert Mountains, fifty
miles distant, showed very distinctly. The channel
between Ellesmere Land and Bache Island was seen to
be nearly closed by a group of rocky islets ; but there
was apparently a northern passage on the westward
side of the island. The islands were named after
Lieutenant Carl Weyprecht, the commander of the
Austrian discovery ship ' Tegetthoff.'

The wind was so strong, and my feet so wet and
cold after climbing up the rugged snow-clad hill-side,
that I was forced to content myself with a sketch and
the most important bearings. Not a particle of water
was to be seen, and the sea between Cape Sabine and
Littleton Island, which four days ago was free from
ice, was now completely blocked.

The high water full and change was found to be at
11 h. 56 m., rise and fall about twelve feet.

The red syenite rock forming Cape Sabine and
the islands in the neighbourhood of Payer Harbour
is sterile and barren to the last degree. During the
three days we were detained there, although parties
from the ships explored the whole of the immediate
neighbourhood, very little animal-life was seen. Six
narwhals were on one occasion observed playing in the
harbour, and a colony of glaucous gulls were found
nesting in a steep cliff on Brevoort Island. A few
eider ducks' nests were obtained, and a large seal (*Phoca*

barbata), the *oo-sook* of the Greenlanders, was shot, also five eider ducks, one or two dovekies, and a little auk, a contrast to the large amount of game obtainable at Port Foulke. Along the margin of the shore of Payer Harbour were several rings of stones marking the summer tents of Eskimo. The fragments of bone scattered about these spots were lichen-covered and friable, showing that they were of great antiquity. Traces of a more recent visit were, however, observed, and a harpoon was found with a tip of wrought iron.

The ice remaining closed during the 2nd, and the light wind holding out no prospect of its opening, I thought it advisable to occupy the time by sending a party round Cape Sabine to ascertain the nature of the coast-line. I also wanted to see whether a twenty-foot ice-boat could be carried on an eight-man sledge, the only one we had ready. The boat having been lashed on to the sledge, I started with Commander Markham, Lieutenants Aldrich and May, and five strong men, but after advancing about a mile, in consequence of the boat being too long for the sledge and the ice encountered being extremely rough, we gave up the attempt and returned on board. The fifteen-foot boat, which fitted the sledge, was dragged easily enough, but it was then too late in the day to start again, as I was in hopes of the evening's flood-tide opening up the ice, and permitting an advance with the ships. The evening, however, turned out calm with a fog, and the ice remained closed.

A light southerly wind on the 3rd, giving hopes of a change in the ice, kept me anxiously looking out from the nearest hill-top. At 9 A.M., the north-running tide having begun to move the ice from the harbour, and slight cracks appearing in the offing, both ships were got under sail, in order to be ready to push round Cape Sabine immediately a passage opened, which I fully expected would be the case. When starting, being only a ship's length from the shore, we calculated on a friendly piece of ice acting as a buffer between the vessel and the rocks; but at the important moment when its services were required, it slipped from the ship's bow, and the tide carried us so close to the shore that the heel of the rudder touched for a moment. By the time we were clear, the cracks in the ice instead of opening had closed, so the ships were kept tacking back and forwards, until high-water, after which, giving up all further hope for the day, we beat back to our old quarters. The constant tacking, and the close shaves between the two ships, as we passed each other, as well as with the rocks occasionally, created much excitement and did good to all. In the evening the wind freshened from the southward and kept a space of water about half a mile in diameter clear of ice near the mouth of the harbour, but off Cape Sabine the ice still remained closely packed.

The wind freshening from the southward on the 4th drifted a quantity of small pieces of ice across to the northern side of the harbour, where the ships were anchored, and prevented our communicating with the shore except by hauling a boat over the ice. At 2 A.M., while I was anxiously watching for and expecting a change to occur with the ebb-tide, the ice off Cape Sabine began to move, drifting to the east-

ward out of Hayes
Sound. A signal was
immediately made to
start under sail, get-
ting up steam in the
meantime. By the
time we were outside
the harbour, a clear
channel had opened
round the cape, and
with lightened hearts
and much rejoicing we
ran quickly along the
land. Our passage to
the northward still re-
mained blocked by im-
penetrable ice ; so that
whether we pleased or
not, an advance could
only be made in a
north - westerly direc-
tion up Hayes Sound.

Very heavy ice was
piled up more than
thirty feet high against
the extreme northern
point of Cape Sabine,
indicating recent se-
vere pressure from the
pack. The ice met
with between Elles-
mere Land and Bache

BUCHANAN STRAIT, HAYES SOUND.

Island had evidently been formed in the neighbourhood during the previous winter, and being in one
unbroken sheet, the water must have been clear of
ice-pieces when the autumn frost set in. It was now
very rotten, had lately broken away from the shore,
and was only waiting for a westerly wind to carry it
off into Smith Sound.

As we advanced under the lee of the land the
wind died away, and rendered steam necessary. We
then ran quickly to the north-west along a slightly in-
dented coast-line, passing Cocked-hat Hill, a very conspicuous landmark, situated on an island close to the
shore. The hills on the north coast of Ellesmere Land
are abrupt and rugged, rising to a height of 1,200 to
1,500 feet, with glaciers here and there descending to
the sea. By 9 A.M., we arrived at the end of the water-
channel, where the ice stretching completely across the
strait effectually blocked any further advance. Ramming the ships into the rotten ice, we endeavoured
to form temporary docks ; but as fast as we pushed our
way into the floes their sides split up.

After waiting about an hour, a narrow channel
opened close along shore, through which a push was
made with only an inch or two of spare water under the
ships' keels. We then gained a large water-space which
carried us a few miles farther up the gulf, but then
the ice, locked in by the Weyprecht Islands, formed
a barrier. To the southward of us we had opened a
long fiord, entirely free of ice, running to the S.W.,
about eight miles in depth and three and a half in
width. Snow-capped hills upwards of 2,000 feet high
with steep cliffs formed the shores of the fiord ; glaciers

occupied the higher portion of each of the valleys, but none of them appeared to reach the sea. This fiord is protected from the entry of any large floes by an island at its mouth, to which was given the name of the Three Sisters, from a similar number of conspicuous conical hills rising from its base.

Wishing to anchor at the entrance of the fiord ready to take advantage of any movement in the outer ice, we sounded our way towards the shore, opposite to a large valley, off which I expected to find a bank with shallow water. Instead of this we obtained no bottom with fifty fathoms at a distance of fifty yards from the beach. Not finding an anchorage, we retraced our course about a mile to a small rocky bay scarcely large enough to receive the two ships, situated at the extreme end of one of the spurs of the Prince of Wales Mountains. I named it Alexandra Haven.

As soon as the ships were secured, the sportsmen started in all directions to explore the neighbourhood. In the valley off which I had endeavoured to anchor, was found what in these regions may be termed a richly vegetated plain extending about two miles back from the coast, and fronting two valleys each containing a glacier. These glaciers coming from opposite directions abut the one against the other, maintaining a constant struggle. Those amongst us who were fortunate enough to visit the locality, which was named Twin Glacier Valley, were well repaid by the grandeur of the scene.

The summer thaw of ice and snow had produced a broad watercourse down the valley, which at this date was occupied by a pellucid stream of some twenty

yards in width.   The flora was surprisingly rich : large
patches of *Epilobium latifolium* were growing on sand-
banks in the dry watercourse, its handsome deep pink
blossoms appearing somewhat out of keeping with the
Arctic surroundings.   Recent traces of reindeer and
musk-oxen were very numerous.   Had we remained
any length of time in the vicinity we should doubtless
have obtained a fair supply of game ; as it was, only

TWIN GLACIER, BUCHANAN SOUND.

three hares were obtained by the men of the ' Discovery.'   It being a fine afternoon the ships' companies
were allowed to wander over the hills : one of the
crew, miscalculating his power of walking in heavy
clothing, had to be carried back on a stretcher.   A
report having spread that musk-oxen were in the
vicinity, the appearance on the beach of the men bearing their sick comrade gave rise to the impression on
board the ships that an animal had been shot.   When

the truth was discovered, the feeling of disappointment at not obtaining fresh provisions considerably lessened the sympathy which would otherwise have been bestowed on the invalid.

Gneiss and syenite seemed to be the prevailing rocks along the northern shore of Ellesmere Land; but at an elevation of 1,500 feet a dense thin-bedded limestone was found capping the rocks. In the Twin Glacier Valley, the stream exposed strata of argillaceous limestone and fine-grained sandstone. No fossils were obtained, but the locality is geologically interesting, as the point of juncture between the sedimentary and granitic rocks on the western side of Smith Sound.

During the night of the 5th the ice opened up a lead to the westward, and by 9 A.M., the end of the ebb tide, the passage was quite clear along shore. Having a fine breeze from the S.W., the ships made a sternboard out of our small harbour, and rounding Three Sisters Island, off which was a rocky bank with shallow water, stood along shore to the westward. In hopes of obtaining a steadier breeze I kept close to the edge of the pack, but the wind shortly died away. At 2 P.M., we had advanced under steam beyond the eastern group of rocky islets. Finding that the strait took a turn towards the westward, I endeavoured to force our way across it to the northward where a pool of water was to be seen near Point Koldewey, from which we were separated by a quantity of rotten ice. This I attempted to force, but after an hour's ramming, we were brought to a standstill and thoroughly beset by ice in such a decayed condition that it was unsafe to

permit men to cross from one ship to the other.
During the night the weather was calm, and the ships
drifted slowly backwards and forwards at the mercy
of the tidal current, but in the main in an easterly
direction.

On the 6th, with the ebb-tide the ships drifted
to the southward towards the open water near the
shore. In the expectation of obtaining a good view
of the strait, Captain Stephenson and I landed by
dragging a boat over the ice to the water. A number
of the officers also went to explore the neighbourhood, but kept within sight of the ships in case of
being recalled. Landing at nearly low-water we had
great difficulty in climbing up the steep and slippery
side of the ice-foot. From an ascent of 1,500 feet we
could not determine the continuation of Hayes Sound,
owing to the interposition of rocky islands; but by
the trend of the mountain ranges the sound or fiord
may be assumed to run for a long distance to the
westward. There is apparently no water connection
with the opening north of Bache Island, unless a communication exists far to the westward. On turning
to the eastward we had the great satisfaction of seeing
that the ice at the entrance of the sound was clearing
out, and that there would soon be a clear water-
passage between Cape Sabine and Cape Albert. We
accordingly hastened back to our boat, deciding to
push to the northward along the east shore of the so-
called Bache Island.

Our sportsmen only obtained a single ptarmigan
(*Lagopus rupestris*), the first specimen procured by us
in Smith Sound. Insects were not uncommon, the

mosquitoes being particularly annoying. Two species
of butterflies, a *Colias* and an *Argynnis*, two kinds of
moths and a humble-bee (*Bombus*), were captured.
The shores of the coast where we landed were studded
with ancient Eskimo dwellings, numerous *caches*, and
marks of summer tents. The bones of a large whale,
no doubt *Balæna mysticetus*, in pieces over five feet
long and a foot broad, had been used as rafters to
one of the igloos or dwelling-places. Numerous
bones of the musk-ox, seal, walrus, and narwhal were
found.

I regret extremely that our short stay prevented
our ascertaining whether Hayes Sound is a channel
leading to a western sea. The flood-tide certainly
ran to the westward inshore ; but Lieutenant Parr,
a very careful observer, reports that on two occasions
when the ship was stationary and he in charge of the
deck, he observed the ice in the offing setting to the
eastward with the flood-tide. This may have been
occasioned by partial winds or an eddy tidal current.
Although we saw no seals in the sound, yet the numerous remains scattered about the old Eskimo dwellings
show that they have been obtained in large numbers in
this locality, and this is seldom the case in an inclosed
bay, where the water is more ready to freeze than in
an open channel. Certainly a large colony of Eskimo
frequented the neighbourhood at one time, and we
may conclude that they travelled from the southward.
It remains to be ascertained whether the route was
along the glacier-lined shore on the western side of
Baffin's Bay, or by a more protected inlet to the westward of Ellesmere Land.

While waiting for the return of Captain Stephenson a sounding was obtained by the ' Discovery ' in forty-two fathoms, the minimum temperature of the water, between the surface and that depth, being 29°·5.

This low temperature was afterwards confirmed by a large number of independent observations.

In Smith Sound, with the exception of a surface film heated during summer, the temperature of the seawater, like that in the Antarctic Ocean, always remains colder than the melting point of freshwater ice. The icebergs floating in a medium of about 29°·5 can therefore only decay in those parts exposed to the rays of the sun, and consequently remain table-topped cubes of ice, with the original surface of the parent glacier floating uppermost, until they drift into Baffin's Bay. There, meeting with water at a temperature above 32°, the submerged portions melt rapidly, and the icebergs, by frequently altering their line of flota-tion, as they decay unequally, assume the fantastic shapes so frequently depicted in views of Arctic scenery. It is remarkable that no icebergs were met with in the western waters of Hayes Sound. This indicates that there are no discharging glaciers on its shores. Probably the Prince of Wales Mountains protect them from the moist south-westerly winds.

CHAPTER V.

RE-ENTER SMITH SOUND—CAUGHT IN THE PACK—ESCAPE—CAPE VIC-
TORIA—FRANKLIN PIERCE BAY—WALRUS—NORMAN LOCKYER ISLAND
—CAPE HAWKS—WASHINGTON IRVING ISLAND—DOBBIN BAY—DOG-
SICKNESS—PERILOUS POSITION OF SHIPS—ROUNDING CAPE FRAZER.

SHORTLY after noon of the 6th, as soon as Captain
Stephenson and I had returned on board our respective ships, we made sail with a southerly wind blowing
off the land, and ran back to the eastward out of Hayes
Sound and Buchanan Strait. As we advanced, the
water-channel between Ellesmere Land and the pack
which rested against the south shore of Bache Island
widened considerably, until off Cape Camperdown only
a few patches of detached floe-pieces remained, where
three days previously not a pool of water existed. To
the eastward there was much water with an ice-blink on
the horizon pointing out the position of the main pack.
Arriving off Cape Albert, a great number of icebergs
and heavy pieces of ice were observed, either lying
aground on a bank or collected together by eddy
currents. The wind dying away, steam was raised, and
we advanced quickly to the northward with light hearts,
looking in vain for the channel reported to run between
Capes Albert and Victoria, dividing Bache Island into
two. We satisfied ourselves that no channel exists there.

Skirting the pack, we were led away from the land to about six miles east of Cape Victoria, but there the edge trended round to the south-east. By retracing our course a few miles I could have entered a water-channel near the shore of Bache Island; there was also a narrow but very tempting channel about two miles long leading directly towards Cape Hawks, with only six or eight miles of ice, apparently open between it and a large water-space stretching out from the south shore of Grinnell Land.

It was now 10 P M., the flood-tide was commencing and the weather was calm. The pack, lately opened and driven to the eastward by the westerly wind, was sure, on the subsidence of the pressure, to work its way back again and in all probability would close up the water-channels. The northern sun, shining brightly and casting a dazzling glimmer on ice and water alike, rendered it difficult to distinguish the most open channels; but with such a prospect of reaching the mainland few could resist the temptation; so at the risk of being beset, I pushed on towards the north through the pack. But, by the time we had reached the end of the two-mile channel the ice had closed everywhere, our retreat was cut off and we were caught in the trap.

No choice was left me but to secure each ship in a notch or bight in the heaviest floe that I could reach, and wait for a change either favourable or otherwise. No one of the floes was sufficiently large to permit the two ships being docked near each other; neither did I deem it advisable, surrounded as we were by numerous icebergs, so to imprison the ships.

After seeing them secured in a fairly large pool of water, I had just entered my cabin when the officer of the watch following me stated that the ice was closing in on every side. On reaching the deck I found that the 'Alert' was surrounded by the ice and drifting towards an iceberg only a quarter of a mile distant.

Signalling to Captain Stephenson, 'Take care of iceberg,' he was able to haul the 'Discovery' a hundred yards ahead; but his ship was then similarly caught in the pack, and immovable either by manual labour or by steam power.

Both ships were immediately prepared for a severe nip; the rudders and screws were raised, the boats turned inboard, the yards braced fore and aft, and all possible precautions taken.

At first the 'Discovery' was apparently in the more dangerous position; but shortly the ice by wheeling round brought the 'Alert' directly in the path of the iceberg, against the side of which the intermediate surface ice was piling itself up as it forced its way past it. Had the pack consisted of ordinary ice from four to six feet in thickness, which would have crumbled up against the side of the berg, the danger would have been even more imminent, but the great thickness of the floe to which the ships were secured proved their safety; for on its advanced edge reaching the iceberg, it withstood the strain without splitting and for the moment checked the main drift of the pack. Very shortly afterwards the accumulating pressure in the rear, exerting its force alternately on either side of the floe as it hung unequally balanced across the face of the berg, broke off large pieces, some of them one hundred feet in diameter. These being heavy enough in themselves to withstand a considerable pressure, became collected in front of the iceberg, and formed as it were a point of heavy ice sufficiently strong to divide and split up the floe, and to act as a buffer to fend off the ship; this it did in our case most successfully. As the ship began to heel over with the increasing pressure, and officers and men working alike had given the last haul to the screw purchases, and when there was nothing left for anyone to do but to look on as calmly as possible waiting for what might happen, the corner of the floe split off and the ship, amidst a collection of débris ice, slid past the side of the berg without damage ; the 'Discovery,' hidden from view on the other side of the iceberg, reading the signal at the masthead ' All safe.' The ships were then secured by ice-anchors to the lee side of the iceberg, where the faster drift of the surface ice left a small pool.

The next thirty hours were spent in constant struggles with the pack, the ships being moved from the shelter of one iceberg to another as circumstances rendered necessary ; and, owing to the unsteady wind and the variable tidal currents, we were never quiet for more than an hour at any one time.

Had I allowed the ships to drift with the ice we should have been carried to the southward deeper into the pack ; there was therefore no alternative but to get up full steam and be prepared to take instant advantage of every change that might occur in our favour. The ships were seldom separated for long, and now, as on many other occasions, they assisted each other. The 'Discovery' was handled in the most masterly and daring manner combined with great judgment, qualities essential in Arctic navigation. She, as well as the 'Alert,' ran not a few hairbreadth escapes. Once in particular when in following us through a closing channel between an iceberg and heavy floe-piece, before getting quite past the danger she was caught and nipped against the berg, fortunately without suffering severely.

Having less beam than the 'Alert,' a finer bow and an overhanging stem, the 'Discovery' proved to be best adapted for forcing her way through the pack. Being backed some distance astern to allow space for the débris ice from a former blow to float away, and for the vessel to attain sufficient distance for the accumulation of momentum with which to strike a second, when forced ahead at her utmost speed she would break her way into the ice for a distance of about twenty feet before the force of the blow was expended. We found that floes up to four feet in thickness and in a soft state, melting not freezing, might be charged with impunity; thicker or harder ice had to be left alone.

It speaks well for our chronometers, and the manner in which they were secured, that their rates were little affected by the frequent concussions on this and on many after occasions.

It must be obvious that the commander of an Arctic expedition can obtain but little rest during the navigable season. In ice-navigation one false decision may imperil the chance of farther advance, he therefore can depute his responsibility to no one, but must be constantly on watch himself. Fortunately for his health an Arctic season lasts only for from three to six weeks.

On the morning of the 8th the weather was calm
and the ice appeared inclined to open, but we made
little advance until the ebb-tide commenced about
4 A.M.   After a large expenditure of manual labour,
gunpowder, and coal. we succeeded in pushing both
ships into more open ice and, by skirting the large
floes as much as possible, we found ourselves at 7 A.M.
in a large pool of water with only one neck of ice
between us and the shore water off Cape Victoria.
On arriving near the barrier I found, to my dismay,
that the floes were closing in as fast as we broke away
a passage.   After half an hour's rather anxious work,
the two ships frequently charging together, and the
' Alert's ' rudder-head being sprung when necessarily
going astern full speed, I observed that the points of
a turning floe would probably offer a chance of escape
in another direction.   Making a hasty flank movement
we arrived just in time to take advantage of the barrier
when at its weakest, and with one charge together, we
broke our way through and escaped, everyone heartily
glad to be in free water once more with no more serious damage than sprung rudders. Within half an hour
there was not a single pool of water in the four miles'
breadth of ice through which we had lately struggled.

The pack, fortunately for us, consisted generally of
ice from four to six feet in thickness ; yet there were
many heavier floés which must have been from twelve
to twenty feet thick ; the surface of these consisted of
a series of mottled ice-knolls of a blue colour, the
melted down remains of former hummocks, denoting
great age.

Previous to our departure from England, although

ice of a similar description had frequently been met with, it was popularly supposed that it was formed only in protected bays which seldom cleared out. One Arctic authority asked me to endeavour to place it beyond a doubt whether it were possible for salt-water ice to attain more than a mean thickness of seven feet; and Dr. Hayes, one of the latest explorers and an undoubted authority, was of opinion that ice soon reaches its maximum thickness by direct freezing; he states, indeed, that he had never seen an ice-table formed by direct freezing that exceeded eighteen feet in thickness. I was, therefore, naturally astonished to see such large quantities of heavy ice.

Now that we know that the ice in the Polar Sea is upwards of eighty and one hundred feet thick, it may be as well to draw attention to the reports of former navigators on this subject. Scoresby describes the ice met with in the Spitsbergen seas as ' consisting of a single sheet of ice, having its surface raised four or six feet above the level of the water, and its base depressed to the depth of ten to twenty feet beneath,' thus making it twenty-six feet in thickness. Sir Edward Parry, in 1820, when he had advanced to the westward of Cape Hay in Melville Island, and was in fact at the entrance to the Polar Sea, remarks with astonishment on the thickness of a piece of a regular floe, which when measured by Captain Beechey was found to be forty-two feet.

Sir Robert M'Clure reports the ice off the mouth of the Mackenzie River and on the west coast of Banks Land as drawing from forty to fifty feet water, and sometimes even seventy-eight feet. All the voyagers to

Behring's Straits report the ice as being from five to six feet high above water, which would allow it to be at least thirty feet in total thickness. Admiral Sir Richard Collinson mentions having observed a floe aground in forty-two feet of water. And Dr. Kane met with ice aground near Refuge Harbour, Smith Sound, 'more like icebergs than hummocks,' one of which 'rose perpendicularly more than sixty feet.'

On our arriving off Cape Victoria, Princess Marie Bay was found to be full of one season's ice, evidently formed there during the previous winter and not yet disturbed. It was very rotten, and in many places the surface water-pools, separated by winding passages of apparently weak ice, had eaten their way through the floe to the sea below.

The main pack and the stationary land ice met each other two miles north of the cape and prevented our farther advance. The ships were therefore secured at the floe edge and Commander Markham landed to ascertain the state of the ice on the opposite side of the bay. A very thick fog and snowstorm, however, obliged him and Captain Feilden, who accompanied him, to return unsuccessful. At Cape Victoria the cliffs are formed of grey limestone resting on a massive conglomerate. The few fossils procured there were of Upper Silurian age.

During the afternoon flood-tide, which set to the westward into the bay, the pack closed in and the thin decayed ice, now covered with thick wet snow, became so pressed together that at one time the 'Alert' was in great danger of being forced on shore. Captain Stephenson keeping farther off shore, was able to force a passage for the 'Discovery' into more open water. As the ebb-tide made, the ice in Princess Marie Bay commenced to drift to the eastward, and water-channels opened between the 'Alert' and the coast of Grinnell Land ; but the 'Discovery' being then surrounded by ice we were delayed for a short time. In crossing the bay the ice was moving so rapidly that the 'Discovery,' although within a quarter of a mile of the 'Alert,' was frequently unable to follow her through the same channels.

Entering by the western side of Norman Lockyer Island, both ships were safely secured to the land ice in Franklin Pierce Bay, on the southern shore of Grinnell Land, at 10 P.M. The ice in the bay being one season old and very rotten it denoted that there must have been clear water along the shore when it was frozen over the previous autumn. To the eastward the pack being tight against the coast effectually prevented our farther advance.

Franklin Pierce Bay would afford fairly protected winter-quarters, but so far as we could judge there is little game procurable in the neighbourhood.

At 4 A.M. of the 9th I landed half a mile east of Cape Harrison accompanied by Captain Feilden and Dr. Moss. A record was placed in a small cairn erected on the spur of the limestone hills forming the west side of Franklin Pierce Bay, two hundred feet above high-water level.

Observing the ice opening in the direction of Cape Prescott, the ships steamed out of the bay, passing between Walrus Shoal and the mainland, but after clearing the shoal a large level floe prevented any

farther progress.   The weather was perfectly calm with
a temperature ranging from 32° to 39°.

While securing the ships at the edge of the floe
three walruses were observed lying asleep at a short
distance from us.   Commander Markham at once started
in a whale-boat with a harpoon gun ; while another of
the party made a short cut across the floe towards
the animals, with a view of obtaining a shot if they
became frightened and made off before the arrival of
the boat.   Beyond occasionally raising their heads and
looking round, they took no notice of our movements
and permitted the boat to approach to within a few
feet of them, when the largest one was easily harpooned, and the other two hit by several bullets.   The
latter, although they were very severely wounded, disappeared into the water and were never seen again.
The animal harpooned was towed back and hoisted
on to the floe.   Its dimensions were, length twelve feet
six inches, girth eleven feet six inches, tusks eighteen
and a half inches in length.

The flesh and blubber when cut up filled five casks
of two hundred and fifty pounds weight each.   The
meat when fried was much appreciated by all of us,
and the liver was pronounced to be excellent.   The
dogs made a hearty meal off the scraps.

The ice remaining stationary, all hands turned out
in the evening on the smooth floe for a game of foot-
ball, the dogs, poor things, also being landed for a run.
Some of them being harnessed gave the novices an
opportunity of practising the art of sledge-driving.

With each dog pulling in a different direction the
starting was a ludicrous sight, and was seldom effected

without the aid of a friend enticing the dogs on with a piece of meat. After struggling on for about half a mile they invariably obtained their own way, dragging their would-be-guiders through many water-pools in spite of the frequent application of the long hide whip which, in inexperienced hands, was more frequently felt by the riders than the dogs.

AMATEUR DOG-DRIVERS.

A sounding was obtained in forty-six fathoms, hard bottom ; the surface temperature was 32°, the minimum temperature between the surface and the bottom being 29°·5. During the night, ice formed on all the water-pools and remained unmelted in shady places during the day.

In high latitudes, during the summer, owing to the height of the sun above the northern horizon, the temperature does not fall much at midnight. Conse-quently the young ice does not form so early in the season as it does in Melville Bay and other southern positions; but when once it begins to form, the sun being lower at noon it does not thaw so readily during the day.

The weather was provokingly calm during the 10th with light rain falling. In our neighbourhood the ice remained perfectly still, although in the offing it was observed to be moving with the tidal currents. A second walrus was harpooned, which gave seven more casks of meat and insured the dogs being well fed for some time to come. During the enforced delay an opportunity was taken to obtain a haul with the dredge and trawl along the bottom, in a depth of thirteen fathoms, which proved to be rich in animal life. Five or six species of fish were obtained: nine or ten species of *Mollusca*; *Echinodermata* were very numerous, and the meshes of the trawl entangled many *Comatulæ* (*Antedon Eschrichtii*). These beautiful crinoids, closing and opening their pinnules when exposed to the atmosphere, reminded us of sensitive plants ; *Echinus drobachiensis* was most abundant. The tangles came up perfectly covered, and it required numerous pairs of scissors and many willing hands to clear them previous to each descent of the dredge. The variety and richness of the captures made us regret that the ever-pressing necessity of advancing northward whenever an opening in the ice admitted, prevented us from using the dredge more frequently.

On the 11th the upper clouds were passing from the N.W., but situated as we were under the lofty cliffs of Cape Prescott, the weather was perfectly calm with fog and a light rain. As we expected that calm weather,

Permanent Woodbury Print.

STOPPED BY THE ICE OFF CAPE PRESCOTT.

combined with tidal movement, would have opened the ice, the delay in our advance was tantalizing ; and with a few the ' social barometer ' commenced to fall rapidly. I landed with an exploring party on Norman Lockyer Island to obtain a view of the ice in the offing. It was with great difficulty that we forced a passage for the boat through the young ice which had formed in sheltered places during the few previous nights.

The low part of the island, for some 300 feet above the present sea-level, is a succession of raised beaches, rising about twenty feet one above the other. The rock, like the mainland, is a compact grey Silurian limestone. On the summit, about 900 feet high, the whole surface of the exposed rock is marked with ice-scratchings in a north and south direction.

Many ancient Eskimo traces were found near the beach with great quantities of decayed seal and walrus bones ; they were particularly plentiful near two small freshwater ponds situated a short distance from the beach.

Before we left the summit the fog lifted sufficiently to enable me to obtain a few bearings. Princess Marie Bay was observed to be half clear of ice, and there was a large pool of water off Cape Victoria, but none towards the N.E. in the direction of Cape Hawks. In the offing there was nothing to be seen but ice. A record was left in a cairn on the summit of the island. A few broods of eider ducks were feeding in the shallow water between the island and Walrus Shoal, the young birds being unable to fly. Three eider ducks, three dovekies, and an Arctic tern were shot. On the island a few eider ducks' nests were found containing eggs still unhatched.

At 8 P.M., soon after high-water, the ice began to set slowly to the southward, and shortly before midnight it opened sufficiently to induce me to make a push towards the east. We succeeded in advancing about half a mile, when the ice closed with the returning flood-tide and obliged me to secure the ships in a very exposed position, one mile distant from the land, which was hidden from our view by a thick fog. As the flood-tide increased in strength each ship was slightly nipped.

On the ice easing at high-water, observing that a crack was inclined to open, I telegraphed to Captain Stephenson to prepare to start ; but the ' Discovery's ' rudder was found disabled, and before I could move the ' Alert ' to take her in tow the ice became stationary again, without having opened a channel. Fortunately the damage to the rudder was slight and quickly repaired.

At 3 P.M., the fog having cleared off, we had the satisfaction of perceiving that although the tide was flowing, the ice in the offing was moving to the southward, which denoted an offshore wind.

At 5.30 P M. a water-channel opened and permitted us to advance by keeping close to the land. The cliffs rose to a height of 1,500 feet; the upper parts being precipitous with a narrow-based talus extending from the water's edge to about 250 feet up their front. Eastward of Cape d'Urville we crossed a large bay, which was named after Professor G. J. Allman, F.R.S., President of the Linnean Society. At its head was a magnificent glacier reaching to within about a mile of the sea, named after Mr. John Evans, F.R.S., the President of the Geological society.

Cape Hawks, forming the west point of Dobbin Bay, is a specially fine headland rising to a height of 1,400 feet. As we rounded it the weather was extraordinarily calm, and every detail of the rich brown of the rocky cliffs was purely reflected in the now broad water-channel, the substance and reflection being picturesquely divided by the white horizontal belt formed by the ice-foot at its base. It was justly comparable to the Rock of Gibraltar. Such was the smoothness of the water that Lieutenant May obtained an excellent meridian

CAPE HAWKS.

altitude of the sun below the Pole at midnight by using the reflected sun in the sea.

After passing through the channel between Washington Irving Island and Cape Hawks a large quantity of ice and many small icebergs were met drifting with the ebb-tide to the southward at the rate of about one and a half miles an hour. Larger floes nipping against Cape Schott and the east coast of the island prevented our progress and obliged me to secure the ships to some icebergs which were lying aground, about a quarter of a mile from the shore, in thirty-two fathoms water. I had intended placing our second large depôt of three thousand rations, for use in the event of a compulsory retreat without our ships, on the island, but the passing ice prevented our doing so without endangering the boats. Accordingly a small protected bay two miles north of Cape Hawks was chosen. There the depôt and a boat were landed while a party visited the island to deposit a notice and obtain a view to the eastward.

On reaching the summit, about 900 feet high, after a laborious scramble up the steep hill-side, we found two ancient cairns far too old to have been erected by Dr. Hayes, the only traveller known to have visited the neighbourhood. They were built of conglomerate and rested on a similar base, which in one case had become undermined by the natural crumbling away of the rock, and in doing so had destroyed a part of the cairn. Lichens which had spread from stone to stone also proved that they were of great age. They contained no records whatever. From our lookout the only water in sight was in Dobbin Bay with an intermediate barrier of ice. To the N.E. the ice was close everywhere, but here and there in the pack a few disconnected pools of water were kept open near the slowly drifting icebergs. On Cape Hawks the recent traces of a musk-ox or reindeer were observed. We could find only the very smallest traces of vegetation; indeed, any but an enthusiastic botanist would call the country perfectly barren.

On again ascending the island at 7 A.M. I found that the channel by which we had advanced was tightly closed. Not a pool of water was to be seen in that direction; but to the northward the ice was fairly open with only a few narrow necks of ice preventing our reaching Prince Imperial Island. During the forenoon, as the ice in the bay was set by the ebb-tide to the southward, a party was sent to clear away these necks by blasting. Steaming up just before the tide turned, we succeeded in forcing our way through and crossed the bay without much trouble. On arriving at the east side a large one season's floe was found pressing against the land near Cape Hilgard. By cutting docks into its northern edge the ships were secured about one mile S.E. of Prince Imperial Island and the same distance from the mainland. Several exploring parties immediately landed, reporting on their return that traces of hares and ptarmigan and a richer vegetation than usual had been met with in the valleys.

On each side of the bay precipitous hills, rising about 1,200 feet, and the very conspicuously coloured stratification, at an uniform incline of 20°, dipping towards the N.W., bear the most striking resemblance to each other. The intermediate area appears to have

been cut away by an old glacier, which has exposed
the correspondence in the stratification of the cliffs
on either side. At the head of the bay the snow-
clad mountains rise to a height of from 3,000 to
4,000 feet. The intervening valleys contain glaciers
in the higher parts, and one of great size extends to
the sea, where it discharges numerous icebergs, a long
string of which were waiting the breaking up of the
last winter's ice, then filling up the bay, to drift out to
sea. The fixed ice extended from Prince Imperial
Island to Cape Schott. Except in the small neighbouring bay near Cape Napoleon, this was the last fixed ice,
left unbroken by the advancing season, which we met,
and doubtless it drifted out of the bay a few days afterwards. The discharging glacier at the head of the
bay, the largest on the west shore of Smith Sound, was
named after the Empress Eugénie, who had shown a
great personal interest in the Expedition.

During the night of the 13th the ice was pressed
up with great violence against Cape Hilgard, raising
a new pile of hummocks twenty feet high on the ice-
foot at the base of the cliffs.

There being no prospect of our making an immediate
advance, and wishing to ascertain what the ice was
doing off Cape Napoleon, I started, with Feilden and
Aldrich and two men dragging the dingy on a five-man
sledge with one day's provisions, over the ice, the pools
on the surface of which were frozen over hard enough
to bear in most places. Dr. Coppinger, Rawson, and
Mr. Hart, with some men, joined the party from the
'Discovery.'

On reaching Cape Hilgard we found a pool of

water a quarter of a mile broad across which we were obliged to ferry, our numbers necessitating three trips with the small boat. We then sledged along the fairly level-topped ice-foot until we came to the pitch of the cape, where the piles of hummocks, pressed up the previous night, prevented our getting on with the sledge except at a great sacrifice of time.

In the bay west of Cape Napoleon a small land floe was still left, kept in its position by some grounded icebergs, and I found that if I could force the ships past the nip, near their present position, there was nothing else ·to prevent our advancing with the next ebb-tide.

The raised beaches in the bay between Capes Hilgard and Napoleon, formed of limestone débris replete with fossils, were very marked and evidently corresponded with those on Norman Lockyer Island. A fine glacier was visited in a valley on the east side of the bay some two and a half miles from the sea. No game of any sort was met with, and the country generally was as bare of vegetation as any I have ever come across. Feilden obtained a considerable collection of geological specimens of Upper Silurian age. Dr. Moss and Lieut. May succeeded in shooting six ptarmigan and one hare near the ship. Three dovekies were also shot out of those feeding in the salt-water.

On the 15th, observing that the water-pool near Cape Hilgard remained free of ice, all hands were employed in endeavouring to clear away the intermediate ice resting against the shore ; but as fast as it was removed the pressure from outside forced in the floe. When the flood-tide made in the afternoon the ice was quieter, and on a number of charges of powder being exploded simultaneously a narrow passage was opened alongshore; but so quick was it in closing that after the 'Alert' had passed through safely, the 'Discovery' scraped along the bottom and for a few moments caused us much anxiety owing to the dread that the ice would force her up on the shore.   As we advanced out of the bay the ice was more open and we rounded Cape Louis Napoleon in a navigable channel half a mile broad.

The pack outside us consisted of very heavy floes closely pressed together, with the edges of each field well defined by a hedge-like line of pressed-up ice. Many icebergs were in the pack : a few grounded here and there alongshore near Cape Frazer now afforded our only chance of shelter should the ice force its way in towards the shore.

Advancing quickly during the 16th with calm weather, a neck of ice checked us for an hour at 1 A.M : but on the ebb-tide gaining strength it opened a narrow channel, and we proceeded, fighting our way alongshore, until we had arrived, at 6.30 A.M., within a mile of Cape Hayes.   At that point we were completely stopped in consequence of the flood-tide having carried the pack in against the land.

The 'Alert' was then secured inside an iceberg aground in thirty fathoms ; but as there was not room for both ships, the 'Discovery' was forced to retreat about a mile to the westward, where she succeeded in sheltering herself to a slight extent behind and inshore of three small bergs.

Shortly afterwards the pack was forced in and we were completely surrounded.   With the boats turned inboard and everything ready for a nip, the ships were left entirely dependent on the icebergs for shelter against direct pressure; but any floe moving alongshore, small enough to pass between the icebergs and the land must necessarily have carried off the ship with it as it forced its way past.

Wishing to see what protection was to be expected near Cape Frazer, Commander Markham, Feilden, and I landed during the flood-tide, during which it was impossible for the ice to open unless assisted by a fresh wind, and walked three miles along the shore to the northward. I found Gould Bay full of pack ice with no protection whatever except what some grounded icebergs might happen to afford. We obtained a few fossils from the talus which fronts the cliffs to a height of about 200 feet. Two ivory gulls were flying about the cliffs, probably near their nests; and on the ice-foot we observed the tracks of a bear.

With the afternoon ebb-tide the ice eased off slightly. There being no prospect of our rounding Cape Frazer for the present, and the icebergs having afforded very poor protection, I decided to secure the ships to a large floe about a mile to the westward, which by resting against two large icebergs was held nearly stationary.

After waiting a short time while the 'Discovery' was effecting her escape, we succeeded in reaching the floe and tried to cut docks. The saws, however, proved to be quite powerless to cut through the ice, which was from twelve to twenty feet in thickness and heavily tongued to an unknown depth beneath.

I therefore secured the ships in a bight in the edge

of the floe as well prepared as circumstances permitted for whatever might happen.

In the event of the ice separating the ships, Captain Stephenson was ordered to rendezvous in Dobbin Bay.

The weather being calm and the atmosphere clear, the sun was extremely powerful during the middle of the day, the temperature rising from 31° at night to 39° at noon. Mount Cary, the highest mountain on the south shore of Hayes Sound, was observed seventy miles distant covered with snow and ice.

About this time the dogs on board the 'Discovery' showed the first signs of disease, owing probably to close confinement, wet decks, and want of natural exercise. Fits were frequent. and a few deaths occurred after symptoms of madness. Doctor Colan and Doctor Ninnis took great trouble to discover the nature of the disease and to arrest it. It was evident that this alarming and very often fatal malady could not be true rabies or hydrophobia, for in several instances the affected dogs recovered.

Although the weather was calm during the 17th and the following day, the pack had a general tendency to drift towards the south-west at the rate of about five miles a day, moving fast with the ebb-tide and remaining at rest during the flood. In consequence of the floe to which we were attached being held stationary the moving pack outside ground its way past, tearing off the exposed corners in a very alarming manner. The dividing line between the fixed and the moving ice was distinctly marked by a hedge-like line of newly raised ice-hummocks, at least twenty feet in height.

As the exposed parts of the border of our floe were broken up one after another the line of nip was steadily but surely nearing us ; but as the same kind of terrific combat was going on a quarter of a mile to the southward, on the other side of the ships, it was unwise to move sooner than we were compelled to.

This was the first time the ice-quartermasters—experienced men in the ice-navigation of Baffin's Bay—realized the vast thickness and power of the Polar ice as compared with that with which they had hitherto been acquainted. The closing together of two Polar floes upwards of fifty feet in thickness may be appropriately compared to the closing of the two sides of a dry dock on the doomed vessel.

As the position of the nip advanced so the two ships gradually retreated before it, losing, much to the regret of all, a portion of our hard-won advance towards the north. By the evening of the 18th we had been forced back into a small pool of water close to the two grounded icebergs, against which our floe was resting with the outside pack nipping against the whole length of its outer edge in anything but a reassuring manner.

The water-pool in which the two ships floated was steadily contracted in size, until at last it became so small that had a nip occurred both must have been destroyed at the same moment. Although the greatest danger was imminent, entrapped as we were, our anxiety was lessened by the knowledge that as human beings we were powerless, and must leave the result to Providence. About midnight when, in endeavouring to keep the ships as far apart as possible, the ' Alert's ' bowsprit was projecting beyond the side of one of the icebergs, the closing in of the outer ice ceased. Shortly afterwards it began to ease off, and at half-past twelve the water-pool had grown so large that I gave the order to raise steam and ship the rudders and screws—heartily glad of a chance to escape from our exposed situation. The ice continuing to open to the westward, the ships were moved about a mile in that direction and secured in a more protected position inshore of three very large grounded icebergs, where, although we had lost ground, we were equally ready to start as soon as an opportunity occurred to pass Cape Frazer.

In endeavouring to connect the 'Alert's' screw some of the ice collected in the screw-well prevented its being lowered to the right depth; consequently the 'Discovery,' whose screw gave less trouble, towed us to our new position.

After the ships were secured, a party of officers landed, keeping within sight of a recall. The young ice in all the protected positions had increased in thickness so much that we had great difficulty in forcing a passage through it for the boat.

I ascended 2,000 feet up the side of Mount Joy, and, the atmosphere being clear, obtained a fine view of the heavy line of icebergs lying apparently aground in Peabody Bay fronting the Humboldt Glacier. In their neighbourhood there were many water-pools.

The summit of the ice-cap on Washington Land, dividing the Humboldt and Petermann Glaciers, eighty miles distant, and estimated as being 6,000 feet high, was conspicuous, presenting a decided peak with the sides sloping down at an incline of not more than two or three degrees.

As I started to descend, I observed that at the last of the flood-tide the ice near the shore showed signs of opening. Expecting this to continue with the ebb, I hurried down and signalled the ships to start, getting up steam as they advanced under sail.

When the steam was ready the water-channels had opened considerably, and by pushing out into the pack for about two miles we entered a channel that led us to the shore again a little north of Cape Frazer.

This cape, where the Polar and Baffin's Bay tides meet, had long been considered one of the most difficult points to pass. On rounding it a fortnight before the end of the navigable season we were all raised to the highest state of hope and expectation.

CHAPTER VI.

DURING the 19th, the water-channel along shore, about
a quarter of a mile in breadth, remained open so long
as the ebb-tide lasted, the pack outside drifting to the
southward at an estimated rate of one and a-half
miles an hour. At 8 P.M., about the time of low-water,
a large floe threatened to block up the water-space, but
after a short delay the passage cleared and by 9.15 P.M.,
we had arrived within two miles of Cape John Barrow.
There the ice prevented farther progress, so the ships
were secured to a floe locked in behind three large
icebergs, lying aground in twenty-two fathoms of
water, and affording protection against the pack.

Although the flood-tide had commenced, the ice
continued to drift towards the southward, proving that
we had passed the neighbourhood where the two
ocean tides meet. While I was taking a short rest,
Commander Markham landed and ascended Cape John
Barrow to watch the movements of the ice. Captain
Feilden and two men accompanied him, and as the
movements of the ice were uncertain, they dragged

the dingy with them.
At this time of the
season the young ice
covering the pools on
the floe was suffi-
ciently strong to bear
the weight of a man.
On Markham ascend-
ing the cape to a height
of several hundred feet,
he observed much open
water to the northward
and along the shore,
and as there was every
probability of the ship
being able to force her
way into it, he ran
back to the boat, much
to Feilden's disappoint-
ment.

The latter had
found an interesting
stratum of limestone
replete with fossils, and
although as anxious
as anyone to advance
quickly to the north-
ward, and knowing
how important every
moment was in ice-
navigation, he yet man-
fully stuck to his prizes.

CAPE JOHN BARROW.

Amid Markham's repeated calls to hasten, he descended the hill, and scrambled over the ice with his load, eventually getting the specimens on board. By the time they had reached the beach the fickle ice had closed in again, and gave them much trouble to haul the boat between, and sometimes over, the newly forming hummocks.

On observing the ice myself I considered its movement so very uncertain as it drifted south that I decided to wait for high-water before starting, hoping that the ebb tidal current would then open up a decidedly clear water-channel. In this I was not disappointed, for on the 20th at 1.15 A.M., about an hour before high-water, I was able to proceed slowly northwards threading our way through the pack. On nearing Cape Norton Shaw the ice opened out from the shore as quickly as it had closed in the previous evening and left several channels for our selection; a very decided and agreeable change in the navigation to what we had experienced since entering the ice off Victoria Head, now left about sixty miles behind.

As we passed the large opening forming Scoresby Bay, the distant shore at the bottom of the bay was so shrouded in mist that we were unable to ascertain with certainty the size of the inlet ; it contained much ice with a large water-pool along its northern shore.

The pack being well open ahead, I left the crow's nest for a short time, pointing out to the ice-quartermaster who took my place a perfectly clear and opening channel. On returning within a quarter of an hour, I found the channel which we had entered not only closing fast but our line of retreat cut off, although on either side other channels were opening. However, after a delay of about half an hour, the 'Discovery' broke a way for us through the moving pack and we were enabled to proceed. In this neighbourhood we had great difficulty in recognizing the land by the chart. According to latitude, Cape Frazer was more than ten miles out of position, and Scoresby Bay sixteen. I have retained these names, as given by Dr. Kane and Dr. Hayes, and published by the United States Hydrographic Office on the chart, without regard to the necessary change in latitude, but at the northern extremity of Kennedy Channel I have kept the names given by Dr. Hayes in the latitudes he adopted.

Arriving at Cape Collinson, I found that a large iceberg, aground two miles distant from the land, had locked in a floe which reached from the south point of Richardson Bay to Cape Collinson. The northern edge of this floe received the whole pressure of the ice drifting to the southward on the western side of Kennedy Channel, and prevented our advance unless I took the ships off into the middle of the strait. Owing to the risk of drifting to the southward if beset, I secured the ships at the southern edge of the stationary floe, in a pool of water near to the iceberg.

To the northward the ice pressing against the southern shore of Richardson Bay was closely packed, but in the offing it was more open although it could scarcely be deemed navigable. It set to the southward during the flood and part of the ebb-tide; for four hours of the latter it remained stationary. As there had been no wind, so far as we knew, to influence it for several days, this may probably be taken as the normal state of the current. The ice drifted about five miles each tide, making ten miles a day, and thus gave us the pleasing prospect of meeting more open water as we advanced north. It also rendered it certain that Robeson Channel communicated with the Polar Sea. We observed that the ice had been forced high up on the shore on the northern side of Cape Collinson, but the southern face of the cape presented no appearance of severe pressure.

During our enforced delay a small depôt of 240 rations was landed on Cape Collinson about one hundred yards inshore and thirty feet above the water-line. These provisions have not since been disturbed. During winter they will be deeply buried in snow, and probably the mark placed over them will have broken down. The opportunity was taken of letting down the dredge in seventy fathoms, and some additional animal forms were added to our list of captures. The tracks of a bear and the recent footprints of a hare were seen, but the gloomy weather, with light snow falling, rendered the land specially desolate in appearance. In the event of the two ships parting company Captain Stephenson was ordered to rendez-vous at Carl Ritter Bay.

At 4 A.M., of the 21st, I determined to try and advance north through the pack in the offing, but, on getting two miles from the land, the channels led us so much towards the south that I returned to the position we had lately left. We then tried to unlock the land-ice from the iceberg with the hope of releasing the ice to the northward, but it is probably fortunate that we did not succeed, as the berg alone was too small to afford protection to both ships. In the

evening the wind having freshened from the northward with a heavy snowstorm, the temperature being
27°, Captain Stephenson and I decided to make
another push for the water which was in sight in the
middle of the strait. Accordingly at 9 P.M., nearly
the time of low-water, we started under steam and
sails, and after an hour's severe struggle succeeded in
forcing our way through the closest part of the pack.
When six miles from the land we entered water sufficiently open to let us choose our own course. Naturally
everyone was in the best possible spirits at our improved prospects; and hopes were entertained by a few,
that having passed the meeting place of the northern and
southern tides, a sea comparatively clear of ice would
be found to the northward. Arriving in mid-channel,
the wind was blowing so strong directly down the
strait that in order to make any progress we were
obliged to work the ships to windward under fore and
aft sails, the ice compelling us to make short boards,
but by tacking as the leads were observed to favour us
we made good way.

The edges of the floes around showed signs of
having been lately exposed to a much heavier sea
than we were then experiencing, large fragments of
well washed debris ice, rounded by attrition, having
been thrown up on the edges of the floes like pebbles
on to a beach.

During the 22nd, as we advanced up the channel,
there appeared to be less ice on the western than on
the eastern shore. Unfortunately the misty weather
prevented our obtaining a good view of the hill-tops.

By noon we were fairly in Kennedy Channel and

CAPE CONSTITUTION.

met with apparently a similar extent of open water to that seen by Mr. Morton of Kane's Expedition in the same locality. Morton's description of Cape Constitution, with the relative positions of Franklin and Crozier Islands, rendered it easy to recognize the spot where his remarkable journey from Rensselaer Harbour terminated in June 1854.

Though our later experiences show that this open water is caused by the rapidity of the tidal movements in a comparatively narrow channel connecting two large basins, yet at the time Dr. Kane wrote, with the incomplete data at his command, he had fair reason to believe in the existence of a very considerable extent of open sea. In justice to the memory of that distinguished Arctic explorer, I extract the following from his volumes, where he reviews Morton's journey, and compares with his discoveries the reported open waters and seas of other Arctic voyagers :

' All these illusory discoveries were no doubt chronicled
with perfect integrity; and it may seem to others, as
since I have left the field it sometimes does to myself, that my own, though on a larger scale, may one
day pass within the same category.'

It not unfrequently falls to the lot of the traveller
to invalidate some of the conclusions of his predecessors
who may not have enjoyed similar opportunities of
observation as himself, but it is equally his duty to
render to those who went before him, the credit when
due, of having given in perfect good faith the result of
their investigations.

In the evening when the two ships were abreast of
Cape Constitution, the wind lulling we took in the fore
and aft sails, and steered onward through the most
open channels, passing to the westward of Franklin
Island. By midnight we were abreast of Hans Island
with perfectly clear water along the eastern land about
John Brown Coast, but streams of ice prevented our
approaching the western shore. Hans Island rises on
its southern face to a cliff about 500 feet high; both it
and Franklin Island showed signs of great pressure
against their northern points, the ice having been piled
up to a height of fifty or sixty feet, while the southern
shores were free.

The land about Cape Andrew Jackson is bluff but
comparatively low, and sinks as it trends to the eastward in the direction of the Humboldt Glacier, the
position of which was very conspicuously marked by a
strong ice-blink as the sun reached its lowest declina-
tion. From Cape Andrew Jackson to Cape Constitution the coast of Washington Land gradually rises,

culminating at the last-named point, and from thence gently sinking towards Cape Bryan. The whole of the coast-line presents an almost precipitous cliff rising to a height of at least 1,000 feet. No deep fiords cut through this long line of cliffs, Lafayette Bay being the only striking indentation, and it does not run far inland. On the western side of Kennedy Channel the noble Victoria and Albert Mountains rear their snow-clad peaks to a height of over 5,000 feet in a series of isolated cone-shaped hills. Judging by the eye, the loftiest portion of this range appears to lie to the south-west of Scoresby Bay, the mountains gradually diminishing in height towards the head of Lady Franklin Sound.

Throughout the day we could not cease wondering why the strong current from the north did not bring down ice to fill up the open water through which we were racing. We were also struck with the paucity of animal life in this region; during the previous twenty-four hours only one seal and about a dozen dovekies were observed, whilst not a single gull or loom was noticed: this is somewhat remarkable if Kennedy Channel remains continuously open during the summer.

At 4 A.M., of the 23rd, steering N.E. by N., the high land about Cape Lupton near Polaris Bay was sighted, distant about fifty miles; the land to the eastward being below the horizon presented the appearance of a channel leading to Newman Bay.

On nearing Hall Basin with a southerly wind, ice was observed stretching across from Cape Lieber to Joe Island, with a collection of stream-ice extending out for three miles from the land on the western shore of Kennedy Channel. After an ineffectual attempt to reach a small bay south of Cape Defosse, the ice-streams being heavy and moving quickly to the northward with the southerly wind and ebb-tide, I steered for Cape Morton to see whether there were a lead to the northward on that side of the channel. Fortunately as it turned out afterwards, the entrance to Petermann Fiord was completely closed. Being thus debarred from advancing along the eastern coast, I left the ‘ Discovery ’ to land a travelling depôt of 240 rations at

BESSELS BAY.

Cape Morton, and took the ' Alert ' back to Hannah
Island, where we had noticed a fairly protected anchorage.   On arriving off its entrance we shortened sail
and came to anchor in eight fathoms on a shallow
bank extending to the eastward of the island.   Nearer
to the mainland there must be a deeper channel
through which the icebergs formed in Bessels Bay
escape to seaward.   The precipitous cliffs on either
shore of the bay are cased in a *mer de glace* from
which glaciers push their way down each ravine into
the sea, and there discharge their icebergs.   This bay
therefore contains a vast assemblage of bergs, and
many lie aground on the shallows near its mouth.
The tide ran with great rapidity over the shallow
bank, and we were obliged to keep our cables ready
for slipping in the event of any heavy piece of ice
being driven against us.

The ' Discovery ' anchored near us in the evening,
having accomplished the task of landing a depôt.
Hannah Island was visited and a cask containing a
notice was placed on the summit of the island, a
second notice being placed twenty feet magnetic north
of the cairn.   From this position the difference between
the eastern and western shores of Kennedy Channel
was very striking.   The summits of the Greenland
hills were buried beneath a nearly level ice-cap, with
each ravine extending from the shore completely filled
by a glacier ; on the other hand, the mountains of
Grinnell Land appeared to be entirely devoid of ice,
their tops only being snow-covered, while the lower
valleys were bared except in sheltered spots where a

few patches of unmelted snow still remained. On the one side the scenery was monotonous and dreary in the extreme, on the other the many bright hues of the stratified rocks varying from black to carmine shades, and wreathed with patches of snow, looked warm and cheerful by contrast. The valleys devoid of snow gave promise of vegetation, and held forth visions of game. Our finding in these latitudes any land uncovered by ice or snow brought back to me remembrances of Melville Island, and its abundant supplies of animal life. It was, perhaps, the joyful feelings growing out of our late success in gaining the more open water of Kennedy Channel that gave birth to these highly coloured reflections, for on a nearer approach to this Grinnell Land shore the following year, the same country appeared to our then more experienced and critical eyes desolate in the extreme.

From the summit of Hannah Island, some 120 feet above high-water mark, I observed the loose ice we had met in Kennedy Channel driving to the northward before a strong southerly wind, and adding to the pack accumulated in Hall Basin, thus giving us but a poor prospect of an immediate advance. The weather being clear we obtained from Hannah Island our first sight of Grant Land, north of Cape Lieber.

It was low-water at Bessels Bay at 10.40 P.M.; the ebb tidal current ceased at 10 P.M.; at 11 P.M. the flood-tide was setting in to the bay with sufficient strength to swing the ships broadside to the wind. In the water round us bird life was abundant, dozens of dovekies nested in the steep limestone cliffs and were constantly flying from the sea with fish in their bills; many broods of eider ducks following their mothers were noticed, and several seals. The dredge was let down in eight fathoms; it came up filled with limestone pebbles, doubtless shed from the bergs; two or three examples of *Trochus* clinging to *Laminaria*, an *Astarte*, a starfish, and a couple of annelids were all the animals obtained. A few Silurian fossils were collected from the massive limestone cliffs that flank the bay.

At 4 A.M., of the 24th, the officer of the watch reported that the southerly wind in the channel was dying away, and hoping that a lead might open near Cape Lieber, I landed and ascended Cape Morton, accompanied by Thomas Rawlings, first-class petty officer, to inspect the condition of the ice. After a very severe climb up the steep sides to the summit of the coast ridge, a height of 2,000 feet, we were amply repaid for our labour and loss of breakfast by the grandeur of the view.

It was a beautiful morning with scarcely a cloud in the sky, the cold sharp wind which had benumbed us at the sea-level was local, for on the summit of the cape it was perfectly calm, and I was able to work without gloves though the temperature was down to 20°. After a quarter of an hour spent in taking bearings, the warmth engendered by our rapid ascent passed off, and our damp underclothing proved anything but agreeable; we were glad enough to put on our warm jackets which we had at first discarded. The panorama was certainly superb. Sixty miles distant in the S.W., were the Victoria and Albert

Mountains of Grinnell Land, fronted by Hans Island showing clear of Cape Bryan, which had Hannah Island nestling at its base. Farther north was the lofty spur from the, main range, which rising between Archer Fiord and Kennedy Channel, forms Daly Promontory, named after the learned President of the United States Geographical Society. Fronting these mountains and apparently separated from them by an extensive valley extending to the northward from Carl Ritter Bay, was the black buttress-shaped cliff forming Cape Back, the southern extreme of a nearly straight-running line of flat-topped coast hills extending for twenty miles to Cape Defosse. From that point the coast land became more hilly and joining the Daly Mountains extended to Cape Lieber, a bluff headland, with Cape Baird a low flat point, jutting out beyond it. Still farther north were the elevated mountains of Grant Land, with the steep cliffs about Cape Union, though seventy miles distant, distinctly visible, forming the western extreme of Robeson Channel. Nearly due north a slight break in the continuity of the land showed where Robeson Channel opened into the Polar Sea. On the eastern side of the strait at a distance of forty miles, Cape Lupton, a notable landmark, terminated Polaris Promontory; then came Polaris Bay, with the low plains leading to Newman Bay. At my feet lay Cape Tyson, and Cape Mary Cleverley, on the northern shore of Petermann Fiord, rising to an elevation of 1,500 feet.

The southerly wind had left fairly open ice in Kennedy Channel between our position and Cape Lieber, with a large space of open water in Lady

Franklin Sound. Robeson Channel, Polaris Bay, and the entrance to Petermann Fiord were closely packed, though a few pools of water could be seen stretching in a disconnected line between Cape Beechey and Cape Lupton.

Offley Island, at the north-western entrance of Petermann Fiord, being within reasonable proximity of the localities where the ' Polaris ' Expedition procured their supplies of musk-oxen, had been looked upon by me as likely to afford good winter-quarters for the ' Discovery,' although the disadvantage of its being on the eastern side of the channel was very great ; but now the condition of the ice preventing any approach to Offley Island left me no option but to take both ships to the western shore.

Hurrying to the boat, the ships were signalled to get under weigh, and I rejoined them as they were leaving Bessels Bay. We ran quickly across the channel under sail, experiencing little trouble with the ice until off Cape Lieber, where the edge of the pack led us round towards the north shore of Lady Franklin Sound. On a nearer approach we discovered a large and well protected bay, inside of an island the outer point of which formed Cape Bellot. There the ships were secured close to the shore at 2 A.M. of the morning of the 25th. Lady Franklin Sound, with its grand precipitous cliffs, which we hoped would prove to be a channel leading to a western sea, appeared, to our regret, to be considerably narrower than it was depicted on the chart.

I at once saw the value of the harbour we had attained as a wintering place for the ' Discovery,' but

in consequence of the quantity of newly fallen snow
lying on the ground, the neighbourhood presented so
desolate an appearance that we could not but com-
passionate her crew having to spend a year, if not
longer, in such a place.

Our crossing from Bessels Bay to the western shore
had given an opportunity for a joke about the musk-
ox grounds having been left behind ; but it was destined
to be short-lived, for on entering the harbour, Dr. Moss,

HEAD OF MUSK-OX.

always on the look-out for game, espied a herd of musk-
oxen near the shore.   They were at first mistaken by
some for black boulders, but soon our doubts were
removed by the animals moving.   Amidst great excitement, half a dozen sportsmen were landed ; being too
eager to submit to much generalship, they had a long
and exciting chase, but at last succeeded in shooting
the entire herd, numbering nine.

Our intense gratification at this result was enhanced

VOL. I.   I

by the news our sportsmen brought back that the country was fairly vegetated, and that numerous tracks of hares, foxes, and ptarmigan had been seen.

No doubt now remained about leaving the ' Discovery ' there, and preparations were at once made for our parting company. Lieutenant Wyatt Rawson and a sledge crew joined the ' Alert,' to strengthen her crew and as far as possible to share the honours of a struggle towards the Pole between the two ships. If the vessels did not separate too far, they were to return to their own ship during the autumn. It was impossible for two ships' companies to have worked together for a common end more harmoniously than those of the ' Alert ' and ' Discovery,' and one and all regretted that duty rendered our separation necessary.

In the evening I ascended a hill on the north side of Discovery Harbour, a height of 1200 feet by aneroid. It was the worst ground for walking over that I ever met with ; the level plots were cut up by the frost into large clods, like a deeply ploughed field with cross ridges ; the whole was covered with a smooth carpet of snow, which while hiding the irregularities from sight was not solid enough to bear one's weight. The footing was so extremely uncertain that several times I fell headlong. It was, however, extremely gratifying to find a loamy soil with abundant sorrel, willow, saxifrages and grasses, instead of hard limestone and gravel plains.

The geological formation of the area around Discovery Bay differs entirely from the massive Silurian limestones of Bessels Bay on the opposite side of the channel. Slates, with thin-bedded hard limestones and indurated shales, compose the surrounding hills. The strata are highly contorted, often assuming a vertical position; veins of quartz and chert were frequently found traversing these rocks. A few species of wading birds still lingered, but as a rule they were in flocks and evidently on their way south; turnstones (*Strepsilas interpres*) were the commonest, but small family parties of the knot (*Tringa canutus*) were feeding along the beach at low-water. Snow-buntings were flocking, and they chirped in a sad disconsolate manner about the frozen streams, trying to extract a little water from chinks and crevices. Residents in temperate climes, who enjoy throughout the year the presence of many birds with their joyous notes, can scarcely realize the feelings of the sojourner in Arctic wilds when the first notes of the snow-bunting, harbinger of summer and returning warmth, awaken in him vivid recollections of the far-off south. With such a one, the snow-bunting must ever remain an especial favourite, and the preparations of this sweet songster for a departure to more genial regions are a reminder of approaching darkness and the monotony of an Arctic winter.

From my look-out hill I noticed that the ice in the strait was much broken up, with a few water-pools here and there; although they were not connected, it was evident that an offshore wind would immediately open a channel by which we could advance.

Owing to our high northern position, although the sun was still above the horizon at midnight, its altitude at noon was too low to affect the temperature much; consequently after August 20th the temperature of the

air remained steadily below freezing point for the
winter, and the young ice formed at mid-day earlier
than it does farther south.   Notwithstanding this,
Arctic navigation is so greatly dependent on wind, that
there was still sufficient of the season left to give us
a reasonable certainty of reaching the northern land
which on the report of the Polaris Expedition had
been placed in latitude 84° N.

On the morning of the 26th, having left my orders
with Captain Stephenson concerning our future movements, the two ships forming the Expedition separated ;
those in the ' Alert,' if the published charts and state-
ments of our predecessors proved correct, having the
cheering feelings of, in all human probability, successfully completing the chief duty assigned us ; those
on board the ' Discovery,' although rejoicing at the
prospects of their comrades, having also the depressing
sensation of being left behind to play what they could
not but consider at the time a secondary part in the
general programme.

On arriving at the entrance of the harbour, the
main pack was found to be resting against the shore
and to have completely filled up Lady Franklin
Sound ; some small floes streaming rapidly into Discovery Bay.   In endeavouring to keep clear of these
the ship touched the ground and hung for a short
time ; fortunately, by lowering the boats and lightening
the ship a little, she floated again without damage.

During the afternoon at low-water the pack, which,
apparently uninfluenced by wind, had been moving to
the southward the whole day, drifted slightly off the
land.

Immediate advantage was taken of the welcome channel to proceed north, but on reaching Distant Cape the pack, which extended completely across the strait, prevented all farther progress ; there was, therefore, no option left me but to return to Discovery Harbour; where the ship was again secured at the entrance ready to advance on the first opportunity.

Commander Markham, with Feilden and Rawson, pulled along shore towards Cape Murchison to watch the ice, but it remained persistently packed against the shore. A small family of terns (*Sterna macrura*) were found breeding on a rock off Bellot Island, and at this late period of the seàson an unfledged young bird was discovered in a nest. A brood of eider ducks unable to fly were also seen.

At this period of our voyage we supposed Robeson Channel to be a narrow strait connecting Hall Basin with a similar sea to the northward, and the difficulties experienced by the 'Polaris' when navigating this channel demonstrated that we could not hope to advance through it except when a westerly wind blew the ice off the western shore. On the termination of the westerly wind, or a shift to any other quarter, the ice would naturally close in again, with the prevailing southerly running current.

This afterwards proved to be the general movement of the pack, except in the narrowest part of the strait between Cape Beechey and Polaris Promontory. There, with a slight northerly pressure during calms, the large floes jammed against each other and blocked the passage. The ice to the south of the block being carried onwards, water-pools were formed under the lee of the pressure, and these occasionally would have permitted the ship to cross the channel, had I wished to do so. A similar occurrence took place with the north running tide; therefore, under a favourable combination of circumstances, a vessel might be navigated from the neighbourhood of Lincoln Bay to Newman Bay.

Our enforced delay within sight of the ' Discovery,' when the season was slipping away so quickly, was most provoking. Naturally there was no want of watchers at the masthead or on shore looking anxiously for a chance of proceeding northward. Light north-east winds prevailed, with clouds resting low on the hill-sides, but a clear sky showed over the eastern land. The pack in the channel continued to move to the south-westward in a compact body, except during the height of the ebb-tide, when it was either stationary or set slowly to the north-east. The different floes of which the pack was composed remained fairly quiet in juxtaposition, except when passing a prominent point; then a momentary disturbance would take place, pools of water would form under the lee of the point until the accumulated pressure behind the floe forced it past the obstruction at more or less expense to its corners; the water-space was then quickly occupied by ice and all would quiet down again. I did not know it at the time, but this ice must have been carried up Lady Franklin Sound, which previous to our arrival had been emptied by a south-west wind. On ascending the hill at 9 A.M., of the 27th, about the time of high-water, the ice was observed moving off from Cape Murchison, but before steam could be got up it had closed again. In the evening during flood-tide, a small pool again formed south of Cape Murchison, but there was no possibility of our forcing a way through the intermediate ice.

The 28th brought in a beautiful morning with a light air from the south-east. At 8 A.M. the wind died away, and the ice seemed decidedly inclined to open. At 11 P.M., the commencement of the north-running tide, we were just about to move when a thick fog enveloped us; hiding everything at more than twenty yards distance, this effectually prevented our starting. Later in the afternoon it cleared off, but it was then low-water, and on trying to move the ship I found that, though afloat, she had settled down with the falling tide into a basin surrounded on all sides by a bank of mud. The ship was immediately lightened by lowering the boats and placing in them such articles as could be readily hoisted on board again. With the tantalizing prospect of an open channel before us, we were forced to wait for three hours, until the rising water enabled the ship to pass over the obstruction. Hoisting up the boats and signalling a final 'good-bye' to the 'Discovery,' we then reached under steam to within a mile of Cape Beechey; where in an encounter with a heavy floe, the rudder-head, which had been badly sprung some days before, became so injured that the rudder itself was nearly useless. Observing that the pack was pressing tight against the cape to the northward of us, I secured the ship inside what at the time we supposed to be grounded icebergs, but which in reality were pieces of Polar floes.

While shifting the rudder the sportsmen, after a

long chase, killed three musk-oxen out of a herd of
five, which were feeding near the edge of a frozen
lake about a mile inland. The coast hills between
St. Patrick's Bay and Cape Beechey are generally undulating and their sides less steep than at other parts
of Robeson Channel, so probably that neighbourhood
is a fair station for game. North of Cape Beechey the
cliffs rise direct from the sea, and except at the head
of the bays offer no feeding ground for musk-oxen.

If ever again travellers visit that neighbourhood,
they would do well to examine the valley leading to the
north-east behind Cape Beechey, which I believe will
be found to communicate with another, descending
into Wrangel Bay. There is apparently another
valley leading in the same direction connecting Wrangel
and Lincoln Bays, behind Mount Parry and Cape
Frederick VII. Land travelling should usually be
avoided, but I suggest this route on account of the
great difficulties encountered on the ice in the channel
by our sledging parties.

The 29th was a calm bright day, and spring-tides
being near there was every prospect of the ice opening.
The barometer falling also gave signs of a breeze from
the southward.

During the forenoon the pack remained close
against the ice-foot of Cape Beechey. After divine
service, Mr. Pullen, Egerton, and I pulled in a boat
along the shore as far as the ice permitted us, and then
ascended the cape by crawling up a steep ravine. On
arriving at the summit I found that we could not see up
Robeson Channel, so we were obliged to walk about two
miles along the hill top through the soft snow before

we obtained the wished for view. Sinking as we did into soft snow up to our knees at each step, the exertion was excessive, and the exact manner in which the footsteps of the leader were followed testified to the severity of the labour. Egerton, who had been chasing musk-oxen all the previous night over somewhat similar ground, was fairly tired before we returned on board. Our scramble bore good fruits, for we had the pleasing prospect of beholding a water-channel extending along shore nearly as far as Cape Union, and also of seeing that the ice resting against Cape Beechey, which cut us off from the channel, was slowly opening. During our excursion we secured our first living specimen of the lemming (*Myodes torquatus*) which we afterwards found to be common in Grinnell Land. Feilden had previously found its remains in the pellets rejected by the snowy owl (*Nyctea scandiaca*), in Twin Glacier Valley, much farther south. I recognized in this lemming an old acquaintance dating from my former Melville Island experiences. The distribution of this little rodent over nearly the whole circumpolar area is a very interesting fact.

Signalling to the ship to advance, we hastened to retrace our steps, and got on board just as the vessel was moving off. Passing Wrangel Bay at 8 P.M., we arrived off the beetling cliffs forming Cape Frederick VII., which rise direct from the sea without any adhering ice-foot. There a very large and heavy floe was driving towards the shore impelled by the southerly moving pack. It was a close and very anxious race to pass it without being crushed against the precipitous cliffs. Lincoln Bay was reached at

10.30 P.M., a little before high-water. The ice would have permitted us to reach a point two miles farther north, but there it touched the shore. Expecting that the ebb-tide would force the pack against the land, I determined to wait for a more favourable opportunity; and it was well that I did so, for very soon after the ice closed in and not a speck of water was to be seen anywhere. The ship was secured in twenty-two fathoms water alongside a floe formed that season, consisting not of newly frozen smooth ice, but of a conglomeration of ice of all sizes interlocked above and below water by pressure and then frozen together, forming an extremely hummocky floe some eight or ten feet in thickness. Already it was so compact as to be extremely ominous of the approaching winter.

During the forenoon of the 30th the flood-tide opened the ice sufficiently for a boat to reach the northern shore of the bay; the opportunity was taken to land a depôt of provisions for travellers, consisting of 1000 rations. The depôt was placed about thirty feet above the sea on a hill-side fronting the first dip in the coast hills from the extreme east point of the bay. A cairn, which can be seen from the ice a mile from land, was built a few yards inshore of where these provisions were deposited. This depôt was not subsequently interfered with by us, and no doubt still remains intact.

At noon, about the time of high-water, the ice commenced to open off shore and set towards the north; we immediately got underweigh and with a little trouble succeeded in getting to within three miles of Cape Union. There the ice inshore was closed, but

outside it was more open, and with the calm weather
gave promise of letting us get round the Cape.
Accordingly I pushed off and ran three miles into the
pack. At 3 P.M. we could advance no farther, and
instead of returning to the shelter of Lincoln Bay, I
waited in a large pool of water in the hope of its
shortly opening towards the north. In this I was disappointed, for at 4 P.M., with just sufficient warning
to enable me to pick out the softest looking place near
us, the ice completely encircled the ship, and she became hopelessly beset in a very heavy pack, consisting
of floes of eighty feet in thickness and from one to
four miles in diameter. The intervals between the
floes were filled with broken-up ice of all sizes, from
the solid hummocks which, grinding past the ship's
side, endangered the quarter boats, to the smaller pieces
which the nipping together of the heavy floes had
rounded, like boulders or pebbles in a rapid stream.
Fortunately for us, intermixed with the pack was a
vast amount of sludge-ice formed during the last
snowfall.

Since meeting the ice off Cape Sabine I had noticed
a gradual but considerable change taking place in the
nature of the floes as we advanced north. The heaviest
that we first encountered were not more than eight or
ten feet in thickness. Off Cape Frazer were a few still
older pieces, estimated at the time as being twenty
feet thick, but evidently that was far short of the
correct measurement. It was now certain that we
were nearing a sea where the ice was of a completely different description to that of Baffin's Bay or
Lancaster Sound, and that we were indeed approaching

the same sea which gave birth to the heavy ice met with off the coast of America by Collinson and McClure, and which sealed up the ' Investigator ' for ever in the Bay of Mercy, after her memorable and perilous passage along the north-west coast of Banks Land.   It was the same description of ice that Parry encountered when attempting to pass to the westward of Melville Island in 1820, and which conquered him and his experienced companions ; that passing down M'Clintock Channel, beset and never afterwards released the ' Erebus ' and ' Terror ' under Franklin and Crozier ; and which streaming along the eastern shore of Greenland destroyed the ' Hansa ' of the last German Arctic Expedition.

As our only hope of pushing north against the general set of the current through such ice (to say nothing of the extreme hazard of remaining in the pack) consisted in regaining the shore, both boilers were lighted and full steam kept ready in order to take immediate advantage of any opportunity that might arise   At 10.30 P.M., the pack, which previously had been drifting in a compact body to the southward, eased a little near the edge of the large and deep-floating floes, in consequence probably of a difference in speed between the surface and undercurrent, but before we were able to clear away a space of water at the stern sufficiently large to enable the rudder to be shipped, the ice closed and obliged us to dismantle again.   A second time at 11.30 P.M., just at the top of high-water, the pack showed signs of opening, but after moving the ship half her length ahead, we were again obliged to unship the rudder.

Fully expecting a change with the flood-tide on the morning of the 31st, with much labour a working space was cleared under the stern, but owing to the rudder being badly balanced we nearly lost our opportunity. At 9.30 A.M., during a momentary slackening of the ice, with steam up to its greatest pressure, we commenced to move. By going ahead and astern alternately, the ship formed an ever increasing water-space and at last pushed her way to where the ice was more open, and shortly afterwards entered a narrow water-channel which led to Lincoln Bay.

Few occurrences are more trying to the temper of the commander of an Arctic ship than an accident which prevents him taking immediate advantage of a momentary change in the ice, on which the success or failure of an expedition may depend. Had the shipping of the rudder delayed us another five minutes, the ship would in all probability have remained in the pack during a heavy gale which shortly after set in from the south, and continued for two days.

When in the pack, I regretted that the ship was not near a floe to which we might have escaped in case of being nipped ; for although a large one was within a quarter of a mile of us, such was the rugged state of the broken-up intermediate ice, that had the ship been destroyed, it would have been quite impossible to have transported any provisions or stores to it, even had we succeeded in reaching it ourselves.

After our late escape all could appreciate Captain Buddington's recommendation, when the ' Polaris ' was placed in precisely similar circumstances, to get out of the Polar pack as quickly as possible. It is either affectation or want of knowledge that can lead anyone seriously to recommend an attempt being made to navigate through such ice. I can answer for all on board the 'Alert' having been most thankful again to reach the land.

During the late struggle, as well as on many previous occasions, it was noticeable how futile the efforts of the crew were to clear away the ice, which impeded the movement of the ship on the bow or quarter, compared to the enormous power exerted by the ship herself when able to ram her way between the pieces even at ordinary speed. Thus, steamers are enabled to penetrate through a broken-up pack which the old voyagers, with their sailing vessels, necessarily deemed impassable. At the same time there is a limit to the risks which are advisable to be run; no ship has been built which could withstand a real nip between two pieces of heavy ice.

Shortly after the ship was secured in her former position to the firm ice in Lincoln Bay, the wind gradually freshened from the S.W., blowing slightly off the land; accompanied with a snowstorm and a threatening appearance of the weather.

So far as we could distinguish through the snow and mist, the main pack was driven by the gale to the northward up the channel; but knowing that it would take some hours to produce a navigable passage past Cape Union, I waited until the morning of September 1, when with steam at hand ready if requisite, we passed up the straits, running before a strong gale, nine knots an hour, between the western shore and the pack, which was driving quickly to the northward, at about three miles distance from the land. By noon, having arrived in latitude 82° 24′ N., a more northerly position than any vessel had ever previously attained, the ensign was hoisted at the peak amid general rejoicings.

With such a strong wind blowing off the shore we enjoyed the pleasing certainty of not being again stopped by ice so long as the land continued to the northward. We therefore had very sanguine hopes that we should at least attain to latitude 84° 20′ N., the reported position of President's Land, without another check. At 1 P.M., we came suddenly and unexpectedly to a block.

On hauling to the westward, at what afterwards proved to be the northern entrance to Robeson Channel and the shore of the Polar Sea, the wind headed us from the north-westward, and then died away. The breadth of the water-channel also considerably lessened, until off Cape Sheridan the main pack was observed to be touching the grounded ice, making farther progress impossible. Running close up to the end of the water-channel, the ship was secured to a large floe which rested against the cape.

The weather at this time remained very misty During a partial clearance we observed every appearance of land due north, and reasonably supposed that we had reached Army Fiord of the ' Polaris ' chart, and that some local cause had prevented the ice being driven off shore by the gale ; our stay was therefore thought to be only temporary. At 2 P.M., finding that the ebb-tide was setting towards the north-west, along the land, and that in spite of it the pack was slowly nearing the shore, I moved the ship to a more protected position inside of some pieces of ice lying aground close to the beach.

Since entering Smith Sound I had remarked the almost total absence of a continuous line of shore hummocks similar to what is usually met with in the western channels of Lancaster Sound. Such a ridge, by protecting the water-space from disturbance that lies between them and the shore, admits of the formation of perfectly smooth ice.

The advantage in sledge travelling of finding smooth ice extending between the shore and a line of outside hummocks is incalculable. I therefore foresaw that when our sledging parties had to journey along these unprotected shores, the daily distances travelled would necessarily fall short of those accomplished during the Franklin Search Expeditions.

In Robeson Channel, except in a few places where the cliffs rise precipitously from the sea and afford no ledge or step on which the ice can lodge, the shore line is fronted at a few paces distant by a nearly continuous ragged-topped wall formed by accumulated ice pressed up by the pack on top of the original ice-foot, and rising from fifteen to upwards of thirty-five feet high. Opposite the large ravines the water carried down by the summer floods melts a way for itself through the barrier and occasionally breaks the continuity of the wall; but immediately the pack closes against the shore with pressure, a newly formed pile of ice is quickly raised and closes up the gap. The débris brought down the valleys, being unable to escape out to sea, is deposited inside of the ice-barrier, forming a raised beach, which, where the land is steadily rising and the incline of the shore favourable, attains a considerable thickness.

To the north of Robeson Channel, where the land trends to the north-westward the coast line loses its steep character, and near Cape Sheridan the heavy Polar ice becomes stranded at a distance of one hundred to two hundred yards from the shore, forming a border of unconnected masses of ice from twenty to upwards of sixty feet in height lying aground in from eight to twelve fathoms water.

Off an open coast, with no more protection than that afforded by such pieces of ice, the 'Alert' was fated to pass the winter. Most providentially during the eleven months she was thus exposed we never once experienced a gale blowing towards the shore.

CHAPTER VII.

CAPE JOSEPH HENRY—HALL'S OBSERVATIONS—SHUT IN BY THE PACK
—RAWSON AND ALDRICH START — MARKHAM LEAVES SHIP—NO
LAND TO THE NORTH—ALDRICH RETURNS—FURIOUS GALE—MARK-
HAM'S RETURN—ATTEMPT TO LEAVE FLOEBERG BEACH—ACCIDENT
TO SCREW—FROZEN IN—DEPARTURE OF AUTUMN SLEDGE PARTIES.

ON the afternoon of the 1st the atmosphere cleared
and enabled Commander Markham and myself to obtain a view of the land towards the north-west from
an elevated station.

The coast line was observed to be continuous for
about thirty miles, forming a bay bounded towards the
west by the United States range of mountains, with
Mounts Mary and Julia and Cape Joseph Henry,
agreeing so well with Captain Hall's description that
it was impossible to mistake their identity. Their
bearing also, although differing upwards of thirty
degrees from that on the published chart, agreed precisely with his original report.

Pack-ice extended close in to Cape Sheridan and
along the shore to the westward, a pool of water being
left on the east or lee side of each projecting point in
the bay; which, however, the intervening ice effectually
prevented our reaching. To the eastward the channel
by which we had advanced was completely blocked

by the return of the ice against the shore; and the ship, lying about one hundred and fifty yards from the land, secured on the inshore side of some large pieces of stranded salt-water ice—afterwards appropriately termed floebergs by Captain Feilden — although in a fairly protected position, was thoroughly embayed by the pack.

The late snowfall had completely covered the land to a depth of from six to twelve inches; and the undulating snow-clad hills, unmarked by any very prominent feature, formed anything but a cheering landscape.

To the northward where it was thought we had ob-

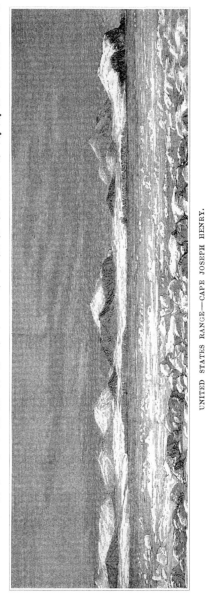

UNITED STATES RANGE—CAPE JOSEPH HENRY.

served land, it was evident that none existed within a
distance of at least twenty miles.

During the evening, with a falling barometer, the
wind again freshened considerably from the south-
west, the drifting snow hiding the land from our
sight.   In a sudden squall the hawsers by which the
ship was secured, carried away and obliged me to let
go a bower anchor ; but before the ship was brought
up she had drifted outside of the barrier of floebergs,
from which the pack was again slowly retreating towards the north-east, being driven off by the gale.

I naturally expected that a water-channel would
open alongshore by which we might advance, but
nothing of the kind occurred ; for although a magnificent sea two miles in breadth formed abreast of
our position, in which a light southerly swell forcing
its way up Robeson Channel was perceptible, yet
the pack remained persistently locked against Cape
Sheridan, only a mile and a half to the north-west of
us.   Even with the ebb-tide, no offshore movement
occurred, the ice being evidently held tight by some
opposing pressure of wind or current.

At work during a greater portion of the night, we
fully appreciated the advantages we enjoyed by the
sun being still above the northern horizon at midnight;
in more southern Arctic latitudes it had long since
ceased to be light at that time.

On the morning of the 2nd the wind shifted
suddenly from S.W. to N.W., causing the ship to drift
in amongst the floebergs, and driving the pack rapidly
towards the shore.

The barometer having indicated the probability of
a change occurring, steam had been kept ready, and

NEWLY–FORMED FLOE–BERGS.
(FROM A PHOTOGRAPH.)

after a considerable amount of manœuvring to clear the cable from the heavy ice about which it had become entangled, the ship was removed from her exposed position.

The protected space available for shelter was so contracted and shallow, the entrance to it so small, and the united force of the wind and flood-tide so powerful, that it was with much labour and no trifling expense in broken hawsers that the ship was hauled in stern foremost. It was a close race whether the ice or the ship would be in first, and my anxiety was much relieved when I saw the ship's bow swing clear into safety just as the advancing edge of the heavy pack closed in against the outside of our friendly barrier of ice.

From our position of comparative security the danger we had so narrowly escaped was strikingly apparent as we gazed with wonder and awe at the power exerted by the ice, driven past us to the eastward with irresistible force by the wind and flood-tide at the rate of about a mile an hour.

The projecting points of each passing floe which grounded near the shore in about ten fathoms of water would be at once wrenched off from its still moving parent mass; the pressure continuing, the several pieces, frequently 30,000 tons in weight, would be forced up the inclined shore, rising slowly and majestically ten or twelve feet above their old line of flotation. Such pieces quickly accumulated until a rampart-like barrier of solid ice-blocks, measuring about two hundred yards in breadth and rising fifty feet high, lined the shore, locking us in, but effectually protecting us from the overwhelming power of the pack.

During the afternoon the wind was light from the north-west, blowing along the land with a heavy snow-fall. So far as we could see through the snow the pack drifted towards the north-west with the ebb-tide, and towards the south-east with the flood, opening slightly off shore in our neighbourhood with the former, but, as before, never leaving Cape Sheridan.

The heavy fall of snow mixing with the salt in the water considerably quickened the formation of the young ice, and before the evening it was so thick we were scarcely able to communicate with the shore by boat.

The temperature had fallen to 18°, our first experience of decidedly cold weather.

While walking on shore my anxiety concerning the security of the ship's position was somewhat relieved by observing that although to the eastward and westward numerous heaps of gravel had been forced up above the high-water line by the ice-pressure, yet in our immediate neighbourhood the beach was perfectly free from any such marks.

The rise and fall of the tide was observed to be very slight and denoted a great change in the configuration of the shore line ; it proved unmistakably that we had passed out of a narrow channel and had entered the Polar Sea.

For the three following days we experienced light westerly winds, with the temperature ranging between 18° and 8°. The pack remained always close against the coast, moving along the land with the tides, but drifting on the whole towards the south-east. Pools of water half a mile long by a quarter broad formed on the south-east side of the larger floes, but they were always completely isolated from each other by several miles of heavy ice.

Although a few large floes could be distinguished in the offing, the pack within five miles of the land consisted usually of floes less than a mile in diameter intermixed with a very large proportion of rubble ice.

The newly formed ice was strong enough to bear us on the 4th. At midnight, on that date, the sun sank below the north horizon.

Although all regular navigation was now apparently at an end, I was naturally most anxious to move the ship from her exposed position before the setting in of winter; but the quickly advancing season warned me that no movement should be made without a reasonable probability of attaining a sheltered situation. Accordingly, Commander Markham and Lieut. Aldrich started on the 5th to look at a bay about eight miles distant to the westward. On their return they reported that it was a well sheltered harbour, thickly coated with newly-formed ice, but that the continuous wall formed by the grounded floebergs across its entrance would effectually prevent our entering.

After this report I decided to commence landing such provisions and stores as were hampering the decks of the ship and which would not be required during the winter should we fortunately be able to move into safer quarters.

Five eider ducks were shot on the 5th, and a flock of ptarmigan seen in a valley three miles to the south-east of our position near Cape Rawson. This headland was named after Lieutenant Rawson, who belonged to the 'Discovery,' but was then on board the 'Alert,' and was destined with his sledge-crew to pass the winter on board of that ship.

The formidable nature of the Polar pack, so different in its character to that I had been accustomed to in my prior Arctic experience, naturally caused me great solicitude. The following in reference to it is extracted from my journal of the 5th :—

'This morning a floe about a mile in extent, floating at least four feet out of water at its lowest part, was passing to the eastward. It is the first piece of Polar ice fit for travelling over that we had seen. The main pack that is usually passing our position, as far to seaward as we can observe, is simply impassable for sledges. What it may be in the spring when the snow banks have levelled off some of the irregularities remains to be ascertained. At present it is quite out of the question venturing upon it. Our hope is, that the land will extend towards the north, and so enable the ship or sledges to get along near the shore. Whatever our travellers do, the work must not be compared with our former Lancaster Sound level floe travelling, the road is so totally different.'

On the 6th we commenced dragging the provisions and stores to the land on sledges over the newly formed ice. The casks piled one on the other formed the sides of a long shed, which was covered by one of the large sails ; it was named Markham Hall, and afterwards formed a valuable storehouse during the winter.

In my journal I remark : 'The temperature remains at 12°, so in spite of our exposed position I have decided to winter here ; indeed the ship is now so firmly frozen in that I have no option left me.   Doctor Moss shot a fine hare last Sunday ; this is the only sign of game belonging to the neighbourhood which has been seen ; indeed, the undulating hills stretching away for a dozen miles are, apparently, perfectly bare of anything likely to attract game to visit us ; a few hollows are vegetated, but very sparingly so.'

It was vexing to observe, as we proceeded northward through Smith Sound and Robeson Channel, that the number of seal met with gradually decreased. We had depended upon a supply of these animals for the support of our dogs, and now their total absence led me reluctantly to the conclusion that we could not possibly provide for all of these useful auxiliaries during the winter.   Nothing having the appearance of meat came amiss to them, but they stedfastly refused to eat the dog biscuit of which we had a small quantity.

For three days previous to the 8th we experienced a heavy fall of snow.   On the 2nd we had noticed how snow falling on the salt water quickened the formation of young ice.   But after the ice was once formed it was noticeable how the snow tends for a time to retard its increase in thickness.

When the young ice, three to four inches thick, became unable to support the accumulated weight of snow two feet in depth, it was borne down until the water percolating upwards had risen three inches above its level.   The superficial covering of snow then afforded such excellent protection that although the temperature of the air was 15°, the water remained unfrozen, its temperature being 29°.   Finding that the ice below the snow and water was actually melting, we were obliged to cease dragging the heavily laden sledges between the ship and the shore.

Though I did not expect any decided movement of the ice to occur during the neap-tides, yet before despatching any travellers to a distance, an ample depôt of provisions was landed for their support in the event of accident happening to the ship, which at the time I considered highly probable. These arrangements having been completed, Lieutenant Rawson with seven men started on a pioneering journey towards Robeson Channel. On the 9th, Lieutenant Aldrich with three sledges and twenty-four dogs, accompanied by Captain Feilden and Dr. Moss, started to explore the land towards the north-west.

Lieutenant Rawson returned on the 10th, having found Cape Rawson impassable by land on account of the steepness of the cliffs, and by sea in consequence of the continual movement of the pack which prevented him venturing on it, even with a boat.

At Floeberg Beach, as the land in the vicinity of the ship was now named, a westerly wind blowing off shore, force 4, combined with an ebb-tide, opened, for the first time since our arrival, a narrow channel extending for half-a-mile beyond Cape Sheridan. On the 11th, the same wind continuing, the channel widened out until it was a mile broad, and extended for six miles to the westward, but ended two miles distant from the shore. As this offered an opportunity of advancing a large depôt of provisions and boats to the northward, Captain Markham started with a strong party of men; having first to draw the boats across the heavy barrier of ice, within which the ship was sealed up, apparently frozen in for the season.

The sky being fairly clear, we were able to set at rest all doubts concerning the northern land reported to exist by the 'Polaris' Expedition. As seen through light haze, the dark reflection in the sky above the detached pools of water in the offing gave a very decided appearance of land when there was a mirage, but after a constant watch, and carefully noting the movements of the darkened patches, I was obliged reluctantly to admit that no land existed to the northward within the limits of our vision.

The absence of any visible land to the northward was extremely discouraging, and the ice that lay before us was of such a nature as to convince me, or any person acquainted with Arctic navigation, that it would be most unadvisable voluntarily to place a ship in it. The following extract from my journal of the 11th expressed my views at the time, and I had no reason to modify them afterwards :—

'It is perfectly evident that the report of "open water" having been seen towards the north from the deck of the "Polaris," when she attained her highest latitude, meant merely that disconnected water-pools were observed, but not that a water-channel fit for navigation existed. In Lancaster Sound or Baffin's Bay a water-pool in the pack may, under favourable circumstances, be expected to open out and become navigable. Here with this decided Polar ice, it is out of the question that any commander should leave the shelter of the land, and force his way into the pack without insuring a retreat if necessary. The term

" open water " is extremely vague. It should only be
used to designate navigable water ; when water-pools
are spoken of, an estimate of their extent should be
given.'

In order to register the temperature of the earth
throughout the winter, a thermometer was buried to
the depth of eighteen inches and then frozen in. This
was the extreme depth to which we were able to
sink a hole in the solidly frozen ground, after three
days' labour. On our arrival at Floeberg Beach we
found a steep bank of a previous season's snow resting
against the northern slope of our look-out hill, which
was 480 feet above high-water mark. Similar patches
were observed in other sheltered positions, showing that
the snow near the sea-level, as well as that on the hill
tops, did not melt entirely during the previous summer.

The 12th brought in a calm day with a temperature
of from 4° to 8°. After divine service, when we took
the opportunity publicly to return thanks to God for
our preservation during our past dangers and labours,
I walked with some officers to Cape Rawson to see the
state of affairs there. The ice was piled up on the ice-
foot to a mean height of about thirty feet, with an
uneven pointed summit, quite useless as a road for dog
or man-sledge. Inside this icy ridge soft snow had collected in undulating banks resting against the cliffs, but
with such steep sides as to necessitate a portage being
made before they could be passed by sledge-travellers.

Wishing to obtain a view of the ice in the offing,
Rawson, Giffard, and I ascended half way up a steep
snow-slope in a gully on the east face of Cape Rawson. Pressing upwards incautiously, it became less

dangerous to go on than to descend; we were indeed fortunate in at last reaching the summit of the cape. I frequently looked at the place afterwards, but no one ever again risked his neck there.

The ice in Robeson Channel was observed to be tightly pressed against the shore, with a few disconnected pools here and there in the offing. In the neighbourhood of the ship the pack had again closed in against the floebergs.

On the evening of the 12th, Lieutenant Aldrich's party returned after an absence of four days. He had succeeded in establishing a depôt of provisions and exploring the coast-line for a distance of twenty miles to the north-west. The travelling, owing to the very rough state of the ice, and the deep snow with its sticky wet foundation of sludge, was found to be unusually heavy; indeed, so bad was it that although only laden with half weights, all three sledges broke down. The few patches of young ice met with were too weak and treacherous to permit sledges being dragged over them; one sledge broke through and was only recovered with much difficulty.

With the fall of temperature that part of the lower deck which was at a distance from the galley fire became damp, but this was at once remedied by the fitting up of an extra stove.

On the 13th and 14th we experienced a strong gale from the south-west with a heavy snow-drift and a low barometer; the temperature rising to 20° and the pack drifting away from the land towards the north-east, leaving a clear water-channel along shore.

On the morning of the latter day the gale was

blowing from off the land, with a decided swell coming up Robeson Channel, indicating much open water
to the southward. From the look-out hill, which I
ascended with difficulty in consequence of the strong
wind, I observed a water-channel leading for ten miles
towards Cape Joseph Henry, but the land-ice was
still clinging to the shore as persistently as heretofore.

By 10 A.M. the swell commenced breaking up the
ice inshore of the ship, and we had barely time to get
the boats which had been landed on board again, before
the ship was left in clear water, all the light ice and
some of the heaviest pieces near us being driven to sea.

During the height of the gale five men in a whale-
boat mistook their orders, and left the ship to pull
to the shore, but being unable to reach it were carried
by the wind to seaward. Fortunately the boat was
brought up against one of the floebergs, about two
hundred yards distant from that against which the
ship rested. The gale was then blowing so furiously
that the men were unable to cross the intermediate
channel. After much work and great anxiety, we
succeeded in rescuing them from their dangerous
position, by veering another boat astern with a long
line and making the distressed men do the same with
a rope they fortunately had in their boat. Then by
sheering the two boats towards each other they met,
and the wearied and half frozen men were rescued.

In the evening it continued to blow fiercely, with
a blinding snow-drift mixed with sand and small pebbles
which were carried by the fury of the storm. While
thinking anxiously over the condition of our travellers
during such a gale, I observed Commander Markham

on the shore abreast of the ship. Although we were so close to the land, it was only by double manning the oars of the cutter that during an opportune lull Lieutenant Giffard was able to establish a hauling line between the ship and the shore, and so communicate with Markham. It appeared that his party had started in the morning with a moderate wind blowing; at mid-day the gale rose, and they pitched their tents with difficulty on a heavy floe. Shortly after tenting, this floe commenced to break up and the party had to beat an immediate retreat to the shore, fortunately crossing the cracks with all their effects before the ice moved away from the land. One man then became so greatly disabled from exhaustion that Markham decided to carry him to the ship. Having reached a ravine that afforded some slight shelter, he tented the main party, and selecting one sledge-crew to drag the sick man, he himself pushed on in advance.

Though desirous of returning to his sledge-party and invalid, knowing his fatigued condition I despatched Lieutenant Giffard and the crew of the cutter to assist the tired men.

After an hour's search in the snowstorm they met the party, and, at midnight, by using the cutter's line as a hauling rope, we had the satisfaction of seeing the sledge-crew ferried across, and the frozen man's life saved. This sledge-crew, who had faced the storm to save their comrade's life, were all so much exhausted that they did not recover themselves for three or four days.

With the morning of the 15th the wind lulled considerably, and the remainder of the travellers, under the

command of Lieutenant Parr, returned, having passed
anything but a pleasant time in their tents during the
gale. On ascending our look-out hill, I observed that
the ice to the westward between the land and the
channel in the pack had drifted to seaward, leaving a
clear road by which we could advance to a place of
shelter. Making a signal to the ship, steam was immediately got ready and the rudder shipped, but on
lowering the screw we found it impossible to enter the
shaft. While raising it again to clear away the ice a
thick snowstorm came on with a blinding mist which,
hiding everything from view, prevented our moving.
Before midnight the gale was blowing as furiously as
ever.

During the night the sea breaking against the shore
became so discoloured by the stirred up mud that the
snow-covered beach over which it broke was darkened
to such an extent that from a distance we mistook it
for the gravel coast-line. On visiting the shore we
picked up a few pieces of seaweed (*Laminaria*) that
had been cast up, and found that the salt water at a
temperature of 29° washing over the snow-bank had
solidified it into hard ice.

The barometer rising on the 16th, I tried to connect the screw ready for a run along the land immediately the gale lulled ; but when the screw-shaft
only wanted an inch of being fixed, the rachet lever
became damaged and the shaft could not then be
moved either in or out. So strong was my desire to
reach what I hoped would prove a more protected
place for wintering, that for a moment I thought of
proceeding under sail ; but we were so hemmed in by

the ice that I was obliged to give up the idea of attempting to beat to windward towards an uncertain haven and along the edge of a pack, to enter which would have been certain destruction.

The forenoon was spent by me in frequent and long visits to the engine room anxiously watching Mr. Wootton repairing the rachet. It was not completed before 11.30 A.M.; on then raising the screw the hole which receives the end of the shaft was found plugged with ice, which was so hard and so much discoloured by rust that when first taken out we all thought that it was the end of the shaft itself which had broken off inside the screw. By the time the screw was fixed and everything was ready for a start under steam the pack was rapidly nearing the land. At 2 P.M., it had reached Cape Sheridan and effectually closed us in for the winter.

After this date the ice never left the shore to the westward of our position, although to the eastward a large space of clear water remained between us and Robeson Channel whenever the wind prevailed from the westward.

On examining the coast-line afterwards, both during the autumn and the following spring, we discovered that there was no harbour sufficiently open to receive the ship, and that the ice at the entrance of each bay was far too thick for us to have cut or forced our way through it before the pack would have closed in. The accident that happened to the screw and our consequent detention at Floeberg Beach, although extremely annoying at the time, was afterwards considered by all a most fortunate circumstance.

During the latter part of the gale, in addition to the bower cable holding the ship, she was further secured by a wire hawser passed from the bow to a second anchor buried on shore. When laying it out it was very readily handled in the cutter, and during the gale, although the strands flattened in the sharp nip at the hawse-hole, the wire cable held on admirably.

The following is extracted from my journal :—

' In the evening, although a strong north-west wind was blowing along the land, it produced very little snow-drift in consequence of there being no more light snow left to fly. A large pool of water remains open off Cape Rawson, which, with this wind, will probably extend as far south as Cape Union. The day before the gale commenced we were preparing an observatory on shore, but fortunately none of the instruments were landed— that is supposing we are still successful in moving farther to the westward into the bay found by Aldrich. I fear we can scarcely expect another favourable gale before the season is quite at an end. A long continuous south-west wind is the only power that will ever open this ice. The " Polaris " had a fortnight's continuous westerly winds at the end of this month, her time of full moon; so we may still have another chance. Were the question of our advance to the north-west only to gain northing, irrespective of any other consideration, unquestionably I could gain ten or twelve miles; but at this advanced season other considerations have to be thought of ; we must be quite sure that we gain a safe wintering place. These hummocks can scarcely be considered a desirable or sufficient protection for the winter. . . . .

'Some step should be taken to guard against the shaft being jammed in the boss of the screw by ice. Mr. Wootton suggests that a hole might be bored through the centre of the shaft, through which a jet of steam could be forced into the screw and the ice readily melted.

'17th.—Barometer rising, temperature up to 30°. Still blowing a fresh gale with squalls from the north-west; the pack ice close against Cape Sheridan. On this side of that point and abreast of our position a narrow water-channel opens during the ebb-tide; but with the flood the pack closes in, moving very fast to the south-east. Aldrich estimates its speed at two miles an hour, but I think one mile is nearer its true rate. The gale conbined with the rise in temperature has completely destroyed the young ice formed on the inshore side of the floebergs.

'Last night, so heavy was the pressure of the pack, I fully expected that our protecting floebergs would give way, and that the ship would be forced on shore. The outer line of our defence was driven in for about one hundred yards, but fortunately the inner line withstood the attack.

'One heavy floe, a fair sample of those composing the pack, which we fully expected would carry all before it, just as it was touching our barrier, fortunately took the ground itself in twelve fathoms water. Three large pieces were then wrenched off, and left behind to add to our protection. The heaviest piece aground, half way between our position and Cape Sheridan, standing at least sixty feet high, has withstood the pressure of the pack for the last ten days; this morning it was thrown over on its side, breaking in two and displaying a fine massive block of blue ice the surface of which was twenty feet above water.

' 18th.—The thermometer last night rose to 36°, a most unusual occurrence, and the upper deck was in a dreadfully wet state from the sudden thaw. The discoloured snow border at the high-water mark on shore, which had been partially thawed, has to-day, with a fall of temperature, refrozen and now forms a broad smooth ice-foot along shore, very convenient for walking on.

' 19th.—The temperature having fallen to 15°, the young ice has formed again so rapidly that Markham, Parr, Aldrich and I had great difficulty in reaching the shore in a boat. From the look-out hill not a drop of water is to be seen anywhere. It is quite impossible that a one-season floe can ever be produced in this sea. In a protected position at the margin of an ancient floe, a small area of young ice might be formed, but no large water-space ever remains long uncovered by heavy pieces of débris ice.

' The ice at Cape Joseph Henry not leaving the land with an offshore wind is a most remarkable phenomenon. If it never does so I can only suppose that the south-west winds blowing off the land are deflected by the United States range of mountains and changed into westerly winds blowing along the coast.

' I have now no longer any doubt that we are on the border of the Polar Sea. Few would credit the great thickness of these floes, and unless we had seen our protecting icy barrier being formed out of the broken-up sea ice, we might have reported that it was

made up of icebergs.   In consequence of the bareness
of the land from snow, the dust has been carried off
by the wind, and has discoloured all the floebergs.
This evidently accounts for the dust sediment left at
the bottom of the water pools on the surface of the
floes, and for that frozen deeply into the ice.

'After three days of constant work, everyone
enjoyed to-day a well-earned rest.'

During the following week the weather remained
calm with a clear atmosphere, and the ship became
firmly frozen in.   Preparations were now made for
the autumn travelling, each man finding full employment in fitting his clothing and preparing the necessary
sledge equipment.   The light sails were unbent, the
running rigging unrove, and the ship made as snug
aloft as possible.   The heavy sails were left bent to
the yards, and did not suffer in the least from their
exposure.   The ship's company's mess deck was en-
larged considerably, and cleared of all the stores and
provisions which had necessarily been stowed there
during our passage from England.   The midship part
of the deck was prepared as the main entrance from
the upper deck, and was also fitted as a workshop for
the artificers and others.   As a greater security against
possible danger, the powder was deposited in a snow-
house on shore.

Owing to the great improvement in ships' galleys
since the time of previous Arctic expeditions, the heat
of the galley funnel was found to be insufficient to
melt snow in sufficient quantities to provide a supply
of water; an alteration was made in the tank for the
better, but throughout the winter, in both the ' Alert '

and 'Discovery,' it was necessary to melt ice in the coppers in addition to the small quantity of water obtainable from the snow tanks.

During the damp and variable weather, the dogs suffered much from cramp, many of them having fits. Their favourite place for lying down was near the warm galley funnel ; this being evidently not conducive to health they were landed, with Frederick to take care of them, until the ice formed sufficiently strong to enable our communicating readily with the shore. So anxious were they to return on board that one was drowned by breaking through the ice, and several narrowly escaped. During Lieutenant Aldrich's journey a dog ran away from the sledge in a fit on September 12 ; it returned to the ship on the 20th, naturally in very poor condition but apparently cured of its disorder.

The darkness by night closed in with unusual quickness. In high latitudes, though longer delayed, the darkness increases daily with much greater rapidity than at positions farther south. A star was seen for the first time since crossing the Arctic circle at midnight of the 20th ; the sun being then six degrees below the north horizon.

With the object of exploring the land about Cape Joseph Henry before the arrival of the main party, Lieutenant Aldrich, with Frederick and two seamen, Ayles and Simmons, started on the 22nd, with fourteen dogs dragging two sledges laden with fourteen days provisions. The dogs were allowanced at the rate of two pounds of preserved meat daily. Michael, the dog that had lately been absent on his own resources, being a willing animal and a good puller, was harnessed in with the rest.

On the morning of the 26th the main travelling party was ready to start, with the object of establishing a depôt of provisions as far in advance to the north-west as possible. The force consisted of two seven-man sledges and one eleven-man sledge, viz., the ' Marco Polo,' ' Victoria,' and ' Hercules,' under Commander Markham and Lieutenants Parr and May, and drawn by twenty-five men ; they were provisioned for twenty days. At 9 A.M., after prayers on the ice, officers and men standing round the sledges, they started off in the best of spirits ; the sledges, weighted to 200 lbs. a man, running easily over the frozen road on the top of the ice-foot. On reaching a place where it was necessary to cross the young ice, which was only five inches thick, the heaviest sledge, weighing 2,200 lbs., proved to be too heavy for it, and after proceeding for half a mile successfully, broke through, wetting most of the gear, but fortunately not the men's clothes. Returning to the ship and equipping a new seven-man sledge, Parr started on to overtake his companions.

The temperature at night fell to one degree below zero, but fortunately it remained calm.

During the 28th the few men left on board were employed in lifting the chain cable from the bottom on to the ice, to prevent its being frozen in during the winter. A second cable was passed from the stern to an anchor buried on shore. The officers were employed in making a survey of the neighbouring coast and in constructing an observatory.

On the 29th, at Floeberg Beach and at Discovery

Bay, a long spell of misty weather set in, with frequent falls of snow, lasting until October 10.

Arctic scenery is naturally expected to be somewhat desolate in appearance, but few are prepared for the utter dreariness which a long continuance of misty weather with a snow-charged atmosphere produces. No shadows or skyline being visible, no measure of height or distance can be formed. The land and the ice-covered sea, masked alike with snow, are indistinguishable, and present a foggy appearance which is only found to be unreal when some dark object intercepts the view.

During the 30th I engaged in snow-house building, with Lieutenant Rawson and four men. We were employed four hours in constructing a dome-shaped house eight feet in diameter, sufficiently large for four men to lie full length, with not too much room to spare. This was a very substantial building and lasted throughout the winter. Doubtless a lighter one could be constructed in much less time when hard snow is procurable; but during half the Arctic travelling season hard snow is not to be obtained in high northern latitudes; and travellers unprovided with a tent would fare badly. Captain Hall, when travelling with Mr. Chester and two Eskimo, Hans and Joe, near Newman's Bay, relates that on October 22, 1871, they were two hours and forty minutes building their snow-house, nine feet in diameter and five and a-half feet in height. This is a long time to keep tired men exposed to severe weather after dragging a heavy sledge for ten or eleven hours.

CHAPTER VIII.

RAWSON'S SECOND START—ALDRICH'S RETURN—HIS JOURNEY TO CAPE
JOSEPH HENRY—HEAVY SNOW-FALL—CONDITION OF THE ICE—
RAWSON RETURNS—FAILURE TO COMMUNICATE WITH 'DISCOVERY'
—MARKHAM'S RETURN—FROST-BITES — RESULTS OF AUTUMN
SLEDGING.

BEING anxious to communicate with Captain Stephenson, if possible before the winter set in, I despatched Lieutenant Rawson on the 2nd of October
with his seven men to inspect the ice in Robeson
Channel and to ascertain if travelling along the coast-
line was yet practicable. Mr. Egerton, who had accompanied Rawson for two miles, reported on his
return that the new ice was still so thin that the sledge
was obliged to take to the land. I therefore could
scarcely expect that Rawson would make a successful
journey. In addition to the thinness of the young
ice, the soft snow which had fallen during the five
previous days formed so great a protection to the
water on the ice which had oozed through from the sea
below, that although the temperature had fallen to 8°
it remained unfrozen. The floe was consequently very
wet and afforded an extremely bad road.

During the 4th, the temperature remaining at 12°,
I was surprised to find that the falling snow crystals,
which are usually very minute at so low a temperature,

were large and downy, resembling those which fall when the temperature is near freezing point.

On the 5th, the weather was still as gloomy as ever, with thick snow falling In the evening Lieutenant Aldrich returned, with eleven dogs harnessed to one sledge on which his light gear was secured. Everything else had been left a few miles behind to enable him to reach the ship before night.

The dogs, sinking as they frequently did in the soft snow up to their muzzles, had proved to be nearly useless, and but for the help of the men the sledge would have had to be abandoned. The dogs had suffered much from fits, one had been shot, and two others had wandered from the party when temporarily mad. Aldrich had succeeded in reaching Cape Joseph Henry, and had spent three days in exploring the neighbourhood. The floebergs and rugged ice piled directly against the precipitous face of the cliffs, with an extremely rough pack in constant motion, effectually prevented sledges being dragged round the cape; but fortunately there was a fair prospect of finding a level road overland to the sea on the other side of the cape in the spring. It was now too late in the season for Markham to attempt it.

Commander Markham's party were communicated with on the 1st, six miles distant from the cape and travelling towards it. The sledge crews had all experienced very hard work, occasioned by the thin state of the new ice having forced them to travel along the land, to follow every indentation of the shore, and to haul the sledges across the hills at the back of the precipitous points. The fact that the travellers continued their advance at all under these circumstances will be fully appreciated by Arctic explorers.

On the 27th September Aldrich had succeeded in reaching latitude 82° 48′ N., a somewhat higher latitude than had ever before been attained, our gallant predecessors, Sir Edward Parry, Sir James Ross, Dr. James Beverly, Admiral Edward Bird, and the coxswain James Parker, in their celebrated boat-journey towards the North Pole from Spitsbergen in 1827, having advanced a little beyond latitude 82° 45′ N.

From the summit of a mountain 2,000 feet high Aldrich discovered an apparently continuous coast-line extending towards the north-west for a distance of sixty miles to latitude 83° 7′ N. with lofty mountains in the interior to the southward. No land was to be seen to the northward for at least eight or ten miles ; misty weather prevented his seeing farther in that direction.

The following extracts from Lieutenant Aldrich's official journal give a description of his journey :—

* * * * *

'*September* 22*nd.*—At 11 A.M. I left the ship, in command of two dog-sledges, seven dogs in each, two blue-jackets (Ayles and Simmons), and Frederick the Eskimo. I arrived at Snow House Point at 4.20 P.M., having been delayed a great deal by several of the dogs falling down in fits, no less than eight of them being thus attacked, and two or three of them twice or three times over.

'*September* 23*rd.*—Shortly after starting I was obliged to cut one of Simmons's dogs adrift, and I was constantly hampered by fits as yesterday. I now had thirteen dogs left. The second sledge gave way in the runner, the tenons of the uprights from being fixtures, make the sledge too rigid and do not admit of enough freedom for passing the rough ice. During the whole of the time I was subsequently away the sledges stood exceedingly well, and among very heavy and bad ice, the uprights being unsupported except by the lashings, and the runner being kept out in its place by a spare batten used as a lever.

' Crossing Black Cliff Bay, there was a large patch of new ice, with no snow on it, which evidently showed where the heavy floes had separated during the gale. I sounded this with an ice-chisel and found it quite strong enough to sledge over, congratulating myself on the rapid progress I was making towards the cliffs ahead. My triumph was short-lived, for as we got well into the middle, I observed the ice bending as we proceeded, and just as I turned round to order an alteration of course towards the old ice between us and the land the second sledge broke through. Beyond the discomfort of a damp sleeping-bag and a stiff lower-robe, I am happy to say nothing of moment resulted, though, from the dogs being very much frightened, it was with some difficulty we hauled the sledge out. The remainder of the afternoon was passed in finding our way over and through the hummocks, with detentions caused by the constant breaking down of several of the dogs, one of which I had on the sledge the greater part of the day.

' *September* 24*th.*—On examining the dogs in the morning, I found one so utterly useless and so ill, that I gave orders to kill it, which reduced the number to twelve.

' A fine morning, with a temperature of 21°, which I should like to have seen lower, as I had nothing to do but try and get across the new ice which had turned me back yesterday afternoon. On reaching its edge I divided the loads, and by making two trips succeeded in getting over all right, the runners occasionally breaking through.

The dogs were free from fits during the day, which promised an improvement much looked for.

' *September* 25*th.*—By aid of drag-belts and half-loads the overland route to Victoria Lake was accomplished, the distance being about a mile, but not enough snow to render it easy work ; in fact, the land was nearly bare, except in patches, which we availed ourselves of as often as possible. On reaching the ice with the first load, I found it to be a solid floe of rounded hummocks, bare of snow, and of great age ; it terminated in a sheet of clear, beautiful ice which I doubt not is of this season's formation, and which was about ten inches in thickness, and over nearly six feet of fresh water. We appreciated the fact of our being on a freshwater lake most thoroughly, and everyone turned out to be thirsty.

' By 3.30 P.M. I had to cut another dog adrift, it being far too constantly ill to do anything ; this left five in one sledge and six in the other. It may perhaps be thought more humane to kill rather than desert dogs ; but I have found from experience that sometimes they follow your tracks, and that they again become useful ; and on my return to the ship last time, a dog by name " Michael " went down in a fit within a couple of miles of the ship ; he was cut adrift and left on the ice, remained away some eight days, during some of which a furious gale was blowing, and then returned to do good service on the present journey. The only harm his absence seems to have done him is to have given him an unappeasable appetite, for he is less particular in what he eats than any other of the creatures ; harness, rope, leather-straps, hide-lashing, painted canvas, &c., have all suffered from his peculiarity ; and on one occasion he investigated the frozen contents of the metal ladle with such eagerness that he bit a piece clean out of it two inches in length.

' On the 27th, accompanied by Ayles, I started off from the tent, in a W.N.W. direction, and at noon reached the summit of a hill near Cape Joseph Henry about 2,300 feet high. The only difficulty was the snow, which was in some places above the knees, but the ascent was generally easy except near the top, which was somewhat steeper.

' The weather did not promise a very good view, and as we got higher I found a dense mist hanging some eight or ten miles from the land between N.W. and N.N.E. Unfortunate in this respect, I was quite the contrary in the place of observation, for instead of a long and undulating plain, which often disappoints one on reaching what is vainly hoped to be the summit, this ended abruptly on its N.W. side in a precipitous descent of over 1,000 feet into the snow-clad valley beneath.

' The hills immediately beneath me prevented my seeing the coast-line for some fifteen miles, but beyond that I got a good view, and good bearing of two well-defined capes.

' Beyond them I saw no land, and as I watched for over three hours, during portions of which time I had good views through the fleeting mist, I am inclined to believe that no land trends to the northward, at all events for a considerable distance.

' *October* 1*st.*—Temperature inside the tent 20° ; snowing heavily in the morning. About 8.30 A.M. it partially cleared. The bag of biscuit and the remainder of our luncheon bacon had been left outside the sledge trough by mistake, and on going out of the tent at 5 o'clock, I had the mortification of seeing that the dogs had eaten all. Fortunately we had the provisions for the day in the luncheon haversack, and the depôt I had left on the lake I knew I could reach in two days. But I was obliged to give up a plan I had intended carrying out of going right round by the coast-line, and endeavouring to determine the depth of the different bays, &c., with more accuracy than can be expected when taking short cuts amid heavy hummocks. At about 1.30 P.M., I heard, " one, two, three, haul ! " and I knew I was somewhere in the vicinity of Commander Markham and his party. From the top of a hummock I found them about a mile distant, making standing pulls across very bad ice, in the direction of View Point. Having attracted their attention, we altered course towards one another and communicated. The route by which I had come being easier than that which they were taking, was adopted by them, but long after we had parted, the " one, two, three, haul ! " showed me that they had not got through the short distance of bad ice previous to getting on to the ice-foot south of View Point. Commander Markham reported all well, in good spirits, and "working splendidly," but that he had found the travelling exceedingly heavy, and had been obliged to resort to standing pulls for the best part of three days.

'We parted about 2.30 P.M., and half an hour afterwards, while eating our luncheon, I saw the Commander struggling back. He had brought us some rum which they could spare, to fill up the deficiency caused by our leaving the ship with eight days' for three men, instead of fourteen days' for four men; we fully appreciated this kindness on his part.

'On the 2nd the weather was foggy, with snow falling. I steered by compass across the bay, making as straight a course as possible by marking hummocks. The increase of snow had entirely altered the appearance of everything, and what appeared before as very hummocky ice now looked like a level floe. It was impossible to pick a road, and very slowly we struggled on, sometimes coming suddenly against a hummock, and at other times falling helplessly into deep holes.

'I picked up my depôt at the entrance to the lake, and pushed on to it, having been looking forward to get water from it for luncheon. The hills at the sides of the ravine, and the ravine itself, were knee-deep in snow, where scarcely any lay when I passed before; the clear and polished floe was covered, and we had a little difficulty in finding out the position of our former water-hole. A pick-axe soon brought us to beautiful water; the ice seemed to have increased in thickness about two inches, or perhaps a little more. While drawing some water Frederick noticed some fish moving about ; on going to investigate I saw some small ones, about six inches in length, swimming close under the ice in the hole. I dropped pieces of biscuit in to see if they would eat it, but they took no notice of it. However, I had a good hour before me during luncheon, and I was very anxious to catch a specimen. This I did with the aid of a bent pin and a small piece of bacon. In an hour and a-half I got three of them. They proved to be a kind of charr, which I packed in snow and brought on board. All the fish seemed to be much of the same size, and I saw none larger than those caught.

' *October* 4*th*.—Snowed a great deal during the night. I vainly imagined on starting we should be on board in the evening. Steering by compass through a thick fog, I went as nearly straight as I could. After luncheon we manned the drag-ropes, and worked with a will to get on board ; but the dogs were quite done up, and insensible to persuasion of every kind, some of them actually dozing off as they sat in the snow ; so again we had to pitch the tent at a distance from the ship as far as I could judge of about five miles. .

' *October* 5*th*.—Breakfast at 8.15 A.M., and under weigh as quickly as possible. Very thick and snowing, calm. The travelling not at all the better for last night's snow. Made small progress, so clapped on the drag-belts ; and, finding that the dogs did not keep steadily at their work, I shifted the principal weights on to one sledge, harnessed all the dogs to it, and the blue-jackets and myself dragged the other one ahead, thus clearing the snow a little for the dogs, who sank sometimes above their muzzles in the soft snow. In this way we proceeded till 1.30 P.M., when we lunched off the remains of the biscuit dust and frozen meat, not caring to wait long enough to cook tea ; after which we again set off, and, as there appeared no chance of our reaching the ship with both sledges, I packed one with the tent, lower robe, coverlet, waterproof sheet, pick-axe, shovel, and snow-saw, and left it on the far side of the nearest bay to the ship, about two and a half miles distant.   We now got on a little quicker,

DOG-SLEDGE.

and in due course I rounded the point, and arrived on board the ship about 8 P.M., finding the ice very sludgy, but far preferable to what we had been travelling over.

‘ Dogs are not of much use when the snow becomes more than twelve inches deep : they are frightened and unable fairly to exert their powers.   On smooth floes they are very rapid, but where men have to lend a hand, the unanimity of action which prevails in a man-sledge is lost, and by no means could we get our dogs to haul when we did. This makes the labour much greater, and it is not agreeable to find, on looking round after a hard struggle in the belt to get the sledge ahead, that some of the dogs are not hauling, and the others helping them ; and yet ordinarily they do a very great deal of work, and if much may be said against them a great deal may be said for them.'

*   *   *   *   *   *

At Floeberg Beach on the 6th. The ice was eight inches in thickness, above it was water one inch in depth, five inches of sodden snow, and on top of all eight inches of dry snow. Owing to this accumulation of snow on the young ice, it suddenly broke away from the ship's side, and sank about six inches, allowing the water to flow over it to that depth, and rendering the surface extremely sloppy ; the water remaining unfrozen notwithstanding the temperature was at $14°$.

On the 7th we experienced a strong breeze from the westward, with snow falling and drifting to such an extent as to hide everything from view that was more than a ship's length distant. I was very thankful that Aldrich and the dogs were safe on board, for the light snow had collected in drifts as high as our hips. On the land it must have been deeper, but our duties did not call anyone in that direction. The upper deck was so deeply buried that it became questionable whether to house it over with the winter awning, but closing it in too early meant shutting out the daylight from below—a very serious loss.

During the evening, the overcast weather clearing

slightly, we obtained a momentary glimpse of the hill-
tops. Although so much snow had fallen lately, the
wind had swept them completely bare, carrying the
snow to the sheltered slopes and on to the sea ice.

I remarked in my journal: '8th.—Light airs and
calms with snow. The floe is in a most deplorable
state; the snow, two feet in thickness, covers more
than one foot of wet sludge at a temperature of 27°.
It was with difficulty that we obtained a sledge-load
of ice from the upper surface of a floeberg about one
hundred yards from the ship. A road was cleared for
a short distance with shovels, but as soon as the snow
was removed the uncovered water a foot in depth
above the floe turned into sludge, but refused to freeze
hard. Matters were little better on shore. After more
than half an hour's struggling over the soft snow on
my knees, I reached the observatory which was about
three hundred yards distant from the ship, but I failed
altogether to reach 'Markham Hall.' A road must be
shovelled away before we can communicate with it
unless we use snow-shoes. This soft snow and so long-
continued a fall of it is a new experience to Arctic
men. The German Expedition on the east coast of
Greenland are the only people who have met with
anything like it. Our travellers must be experiencing
very hard work, but fortunately they have plenty of
provisions. It is difficult to say which is worse, the
soft snow or the continuous misty weather. The dogs
can do nothing in it, and it is quite impossible to put
them into snow-shoes.

'Yesterday's wind forced the pack off the land from
Cape Sheridan to Cape Rawson, leaving a water channel

from two hundred to three hundred yards broad, open for several hours. The pack still works alongshore with each tide, but does not move so quickly as it did.

' 9th.—This morning the weather has completely changed and the temperature has fallen to minus 10°. Everyone felt as if a weight were being removed as the mist rolled away before a light northerly wind, giving place to a cloudless sky. The travellers will be very thankful for the change and the fall in temperature, for we may soon expect a dry floe and hard snow.

' The sun was seen at 8h. 45m. A.M. for a few minutes, rising above the Greenland hills, and yet so slightly is its pathway inclined to the horizon that at noon it was not more than one degree high. The hills south of us, being elevated three degrees, hid it completely from view. It remained more than six hours above the horizon, nearly as long as during the shortest day in England, in three days it will have left us altogether for the winter. To-day we commenced housing the ship in ; the snow, accumulated on the upper deck during the last fall, has been levelled off ready to be covered with gravel when the housing is complete. At midnight the northern sky was quite bright with an orange tint which at first was thought to be an aurora, but as the sun was only ten degrees below the horizon it was certainly the reflected twilight.

' 10th.—Wishing to place a dark object on Cape Sheridan to guide the sledge travellers expected back in a day or two, a cairn built of casks, with a pole, has been erected there, which will give them something to steer for should the misty weather return. In the evening the temperature again rose above zero.

'12th.—A strong wind blew from the north-west during the night, but it has turned out a truly magnificent day. Not a particle of cloud or mist in the orange-coloured sky. At noon the sun, nearly at its lowest altitude, was shining, on the southern slopes of the Greenland Hills and United States Mountains, and gilding the summits of the lofty hummocks three and four miles north of us. It is as agreeable a contrast to the late misty weather as anyone could wish for; and except for the sake of our absent travellers, we should forget what is past. To-day I obtained astronomical observations at this position for the first time. On our first arrival here, no stars were visible, and the sun itself was at too low an altitude. Since it was dark at midnight we have only seen one star and then only for a few moments.

'During the afternoon Rawson returned from a ten days excursion to the southward, having, as I fully expected, been unable to force his way along the coastline beyond a cliff about twelve miles from the ship. He found the broken masses of ice forced up on top of the ice-foot and resting against the cliffs, in many places more than thirty feet high; this and the accumulated deep snow-drifts fronting the valleys caused more than usually laborious travelling and finally stopped him altogether. The ice in the channel was in constant motion; hence it was out of the question to trust his party on it even with a boat.

'Having built a snow hut with much trouble caused by the difficulty in obtaining hard snow—one of a chain of huts which I hope to construct for the use of travellers journeying between the two ships—he passed the gale of the 7th in comparative comfort. The only draw-back was the heat inside the hut, which rose from 15° outside to 45° inside, and naturally melted the roof. Although the door and a ventilating hole in the upper part of the dome were both open, the drip from within could not be stopped.

' So soft and deep was the snow, that on the return journey the party were obliged to cut a road for the greater part of the distance, and only travelled about one mile a-day with a nearly empty sledge. On two different occasions Rawson while travelling in Robe-son Channel experienced strong southerly winds, while at the more protected position near Floeberg Beach, only a few miles distant from where he was, the weather was nearly calm.

' 13th.—Again a beautiful clear calm day without a cloud in the sky. Walked to Cape Sheridan with Feilden in the hope of meeting the travellers, but we were disappointed. The snow-clad United States Range, tinted a pink colour by the sun, looked very grand.

' The strong wind on the 7th having blown away the snow-blanket covering the sloppy floe, the cold weather has at last been able to exert its power. The wind on the 12th removed what dry snow remained. and to-day we have a hard frozen surface of ice, at which everyone rejoices. The upper surface of the ice which was originally formed by the sea freezing, is now, by measurement, buried ten inches below the surface of the present floe ; the salt water which oozed up through the weighted ice produced on mixing with the snow, salt sludge ; this by freezing has added a stratum of salt or brackish ice above the original upper surface.

When a heavy fall of snow occurs during the autumn, thin ice is thus ever increasing in thickness superficially, consequently any article which may be left lying about becomes frozen in and buried. An old floe being able to support the weight of the snow, and not admitting of percolation from below, does not add to its upper surface in the same manner.

' Although we are surrounded by large pieces of sea-water ice, of great age, it is difficult to obtain any that is perfectly free from salt. In many places the ice when melted is sufficiently pure to drink, and the salt contained in it cannot be detected by tasting, but Dr. Colan will not admit it as perfectly pure water. The ice we have been using for drinking purposes is obtained from the surface of a gigantic flat-topped floeberg, eighty feet in thickness, which is lying firmly aground, after having been forced up the incline of the sea-bottom and raised about eight feet by the pressure of the outside pack. At the bottom of the coating of hard compact snow which lies on its surface, and which appears to me to have withstood the last summer's thaw, is a thin stratum of crystallized snow one inch and a quarter thick. Beneath is a thickness of from ten to twelve inches of perfectly pure ice lying above the brackish ice of which the rest of the floeberg consists. There is a horizontal dividing line between the fresh and the salt ice, the pure ice being the whitest of the two ; but the pieces of ice chipped off from the two parts are precisely alike as regards transparency. Dust spots are plentiful in the salt ice lying at various depths, but generally in connected layers ; the fresh ice contains none. Occasionally at the dividing line there is a layer of granulated ice less solid than that above and below it. After carefully examining many floebergs, I conclude that all the pure ice has been formed from the melted snow being gathered into pools on the old floes and refrozen. The dust which was originally intermixed with the snow eats its way down into the brackish floe-ice at the bottom of the freshwater pool during the heat of summer.'

On the 14th, Dr. Moss walked out to Dumb-bell Bay on snow-shoes, and there met Commander Markham and his three sledge crews, struggling homeward through the deep snow.

I did not expect Markham on board until the following day; but so great was the discomfort of passing another sleepless night in the stiff and shrunken tents and hard frozen blanket-bags and clothing, that he made a forced march to get on board, sending Lieutenant Parr in advance to report his intention. I ordered a hot meal to be prepared, and all hands from the ship walked out to meet the travellers. They fell in with them at Point Sheridan, as they were struggling through the last of the deep snow before reaching the mile and a half of hard ice leading to the ship; this was the first level ice they had met with throughout their journey.

The men were in wonderful spirits, but although all were able to walk, several were severely frost-bitten. The journey had been most severe; but Markham had nevertheless succeeded in establishing his depôt of provisions at Cape Joseph Henry. All made light of the numerous unavoidable hardships they had undergone, remarking laughingly but truly, 'We could never have learnt our work except by the actual experience we have gone through.'

Sledge travelling during the autumn is necessarily accompanied by greater hardships and discomforts than that during the spring, to say nothing of its being usually undertaken by inexperienced men. During the spring the weather, and consequently the travelling, is constantly improving, and the equipment, moistened during the earlier days, can usually be dried before it becomes very bad. During the autumn the temperature, too warm at first, steadily falls, and each day adds its modicum of dampness to the tent, blanket-bags, and clothing, until at last they contain so much moisture and become so frozen and contracted in size as to be almost unserviceable. The sodden blanket-robes frozen as hard as boards can scarcely be unrolled, and the stockings and foot-wrappers, put on damp in the morning, are by night frozen so hard into the canvas boots as to refuse to separate unless cut apart or melted inside the blanket-bag by the heat of the body.

Markham's journey of nineteen days was accompanied with the usual hardships and sufferings. The deep soft snow, reaching sometimes above the knee, was nearly impassable ; being a totally new experience the travellers were unprepared for it. In the daily endeavour to advance, the three officers walked in front of the party, treading down a road through the snow ; and as the most severe labour devolved on the sledge which happened to be in front, its crew was augmented. The order of march was changed daily as well as the leading men on the drag ropes ; when the snow was very deep, the whole party of twenty-one men had to drag

the sledges forward one at a time.   The newly formed
ice was so weak that it became necessary to cross it
with half-loads, and the unfrozen water-spaces near the
shore were so frequent that land travelling along every
bend of the coast-line had to be resorted to.   A large
water-pool in the neighbourhood of Cape Richardson
obliged the travellers to cross a hill 250 feet high.

Out of the party of twenty-one men and three
officers, no less than seven men and one officer returned
to the ship badly frost-bitten, three of these so severely
as to render amputation necessary, the patients being
confined to their beds for the greater part of the
winter.

The sledges with their cargoes on four occasions
broke through the ice, and individual men frequently :
these being made to change their clothing escaped any
bad consequences.   The frost-bites were attributable
entirely to the wet sludgy state of some of the ice that
had to be crossed.

The water that had oozed up through the ice
remained unfrozen, although the temperature was
upwards of forty degrees below freezing point; consequently whenever the travellers, inexperienced as
they were at the time, were forced to drag their
sledges over a road of this nature, their feet became
wet and frost-bitten a considerable time before they
discovered it when changing their foot-gear in the
evening; by which time the mischief had attained such
an advanced stage as to defy all restoration of the
circulation.

The sledges proved to be too rigid ; but by taking
out the metal pins connecting the uprights to the
upper bearer, and depending upon the hide lashings

alone, they afterwards stood the unusually heavy work admirably.

There was not one day while Markham was travelling that he could have obtained snow of sufficient consistency to enable him to build snow-houses for shelter by night.

Subjoined is the weight of the sledge equipments before starting and on the return of the party; the change is due entirely to the constantly increasing moisture of the articles. The contracted dimensions by freezing was considerable.

Description	Before Starting		On Return
	lb.	oz.	lbs.
Tent	31	14	55
Sail	9	1	17
Coverlet	21	1	48
Lower rope	18	4	40
Floorcloth (waterproof) . . .	11	4	29
Sleeping bag	8	2	17
Knapsack	7	4	10

Five hares were shot by Lieutenant Parr on Cape Richardson, and traces of ptarmigan were seen there and at Cape Joseph Henry.

The temperature ranged between 15° above and 22° below zero. The party was prevented travelling on two days by gales of wind; and it is remarkable that on one of these days, October 3, when they were detained by a northerly gale at Cape Joseph Henry, we experienced a calm at Floeberg Beach.

The fall of temperature which was experienced on board the ship on the 14th appears to have occurred several hours previously at a position only eight miles distant towards the north-west.

The usual ration of spirit at lunch was changed for

tea, and this alteration in the diet was reported on favourably by everyone without exception. Doubtless tea is preferred by the men, but the long halt of at least an hour, required for boiling water and preparing the tea, must completely chill the sledgers, and cannot, in my opinion, be advantageous. On this journey attention was drawn to the fact that the barrels of the breech-loading fowling-pieces became contracted by the cold to such an extent that the paper cartridges which at a higher temperature fitted well could not be inserted until the outside paper had been stripped off.

Markham reported that during the return journey one of the Eskimo dogs that had been abandoned by Lieutenant Aldrich joined his party, and prowled about at a distance of from four to five hundred yards, but nothing would induce her to approach nearer during the day. This dog remained near them until the day before they arrived on board, when she disappeared and was not seen for several weeks.

The results of the autumn sledge journeys were, the advance of a large depôt of provisions for use in the following spring, an invaluable additional experience in Arctic travelling, and further, by our greater good fortune in finding continuous land over or near which to travel, we succeeded in wresting from Sir Edward Parry and his companions their gallantly achieved distinction of having advanced the British Flag to the highest northern latitude.

The names of Sir Edward Parry and his followers have been given to the newly discovered land to the westward of Cape Joseph Henry in about latitude 82° 45′ N., the parallel to which they attained in 1827.

CHAPTER IX.

PREPARATIONS FOR WINTER — DOG-SICKNESS — SNOW-HOUSES —VENTI-
LATION OF ARCTIC SHIPS — ARCTIC CLOTHING — ASTRONOMICAL
OBSERVATIONS — FIRE-HOLE — AURORA—THE MOON—THE 'LADIES'
MILE '—ROYAL ARCTIC THEATRE—PARASELENA—ARCTIC DARKNESS
—HIGH TEMPERATURE—CHRISTMAS—END OF THE YEAR.

THE sun having bidden us farewell, our preparations
for the long winter were actively pushed forward. The
pack-ice outside of our barrier of floebergs still continued in motion, indicating that the ice in Robeson
Channel was unfit for travelling on. I was therefore
most reluctantly compelled to give up all hope of
communicating with Captain Stephenson at Discovery
Bay until the following spring. I accordingly informed
Lieutenant Rawson and his sledge crew that they were
to pass the winter on board of the ' Alert ' instead of
returning to their own ship. Having left the ' Discovery ' with the belief that they would only be absent
from her for a few days, they were unprovided with
winter clothing, but the articles I was unable to
provide out of the ship's stores were readily made up
to them by the liberality of their companions, and they
passed as comfortable and happy a winter as any on
board our ship.

With the exception of the cases of frost-bite the

health of all was excellent. The frost bites certainly would not have occurred had the travellers been more experienced. Precept and admonition are of little avail beforehand ; experience alone will teach men that a long journey can be performed after the feet have lost all circulation. The face also may be frost-bitten without a person being aware of the fact until informed by a companion that his nose, cheeks, or ears have become a dead white. So long as the stinging sensation of being cold is felt all is safe. One of our worst cases occurred in consequence of the traveller neglecting to remove his solidly frozen foot-gear, trying instead to thaw it off inside his blanket-bag.

By this time a heavy mortality had occurred among our dogs, fifteen out of the thirty originally embarked having succumbed to disease, run away, or been neces-sarily destroyed. Though the animals had been selected with great care from districts in North Green-land supposed to be uninfected, the mysterious disease which of late years has prevailed amongst the dogs in the Danish settlements soon made its appearance in our packs. Apparently healthy dogs were suddenly seized with this strange disorder, generally falling down in fits not unlike epilepsy. The spasms of the poor animals in these cases were most painful to witness. During the intervals between the frequent fits they roamed about unconscious, foaming at the mouth, and snapping and biting at the other dogs, or at anyone who came in their way. When in this condition they would go overboard into the water, or try to run on thin ice, which in their healthy state they would never have ventured on. The Eskimo dog has a great horror of getting into the water. I have seen an animal resting on a sloping snow-bank near the sea suddenly taken with a fit. Evidently aware of what was coming, it made the most desperate efforts to escape up the incline, and howled dismally as its limbs refused to perform their office. Finally dropping into the water, it would have been drowned had it not been rescued. The medical officers of the Expedition, Doctors Thomas Colan and Belgrave Ninnis, paid the utmost attention to the outbreak, and in several instances animals that were severely afflicted with fits recovered under their treatment, and afterwards did good work. Dr. Ninnis has officially reported on the disease. We are, I regret, unable to throw much light upon the origin of this mysterious malady, which in some of its phases is not unlike the description given of rabies ; but there is no instance recorded in Greenland of human beings who have been bitten having suffered from hydrophobia, and the recovery of the animals in some instances is entirely opposed to the recorded experience of true rabies.

After consulting with Doctor Colan regarding the scale of diet which our stock of provisions would permit us to issue during the winter, the allowance of preserved meat was slightly increased, and the ration of salt meat correspondingly diminished. Our supply of fresh musk-ox flesh was sufficient for about twenty days' allowance. Fresh baked bread was issued three days out of four, biscuit on the remaining day. With this ration the whole allowance of biscuit was seldom consumed. As the travellers in the spring could not possibly carry bottled fruits while absent from the ship, the winter ration of that article was increased; an arrangement that was much appreciated by everyone.

Substantial snow-houses were built on the floe and on shore in which to store the salt meat. So long as the temperature did not fall much below zero the brine in the meat remained unfrozen and continued to drip, thus ridding the beef of a large portion of the salt. This plan proved a most excellent one, the meat retaining more flavour than when soaked in water. Mr. Kennedy, when wintering in North Somerset during 1851–52, adopted a somewhat similar mode. He remarks: ' On the suggestion of one of our officers, we have for some days been trying an experiment to ascertain how far the exposure of our salt provisions to the frost, and burying them in the snow, would have the effect of freshening, that is, drawing the salt from them; but we have had no reason to put any faith in it.' They probably did not protect the meat in a snow-house from too severe a temperature.

The banking up of the ship's sides progressed but slowly, for the snow within a reasonable distance was soon exhausted, and it was found necessary to drag a great quantity on sledges from the shore. Large and substantial magnetic and astronomical observatories were constructed on the land, and were at once named by the men Kew and Greenwich. Fortunately for the architects, the gales in the middle of September had formed hard snow-banks, out of which a compact building material was readily procured; but the heavy fall of snow early in the month had covered this completely; consequently the accumulation of discarded material round each building was consider-

able, and for a long time presented anything but a
tidy appearance. Some of the officers also constructed
smaller snow-houses in which they stored their superfluous gear, thus giving themselves more space in their
cabins.

The floebergs forced on shore in our neighbourhood
were as a rule solid masses of sea-water ice; but
in one large one a cave three feet high and six
deep was left, hollowed out of the side below the
former line of flotation. Long after the temperature
had fallen below the freezing point of salt water, icicles
continued to form, hanging from the roof of the cave.
These increased in size and length and continued to
drip while the temperature remained above minus 15°
The brine appeared to percolate downwards through
the seemingly solid ice, and while a somewhat purer
portion became frozen and formed the icicle, the saltest part of the liquid continued to drip from the end.
When the temperature fell to minus 19° even the saltest
part became solid. Throughout the winter whenever a
rise in temperature above minus 19° was experienced,
these icicles commenced to drip, and to contract in size
as the increasing warmth of the atmosphere melted the
purer ice in the middle. The size and degree of salt-
ness of the icicles thus varied as the temperature of the
air rose or fell.

As the season advanced and the temperature decreased, the usual troubles of Arctic ships were experienced. The descending cold draughts through the
stove funnels increasing, caused them to smoke badly
and necessitated the removal of the long horizontal
parts which were led under the deck beams for the

purpose of economising the heat. By introducing tall
upright funnels this annoyance was removed. The
moisture formed by the
meeting of the hot and
cold air inside the funnels
froze and gradually col-
lected sufficiently to lessen
the draught. At the
top of the funnels icicles
formed, blocking up the
apertures and hanging
down outside; these if
permitted to increase,
would at last close the
funnel entirely. It was
difficult to remove the
ice that accumulated in-
side, except by allow-
ing it to melt naturally
and run out through the
joints in the funnelling, where it was collected in buckets.

The greatest annoyance of all, and which has never
yet been completely avoided in Arctic ships, was the
moisture which collected on the beams of the mess-
deck, to such an extent as to necessitate their being frequently sponged in order to prevent it dripping. The
immediate neighbourhood of the entrance hatchways
and the 'downtakes,' where the rush of cold outer
air caused vapour to form, were the dampest parts.
The steam from the coppers during cooking times also
added considerably to the evil. A thorough mode of
warming and ventilating the lower deck of a ship is

an extremely difficult matter at any time ; in the Arctic regions, where the inside temperature of the ship differs from fifty to over a hundred degrees from that of the outside air, the difficulty is considerably increased. Every precaution has to be taken to prevent the cold descending air mixing directly with the warm and rarefied atmosphere of the mess-deck; for wherever this takes place the air becomes vaporized and the moisture is deposited. To effectually warm the fresh air would consume more coal than an Arctic ship could possibly carry. If the question were one of ventilation alone no difficulty would be experienced; for with a difference of temperature of fifty degrees the down rush of fresh air is so strong that the supply has to be regulated.

Sir Edward Parry, after his third and last voyage to the Arctic seas, observes :—

' No means for the production of internal warmth will prove sufficient, without the most minute attention to the stopping of every crevice communicating with the external air. There should, on this account, be no openings whatever, but those for the stove pipes and the two ladders. . . . I have heard a doubt expressed whether, with all these precautions, there is not a risk of not admitting *enough* fresh air for healthy respiration and to afford draught to the fires. But I do not think there is any apprehension : enough, and, without great care, more than enough, for these purposes will always gain admission by the frequent opening of the doors ; for it should be remembered that the more warmth is produced below, the more forcibly will the cold air from above find its way in to supply the place of that which is rarefied.'

With a greater cubic space per man in the 'Alert' than in any former Arctic discovery ship excepting the 'North Star,' I hoped that with care the dampness would be lessened. In this I was not disappointed, but although every means in our power was taken to reduce it to a minimum, it still existed to a considerable extent.

The object in both ships was to increase the size and height of the mess-deck as much as possible, by building snow-houses with wooden roofs over each hatchway; also to enlarge the entrance porches at the top of each communication hatchway. In the 'Alert' a snow-house was erected on the upper deck above the galley hatch, fifteen feet long and nine broad; this acted admirably as a condenser, collecting the steam as it rose from the boilers below. The porches on the upper deck were doubled in size, forming rooms eight feet square. The walls being composed of hard snow-blocks and having ventilating holes in them, the temperature of the descending air, by passing through the warmed snow-chamber, was by this means raised considerably before it reached the lower deck.

The washing and drying room at the extreme end of the lower deck was kept quite distinct from where the men lived; the forecastle above it being converted into a snow-condensing chamber, the damp air from the washing room below ascended into it and passed out through a ventilating tube.

In our endeavour to get rid of the rarefied air from the ship several 'uptakes' were introduced, but only those above the hatchways answered the purpose satisfactorily; many of the rest, being more frequently 'downtakes,' had to be closed up again. Openings made in the stove funnel near the beams were constant and most valuable ' uptakes.'

On the lower deck everything that prevented the free circulation of the air was removed, the dividing bulkhead shifted farther aft, and free communication arranged for between the fore and after parts of the deck.

After these improvements were completed and the upper deck covered with a layer of snow two feet in thickness, the lower deck beams were fairly dry in all ordinary weather : but in the immediate vicinity of the ventilating hatchways and in the parts most distant from the warming stoves, and more especially during the coldest weather, constant sponging was necessary. Although the captain's cabin and the wardroom were perfectly dry, the officers' cabins opening into the wardroom, not permitting a free circulation of the air, were as usual the dampest parts of the ship, and each officer was obliged to construct a waterproof covering over his bed to catch the frequently falling drops. The only remedy appears to be to remove as many bulkheads as possible.

It has been proposed that the air necessary for ventilating the ship should be passed through a warmed chamber attached to the stoves ; but when it is considered how quickly all air-tubes become choked with the accumulation of frozen moisture, it will be understood how difficult such an arrangement would prove in practice.

A stove fitted with water-pipes was tried on board the ' Discovery ' with an excellent result, the warmth being distributed and conducted to a distance from the fire by means of the piping.

Whenever the difference of temperature between the outside and inside of the ship was greater than fifty degrees, the ascending rarefied air from the deck below, on escaping from the top of the ventilating funnel, became visible on condensing, and appeared like steam escaping from a boiler.

During the month the temperature of the lower deck ranged between 35° and 55°; that of the outer air being between 21° and minus 32°, a mean difference of about 55°.

The clothing in wear when on board the ship was a thick under flannel and pair of drawers and socks; a thick woollen shirt with a turn-down collar and a naval black silk handkerchief, a knitted waistcoat and a box-cloth waistcoat with sleeves, a pair of seal-skin trousers and box-cloth shoes; the ship's company wore knitted jerseys instead of the waistcoats.

When going on deck or on to the ice, a duck jumper, or a seal-skin jacket, was worn in addition, with a naval blue comforter round the neck, a thick pair of fisherman's stockings, duffle knee-boots with thick soles, and a leather cap with ear-laps lined with lamb's skin, with mits as necessary. When the temperature was below minus 30°, Welsh wigs or the ' Eugenie ' woollen head-cover and seal-skin caps were worn, with large hanging mits suspended from the shoulder. A suit of chamois leather underclothing was worn by some of the officers when they were taking observations and thus prevented from taking quick exercise.

The rough duffle cloth leggings on the boots were

found to catch the snow badly. Except during very cold weather the snow turned into ice from the heat of the leg, and by clinging to the hairy cloth gave much trouble in removing it.

Very early in the autumn it was found that when the hammocks were carried from the lower to the upper deck daily they became so thoroughly cold that on being taken down to the warm deck the bedding became quite damp from the difference in temperature. In order to guard against this the hammocks were necessarily always kept below during the winter.

In fixing up the transit instrument, Lieutenant Parr observed that owing to the excessive cold, the spirit in the levelling tube had contracted to such a degree that the air-bubble extended the whole length of the tube and was therefore useless for levelling the instrument.

Throughout the cold weather we were much troubled by the moisture which collected on the astronomical instruments from the condensation of our breath and from the warmth of the eye dulling the telescope glasses. To remove the moisture we found it best to apply the warm finger, which melted the film of ice and also dried the glasses ; but as the temperature of the glass fell again a new film of ice would collect. Anything is better than trying to remove it by rubbing, as that puts the instrument out of adjustment. In fact it was found necessary to obtain the error of the sextants with each observation.

The fire-hole cut through the ice near the bows of the ship was domed over with a large snow-covering, both to keep the drift-snow away and to protect the water from the cold temperature. The temperature of the snow-house being twenty degrees warmer than the outside air, the layer of ice newly frozen each day was considerably reduced in thickness.

The fire-hole was left open in case the pumps should become frozen; but as the supply valve was situated below the water-line, they remained free from ice and serviceable throughout the winter; the fire-hole was therefore really useless except for making tidal observations.

For the daily occurrences throughout the winter it will be more convenient to quote from my journal :—

' 22nd.—The young ice is nineteen inches thick. Ten of these are due to increase on the upper surface from frozen sludge. On the 1st of this month the ice was eight inches thick; therefore the increase by freezing below the surface, when the ice was protected by snow, has been only one inch against ten inches of increase upwards.

' 23rd.—The temperature rising from minus 25° to minus 10°, with calm weather, the air is so sensibly warm that the crew are able to work on the ice with their hands uncovered. Some officers building a snow observatory worked without their outer coats and with merely ordinary black silk handkerchiefs round their necks for two hours without feeling cold.

' 24th.—Last night the tide-pole becoming frozen to the ice was lifted off the bottom by the rise of the tide. The observations will be now discontinued until another register is fitted in the fire-hole.

' 26th.—A perfectly calm morning. The magnificently clear weather we have experienced for the last fortnight somewhat repays us for the previous misty weather.

'With the sun five degrees below the horizon the Greenland mountains thirty miles distant, lighted with a glorious orange-tinted sky, were distinctly visible. Last night there were flashes of bright colourless aurora bearing S.E.

This was the first sign of an aurora seen from either the 'Alert' or 'Discovery.'

'27th.—As the spring-tides approach, the ice-hinge formed between the main part of the floe and the grounded ice rises and falls with each tide; the end resting against the floeberg being forced up higher daily as the water freezes in the ever-breaking joint.

'Stars were visible to-day at noon.'

'31st.—Since the 21st there has been no movement in the pack in a line parallel with the shore. The 17th was the last day that any additional floebergs wrenched themselves away from the parent floes and by grounding outside contributed to strengthen our position. A few water-pools have been seen lately in the offing and yesterday the increased tidal motion opened two large pools, about one hundred yards in diameter, a quarter of a mile outside of us. To-day they are nearly closed again; so we may conclude that no great alteration will take place in the pack before it breaks up next season. I am still anxious about the effect of a heavy onshore gale; it would certainly force the floebergs and the ship high up on the land. The fact that we are wintering on a perfectly open coast, protected only by a line of salt-water ice-pieces, will enable others to realize the heavy nature of the ice better than anything else. Whatever results may happen from our wintering in this exposed manner, other voyagers should not follow our example. Walked with Dr. Moss and Aldrich to Cape Sheridan : light wind, temperature minus 15° ; it was rather stinging to our faces while crossing the land ; but near the ship our walk along the floe was more protected, and we scarcely felt the cold at all.

' The upper deck having been completely housed over, the thermometer screen has been removed from its position inboard to a snow pedestal, twenty-three feet from the ship, raised four and a half feet above the floe.

' *November* 1*st.*—After the monthly medical inspection to-day, Dr. Colan reports everyone in perfect health with the exception of one man, the wardroom steward ; he should never have been brought here. A glass of beer is now issued in the evenings twice a week. On the other five evenings a second allowance of rum will be issued during the winter.

' The dinner-hour has been changed from noon to 1 P.M., in order to keep the ship's company out on the ice during the lightest part of the day.

' On Sunday church is over by 10.30 A.M.; all hands are then started off for a walk. School was commenced this evening on the lower-deck, all the crew attending. Commander Markham, and Mr. Pullen, have the general superintendence ; all the officers are instructors when other work does not prevent their attending. The lower-deck is dry and very comfortable. Only three men in our crew can neither read nor write; these are instructed by Dr. Colan, who certainly has the most monotonous work of all.

' 3rd.—Yesterday an unusually high barometer, 30·65 inches, beginning to fall, accompanied with a rising temperature and a cloudy sky, foretold a wind from the southward.

' At 10 A.M., as soon as it was sufficiently light to see any distance, I ascended the look-out hill, and observed a large pool of water a quarter of a mile in breadth, extending from Cape Rawson to Cape Sheridan.

' The outer edge of the fixed ice formed a continuous curve from one point of land to the other, and extended to a distance of half a mile from the shore abreast of the ship. This movement of the ice proves that there must have been a southerly wind during the night, although in our protected position under the land we only experienced a rise in temperature. As the light increased we found that the snow had been blown from the unsheltered brows of the hills about Cape Rawson. At noon snow was observed drifting off the top of the cape from the southward, and very shortly afterwards the gale reached Floeberg Beach, accompanied, as was anticipated after calm weather lasting for more than three weeks, by a very heavy snow-drift. Captain Markham and Giffard, who were observing in the magnetic house, were snowed up and obliged to break the door down to effect their escape. The temperature rose thirty-four degrees above what it was yesterday; there is probably water in Robeson Channel.

' This morning the screw was raised and secured for the winter. The ice formed in the screw-well protected from snow-drift was twelve inches in thickness.

' In consequence of the increasing darkness the maximum and minimum thermometers were removed from the shore and placed on a pedestal four and a half feet above the ice level and seventy-seven feet from the ship.

' 4th.—A calm morning ; the outer pack has closed in again and the temperature has fallen. A row of casks, about twenty feet apart, has been established in a line between the ship and the Greenwich and Kew observatories. In a thick snow-drift, owing to the tendency to keep one's head down to avoid facing the sharp snow and cold wind, these marks are of less use than might be supposed. The black links of the chain cable between the stern of the ship and the shore are the best guiding marks in a heavy snow-drift.

' The moon being entirely absent we have only the mid-day twilight to lighten us. At noon, it was light enough to put out all the stars except those of the first magnitude. The clouds in the southern sky were tinted with a dark brick red. This is probably the last glimpse of the poet's " blush of dawn " which we shall experience for a long time.

' 5th.—A fresh breeze from the S.W. during the night has again formed a few water-pools in the offing ; but it would appear to be now incapable of producing a long continuous water-channel. Shut up as we are, there is a great difficulty in finding suitable prizes for winners in games of chance ; one does not wish to stop cards, backgammon, and other games amongst the crew; in fact I encourage these pastimes; but whereas the officers can establish a score book at one penny a point, the men, I fear, cannot so readily institute a recognized stake. How great a need there is for some article of currency is shown by games being played in the wardroom jokingly for lucifer matches. Candles have been thought of; but they are of too much importance for their loss to be risked.

'In the evening Guy Fawkes, with a blue light in his mouth, mounted on a sledge and escorted by the band playing the "Rogue's March," was dragged to the top of one of the largest floebergs. Being placed on a tarred barrel he was set fire to, and after being dismembered, as crackers blew his limbs off one by one, his miseries were finally put an end to when the fire reached some powder in the interior of his body. What Frederick the Eskimo thought of the proceeding I could not discover.

' 9th.—The Prince of Wales' health was drunk with great enthusiasm after dinner. His Royal Highness's thoughtful present to the officers and crew of both ships of a library of books has been most fully appreciated.

'For the last week the temperature has been unusually high. To-day it has again fallen below zero. With the sudden decrease in temperature to minus 5° the air feels raw and much colder than when the weather is settled at minus 20°.

'The temperature inside the snow-house situated above the after hatchway is 35°; that of the deck below ranges between 43° and 55°.

'The snow house over the galley hatchway, receiving the heated air from below, has melted considerably and requires frequent repairs. The snow blocks forming the walls have changed into a continuous sheet of ice. Had we sufficient plank it would be advisable to form an inner lining of wood.

'The snow has become decidedly harder since the

gale ; we can now cut blocks a foot and a half thick
from the snow-drifts collected on the floe. This is the
first time that we have been able to do so.

'Yesterday, at noon, it was as dark as any previous
English expedition had experienced. With a perfectly
clear sky the noon twilight was insufficient to enable
us to make out the words in a " Times " leading
article, when the paper was held up facing the south.
We have yet eighty-seven days of more intense darkness to pass through.

'To-day the moon reappeared above the southern
horizon. Her movements are so important to us that
a monthly bulletin is published giving the precise
account of when she will appear and when depart.
She is truly the " presiding goddess " of the long Arctic
night ; reflecting to us, during each of her visits, the
light of the totally absent sun for ten successive days
and nights as she circles round the heavens without
ever setting. During some period of her stay full
moon occurs, and she displays her greatest beauty. At
the time of new moon, when her light would be of the
least value, she is absent in southern latitudes. Thanks
to her we can never realize what existence would be if
totally deprived of light.

'10th.—The temperature has fallen to minus 27°,
showing that the disturbing southerly wind has ceased.
The snow beef-house built on the ice continues at a
steady temperature of 12° unaffected by the changeable temperature of the air ; the beef consequently
must be quickly ridding itself of salt. To-day we
tasted a piece that had been dripping for ten days ;
it was perfectly good and appeared, as already observed,

to have more flavour than if it had been soaked in
water.

' We are still at work embanking the ship and building houses on deck.

' 11*th*.—To-day a course of lectures, with popular
readings and songs in character, to last about two hours
on each Thursday evening, was commenced. I opened
the course by a lecture on astronomy. At the end
it was scarcely necessary to remind such a steady
thoughtful body of men, that astronomical subjects lead
us to consider how God employs the numberless
objects around us to contribute to our wants, and how
after creating the sun, moon, earth, and stars—" God
saw that it was good."

' 14*th*.—Misty weather enables us to realize how
very dependent we are on shadow, whether cast by the
moonlight or sunlight. When shadows are prevented
forming, the snow tints are so similar and the lights so
blended that there is an anxious uncertainty attending
each step, similar to that experienced when walking in
the dark, and it is impossible to be sure whether the
next step will not lead one straightforward on the level,
directly against an obstacle, or headlong over a pre-
cipice. In this manner Rawson stepped deliberately into
a chasm some ten feet in depth during his last journey.
In the evening the mist cleared off ; we could then read
the newspaper with ease by the light of the full moon.
The shadow of the ship showed every rope and spar
distinctly on the pure snowy ground.

' The frost-bitten patients are all going on well, but
continuous darkness, or rather lamp-light, is evidently
not the best restorative for invalids.

'Michael, the Eskimo dog that was lost for eight days during the autumn, was found dead yesterday. He was a very willing strong dog, but always most unsociable with the others. He held himself aloof from the rest of the pack, and they apparently agreed to keep him in "Coventry."

'15*th*.—In anticipation of the expected darkness when the moon leaves us on the 20th, a large depôt of fresh ice is being collected near the ship sufficient to last until her next return. The ice quarry being 300 yards from the ship and the roadway extremely rough, it is not advisable to send men amongst the heavy hummocks during the darkness; moreover, when quarrying by candle-light they would probably strike too deep and give us salt ice instead of fresh.

'The uptakes in the snow porches are a great success. From the accumulation of frozen moisture constantly collecting on the inside of the pipes they must also be downtakes, the warm air passing up the middle of the pipe and the cold air down by the sides. Thus the cold air becomes warmed before reaching the lower deck. Frequent brushing is necessary to keep the pipes clean. The wardroom is the only part of the ship where there is a continuous downtake; it is a large tube leading from eight feet above the upper-deck to the floor of the wardroom; it freshens the air considerably but makes the wardroom cold. As this ventilator acts only as a downtake, no accumulation whatever collects *in*side; but owing to its conducting the extremely cold air through the warm atmosphere of the wardroom, the frozen moisture collects on the *out*side of the chilled pipe, forming a white mass of efflorescence

at least two inches in depth, which rendered it so unpleasant and cold a neighbour when placed in the middle
of the wardroom, that it has now been moved and cased
round with wood.

' The snow on the land is at last sufficiently hard to
allow us to extend our walks on shore to wherever we
please ; but the darkness and cold combine to keep us
from straggling far.   From Observatory Hill we can see

THE LADIES' MILE.

one small pool of water at the entrance of Robeson
Channel about two miles distant from Cape Rawson.

' Dr. Colan has marked out a level walk half a mile
in length with piles of empty preserved meat tins placed
thirty feet apart.   This forms an excellent exercising
ground and has been named the " Ladies' Mile."

' During this calm moonlight weather, although the
features of the land cannot be distinguished, the sharp
definition of the hill-tops against the thin streak of

pearly twilight in the southern sky at noon is very clear and decided.

'18th.—Instead of the usual Thursday readings and songs, the Royal Arctic Theatre was opened this evening, after a close, I believe, of twenty-three years. Owing to the large size of the lower deck we are enabled to erect the stage there with the temperature of 50°, an advantage appreciated by both actors and audience. A representation held on the upper deck, with a temperature of about twenty degrees below zero, leads everyone to long for the finale at an early hour.

'The acting was excellent, and everything went off well. Aldrich's frequent and pleasant performances on the piano have quite put a stop to the intended formation of a band. He very kindly plays dance music on Thursday evenings after the usual gathering, much to the delight of the numerous dancers. The drop scene was embellished with a representation of Austria, America, and England struggling for the Pole.'

Owing to the small size of the ' Discovery's ' lower deck a large snow-house was constructed on the floe, which served as a theatre and lecture-room.

19th.—At 11 A.M. the magnetometer and electrometer both showed a disturbance. At 6 30 P.M. there was a fine clear paraselena, the arch being forty-four and a half degrees in diameter. Three mock moons were visible, one above and one on each side of the moon. The prismatic colours were very decided in the halo passing through the horizontal mock moon, showing red towards or nearest to the real moon. The upper vertical reflection was not clearly defined, being merely a bright blur. The vertical and horizontal reflection forming a cross passing through the moon was very clear.

' Sailors being more accustomed to using a hand-spike than to digging with a spade, cannot resist the temptation of using the latter as a lever before the block of snow has been disconnected from the snow bank ; consequently our few available spades are all more or less damaged, giving constant work to the blacksmith, whose forge is erected on the forecastle.'

The ' Discovery ' improved upon this arrangement and constructed a convenient snow smithy.

' 22nd.—Temperature minus 37°. The after part of the lower deck is dry overhead ; the fore part fairly so. The officers' cabins are still bad : the moisture collecting and freezing when it is cold, thaws and drops at other times. To-day there was a light air from the N.W., force 2. A few cheeks and noses were frost-bitten, but not sufficiently to stop the work outside the ship. We are still in want of snow for banking up against the ship's side : since the heavy snowstorm in September very little has fallen, and owing to the calm weather deep snow-drifts have not collected near us.

'Last night a bright streak of aurora was seen stretching through the zenith in a north and south direction.'

About the same time a faint aurora was observed at Discovery Bay.

' Yesterday, the low mist through which Aldebaran was glimmering made it appear to move up and down, or ' jump,' as several reported ; it was about six degrees above the horizon and the refraction very changeable ; this evening there was little or no refraction : the crescent of the moon skirting close above the southern hills was so slightly distorted that it appeared in its true form until the points of the upper horn sank behind the land, not to return to us for thirteen days.

'23rd.—A cold day with a clear sky. Mercury frozen for the first time: temperature down to minus 45°. Being calm, there were no ill effects from the extreme cold, the work outside the ship being carried on as usual.

'The cracking noise mentioned by former voyagers has only lately been heard on board; as the spring-tides approach the noise increases in frequency; it is evidently due to the movement of the ice in close contact with the outer skin of the ship.

'Taking advantage of the cold weather, we compared a number of spirit thermometers with each other; although their readings were widely different, yet when the Kew correction was applied each agreed fairly with the general mean.

'26th.—This morning we experienced a southerly wind. During the afternoon the weather was very squally, but the wind never exceeded force 5; the temperature, however, rose nineteen degrees, proving that a gale was blowing in our near neighbourhood.

'A band of smoky-looking clouds has collected above Robeson Channel; remaining stationary, they denote that the wind does not extend to any great height above the hills. I could see no water or water-smoke at noon from the look-out hill, but by the temperature rising forty degrees there is probably some water in Robeson Channel. Immediately the wind changed from S.S.E. to W. the temperature fell twenty three degrees.'

We afterwards learnt that during this period the 'Discovery' in her protected position experienced calm and cold weather, only one light puff of wind from the south-east reaching her at noon of the 26th. As her highest temperature was minus 10°, I conclude that the warm blast of air which raised our temperature to 19° passed up Robeson Channel from the southward without entering Discovery Bay.

'During the forenoon a streak of aurora was observed passing through the zenith in a north and south direction; it consisted of a continuous straight ribbon of fairly bright diffused light with distinctly marked edges extending to within about eight degrees of each horizon. The stars shone through the aurora as plainly as those in any other part of the heavens, and the sky at the border of the ribbon was not darkened in appearance.

'27th —The weather having become settled, leaving an unusually clear sky even for this cloudless region, with calm weather and a temperature of minus 15°, everyone was induced to prolong his usual walk.

'28th.—At 1 A.M. a bright streak of aurora, composed of detached feathery streams, stretched across the zenith in a north and south direction, extending to within about twenty degrees of each horizon. At the same time, bearing S.E., there were several bright flashes forming an arch with a darkly shaded sky below.

'The streams in the zenith, judging by their lateral motion as they passed overhead towards the south, were apparently not far from the earth; in passing they partially hid the stars from view, somewhat in the same manner as a fine cumulus cloud would have done.

'This is the brightest aurora we have experienced

but we could detect no disturbance in the magnetometer. Contrary to the popular belief, the aurora
gives us no appreciable light.

'30th.—With the exception of the "Polaris" we
have now experienced a greater degree of darkness
than any of our predecessors. To-day, with a perfectly
clear sky, from a distance of half a mile in a southerly
direction, the ship was distinctly visible from 11 A.M.
to 1 P.M. At noon, just topping the southern hills,
was a faintly tinted pearly green sky, through which
stars of the first magnitude had a difficulty in shining;
above, it toned off into a slightly brightened light blue
which extended to the zenith; from thence to the
northern horizon was a distinctly brightened dark
blue sky. When the twilight, after lingering for eight
hours, has left us, the reflection from the prevailing snow
is sufficient, even at midnight, to brighten the heavens
and to render the stars in the "Milky Way" very faint;
in fact that glorious band, only apparent on dark nights,
is here scarcely visible. When mist or snow-drift
obscures the stars then only is the darkness intense;
it is never equal to the black gloom of a coal mine.
The continuousness of the darkness, rather than its
intensity, is the depressing accompaniment of winter in
the Arctic regions.'

After the ship was fixed in winter-quarters an attempt was made to train the carrier-pigeons to return
to the vessel. In doing so one was lost, and the three
remaining were then left to fly about the ship and
accustom themselves to the neighbourhood. As the
cold increased they preferred remaining in their house;
consequently they were berthed below on the lower-

deck. Afterwards appearing to be sickening they were again taken on deck, to ascertain if they could withstand the cold weather which they would have to undergo if they were to be of any use to us; but they were so sluggish in their movements and so helpless that the Eskimo dogs caught two of them : the last survivor was then killed and added to the larder hanging in the mizen rigging. Capt. Stephenson succeeded in keeping one alive throughout the winter. In July, when the temperature was above the freezing point, it was released five miles distant from the ship, but was never seen again.

These pigeons were sent on board with the belief of many, that when liberated from captivity from any distance they would return home; but in reality, homing pigeons, like other creatures, have to be taught what is required of them. After becoming well accustomed to one neighbourhood, they must first be taken a short distance from home in the direction of the place whence they are wanted to make their final flight. The distance has then to be gradually increased, until at last they know the whole country above which they have to return. They are of little or no use during fogs, strong winds, or heavy rains. Pigeons are therefore practically useless for explorers advancing over a new country.

'December 1st.—Another magnificent day; calm, with a bright clear sky overhead and a temperature at minus 10°, which, after taking one turn along the Ladies' Mile, made us so thoroughly warm that we could have dispensed with our inner waistcoats.

'The men are working outside the ship with their

sealskin jackets off, cutting out the chain cables from
the ice in which they became buried by the sludge and
snow freezing over them in September.

' As the ice is constantly cracking with the tidal
motion and contracting from the cold, I am afraid that
the links of the chain, solidly embedded as they are in
the ice, will be unable to stand the great strain to
which they must be subjected at the parts where the
cable crosses the cracks.

' At the monthly medical inspection to-day Dr. Colan
reports that everyone is in perfect health with the exception of the wardroom steward, who is very ill.

' Many of the officers are experiencing a loss of appetite ; a few of the men are also similarly affected, but
as they have more regular outdoor bodily labour to
undergo, they are not so liable to feel the change as
the officers. With the increasing darkness we become
more dependent on each other for companionship, and
it requires more than the usual determination to take
a solitary constitutional walk. The snow embankment
round the ship is at last nearly completed, but owing
to her bow being so high out of the water the weight
is too heavy for the ice, which has settled down so
much that the water has overflowed the fire-hole and
requires to be dammed off to prevent it flooding the
surface of the ice.

' 2nd.—A misty day, light northerly airs with a
temperature minus 8°. The moon being absent we can
scarcely see our way along the Ladies' Mile, the marks
thirty feet apart being barely visible from one to the
other. Except by moonlight, it has long since been
quite impossible to identify anyone, or to distinguish

officers from men, except from some peculiarity in
height or gait. It has been suggested that we should
decorate our seal-skin caps with a distinguishing mark
like the knights of old.

'With the present comparatively high temperature
the roof of the snow-house over the galley is continually
dripping, and has to be rebuilt or patched up about
once a week. By incessant care and attention, the
ventilation of the ship has been much improved, and
there is little now left to wish for except in the officers'
cabins. They are so full of gear that the air cannot
circulate freely, and are therefore very damp. The
mess-deck is ventilated through the midship part of the
lower-deck, where there are three stoves constantly
burning.

'The total consumption of coal is 18 cwt. a week.
The galley fire burns 105 lbs a day ; captain's fire,
25 lbs. ; ward-room, 28 lbs. ; three midship lower-deck
stoves, 28 lbs. each ; small stove before the galley on the
mess deck, 25 lbs. ; and the washing-room stove, 15 lbs.
With this consumption, the average temperature of the
lower deck is 49°.

'3rd.—To-day the barometer was falling slowly
with a light breeze from the S.S.E., and a very unusual
rise in the temperature to 25°. I supposed that this
denoted that a strong gale from the southward had
broken up the ice in Kennedy Channel, and that the air
had become raised in temperature by passing over the
uncovered water ; but at 2 P.M. it was reported that the
temperature had risen to 30° ; as this was much higher
than the known temperature of the seawater below the
ice, 28°·5, I looked at the thermometer myself to confirm

the observation ; but in the meantime the temperature had fallen to 28°. On going to the observatory I found that the maximum thermometer, which had been set at noon at 29°·2, had registered during the interval 34° ; this corroborated the report, but I thought that a combination of accidents might have introduced some error. I then reset the register at 28°, and particularly observed that it was fixed in its proper position and immovable by wind or any shaking cause.

' During the afternoon the temperature was extremely variable, with squally weather from the S.S.E. At 8 P.M., a second warm blast was experienced. It fortunately happened that Dr. Moss, Lieutenant Giffard, and I were comparing some thermometers with those in general use, and while doing so each of the five registered 30°. On going to the observatory the two thermometers there registered the same degree of temperature, thus giving seven independent observations. Moreover the maximum thermometer set at 28° at 2 P.M. had registered a temperature of 35° in the interval.

' This proves that the rise in temperature could not be wholly due to the air passing across open water.

' The gale must undoubtedly have travelled to the northward from Baffin's Bay, perhaps from the Atlantic ; the warm air is at a higher temperature than any water within 600 miles of our position.

' Subsequent observations taken by Dr. Moss, showed that the temperature at the masthead, apart from the cooling influence of the cold ground and ice, was two or three degrees warmer than that below.

' At 10 P.M. the wind changing to the northward

lowered the temperature immediately; by midnight it had fallen to 4°.'

We subsequently learnt that this very warm blast of air from the southward passed the latitude of Discovery Bay without affecting the temperature there, the highest registered being only 4°. While we experienced southerly winds the 'Discovery' had light north-westerly airs and calms.

' 4th.—At 6 A.M., after calms and light airs from the southward for the five or six previous hours, a southerly squall of half an hour's duration was experienced, the temperature again rising to 23°. After 8 o'clock the weather was calm and the temperature below zero. While walking for exercise, although the temperature was only minus 12°, everyone complained of the stinging cold air; when only three days ago, with the same degree of cold, but after a rise in temperature, we were actually complaining of the warmth.'

The 'Discovery' experienced a similar southerly squall affecting the temperature to the same extent, but, curiously enough, the disturbance took place there four hours later in the day.

' Owing to the weight of the snow that has accumulated during the gale in a bank near the bows of the ship, the ice has sunk down and the water has flooded it to the depth of six inches.

' As the ice has increased in thickness, so the ship's situation, only twenty feet distant from a large floeberg, has caused us annoyance and extra work. Before securing her for the winter, this trouble was foreseen, but owing to the shallowness of the water and the proximity of the land I was unable to move farther away from our disturbing neighbour.

'However cold the temperature may be, the ice which is subject to the rise and fall of the tide, must always remain separate from any fixed object such as the shore or a piece of stranded ice. The sea surface being greater at high than at low-water, the ice frozen during the rising tide acts as a wedge to force objects apart during the falling tide. The ship is thus being steadily forced away from the floeberg, the pressure causing her to heel over, away from the berg. The ice has lately cracked within a few feet of the ship and formed a hinge-piece which alters its angle as the tide rises and falls. Consequently the snow embankment on that side of the ship falls away during the spring-tides and requires constant repairs.

'6th.—Owing to the extraordinary rise in temperature a few days ago, the air, being warmer than the wood and ironwork of the ship, congealed into soft feathery snow-crystals, forming a beautiful efflorescence attached to the ship's side and on the bolt-heads. Until the ship itself became of an equal temperature to the air, these grew in length, without turning into pure ice, as the similar formation does which at other times occurs inside of the ship, but which is affected by a temperature of about 50°.

'Yesterday, when the temperature fell to minus 20° the efflorescence gradually evaporated, and to-day the surface of the ship's side is perfectly clean again. Owing to the thick embankment of snow outside of the ship and that on the upper deck, the temperature of

the lower-deck was not much affected, although every
door was freely open.

' 7*th*.—A calm day, with misty weather, temperature
about zero, everyone complaining of the warmth. The
men working outside the ship and the officers walking
on the ice were obliged to take off their seal-skin coats,
even feeling warm and uncomfortable after doing so.
During very cold weather seal-skin dresses, invaluable
for common wear, cannot be used by anyone engaged
in hard manual labour. When taking violent exercise, or undergoing hard work and perspiring freely,
the warm emanations from the body, being unable to
pass through the skin-dress, collect inside, wetting all
garments alike, the seal-skin amongst the number.
When resting, the then damp outer skin-dress becomes
frozen, hardening like a board, in which it is impossible
to move.

' 13*th*.—Temperature minus 28° and calm weather.
A glorious day, or I suppose we ought now to say night,
for were it not for the full moon shining brightly in a
clear sky we should be in total darkness. The floe is
lightened up considerably, and the shadows thrown by
the ice hummocks and snow-ridges permit us to walk
forward with confidence. The lumps which we have
been stumbling against during the absence of the
moon are being smoothed down. The temperature of
the beef-house on the ice has remained steady at 12°
for some days. Owing to the brine dripping from the
unfrozen beef on to the ice below, the surface of the
ice has itself become sufficiently salt to thaw at that
temperature ; consequently, under the grating on which
the beef is placed there is a pool of water—a very

unusual sight during the winter in these regions. During the spring-tide last night the water forced its way through the crack in the ice near the ship, and overran the floe on the starboard quarter to the depth of at least a foot. Yesterday the ice newly frozen this season was forty and a half inches thick ; the upper surface was two inches above the water-level, with five inches of hard snow lying on top of it.

' The weather has now apparently settled. Any force that can put in motion so vast a body of air as must be necessary to affect our temperature fifty degrees, raising it from minus 20° to 35°, and keeping it above the average for eighteen days since November 25, must have been very considerable, and I cannot but expect that very severe weather has occurred even in the Atlantic.'

After our return to England I learned, through the investigations of Captain N. Hoffmeyer, Director of the Meteorological Institution, Copenhagen, that each of the observing stations on the west coast of Greenland between Ivigtut and Upernivick had experienced warm south-easterly winds between November 19 and December 12, agreeing precisely with the warm temperature we experienced during the same period, and proving that the disturbing cause travelled over the intervening district, embracing an area of at least 1,300 miles.

' 14th.—From the look-out hill we can observe a small crack in the ice about a mile to seaward, from which frost smoke is rising every here and there.

' Since the winter set in there has been no collection of " barber " on the yards or rigging. The little that may collect on the thermometers or ship's side never attains any great thickness, and has always disappeared by evaporation on the following day.

' In September and October it was far otherwise. Each rope—even the perpendicular ones—became incased in frosty ice, and increased to three or four times its natural size. The absence of this now is probably due to the great dryness of the atmosphere.

' 17*th*.—As the moon sank towards the northern horizon a misty paraselena formed, of the usual diameter.

PARASELENA.

Observing that the reflection was between us and the land, I walked until it fell directly on the ship, my position being 250 yards from the reflection. Objects at a greater distance were mistily hidden from view by the lighted part of the atmosphere ; while other objects at the same distance, which were seen through the same misty but unlightened atmosphere, were quite distinct and presented sharp outlines.

'The magnetometer has been disturbed slightly for the last two days, but we have seen little or no appearance of aurora. Probably the moonlight is too bright to permit such faint auroras as we experience to display themselves.

'Yesterday our usual Thursday evening's gathering was somewhat changed by Commander Markham appearing as the "Wizard of the North." His having taken lessons in the art of legerdemain, and provided himself with the necessary apparatus, had been kept secret, and few of us knew who the wizard was until the drop curtain was raised. All the frost-bitten patients attended the entertainment. Their recovery has been slow. With the exception of these and the steward the doctor's hands have been free all the winter. With the extremely dry atmosphere no one complains of colds, coughs, or rheumatism.

'22nd.—The sun attained its most southern position this morning, so our first winter is half over. Although we are only 453 miles from the Pole, it is still no misnomer to call this the shortest day, for at noon there was an indistinct greenish tint brightening the southern sky, and as there was a low bank of mist to the northward the light was reflected across to that side of the heavens. The twilight was sufficiently strong to put out the stars forming the Milky Way within thirty degrees of the north and south horizon, and only allowed those overhead in the zenith to be faintly distinguished. To escape completely beyond the limit of twilight we must yet journey northward one hundred and twenty miles before the sun sinks eighteen degrees below the horizon, the measure by which the garrison twilight-gun is fired throughout the world.

'There is a decided change in the complexion of each of us in consequence of the want of sunlight ; in a few instances noticeably so.

' 25th.—Apart from the absence of the sun it was a splendid Christmas Day, with a perfectly clear starlit sky, the faintest twilight glimmer at noon, and just sufficient movement of the air to render our walk on the ice the more bracing, with a temperature at minus 34°.

'Shortly before our departure from England a box arrived from Queenstown, containing presents for every one in the Expedition, from Mrs. Coote and her friends, and other members of Sir Edward Parry's family. Unfortunately, one parcel had been stowed in a damp place, and I was obliged to distribute its contents a few weeks ago ; the rest of the presents were given out to-day, and, expressing as they did the kindly fore-thought and interest of the donors, I need scarcely say how greatly they were appreciated.

'The lower-deck was appropriately decorated, the dinner tables being laden with as good and ample a meal as any could wish. Each mess had a joint of musk-ox or fresh mutton, and an unrestricted allow-ance of the usual provisions. The fattest musk-ox had been naturally kept for this dinner. The fat on the outside of the loin was two inches thick by measure-ment ; no meat could have been more tender or juicy.'

The ox referred to was killed at the end of August ; but those killed the following year in July had very little fat on them.

' Since the temperature has ranged between minus 30° and minus 40° the ceiling between the beams on the lower-deck, near the entrance hatchway, has been damp. It is merely a question of quantity of coal, of which we have little enough. As no one is living or sleeping there, I have merely directed increased attention to sponging off the dampness, and drying the beams with cloths.

' Dr. Colan is, I think, correct in considering that a temperature of minus 30° is about the limit of cold bearable unless the weather is calm. When the temperature is lower extra precautions have to be taken.

' The frost-bitten men are now nearly convalescent. They have had a weary time of it, confined to their beds for so long a period without sunlight.

' One of the dogs left at a distance from the ship by Aldrich in October, returned early in December in a most deplorable condition. She had been seen occasionally wandering about in the neighbourhood, but would not permit anyone to approach her; the other dogs, as in the case of Michael, evidently conspired together to put her in 'Coventry.' Being at last captured she was placed on a diet of one pound of preserved meat a day and what else she could obtain through compassion, and now is so fat that her extra allowance is stopped. So great is the change in popular opinion consequent on her improved condition that society has taken her into favour again, and the other dogs now permit her to mix freely with them.'

This animal afterwards became queen of the team, and one of the best pullers of the whole pack.

' During the early part of the month we lost a very

fine puppy by cramp, the only one which managed to survive for a time out of six. An Eskimo is anything but a good nurse, and although Frederick is a valuable man in other ways he cannot be induced to take sufficient care of the young dogs. A female before pupping can be readily enticed on board and placed in a kennel; but at no other time can an Eskimo dog be induced to sleep in a covered-in place. Two females are domiciled comfortably enough at present in casks on the upper-deck.

'The temperature of the land a foot and a half below the surface is minus 3°, that of the snow-huts is minus 5°; and the snow-protected fire-hole remains upwards of 20° warmer than the outside air.

'It is difficult to keep the heels of the cloth boots from slipping; consequently the heels of the socks and boot-hose wear out very quickly. The officers walking briskly can wear blanket wrappers and moccasins without feeling cold in the feet, but the crew while at work, having to stand about a great deal, are necessarily unable to wear the thin-soled moccasins, and are obliged to keep to the warm but clumsy cork-soled cloth boots.

'As is usual in Arctic ships, all expected that during the winter there would be ample time for reading and writing; now the general complaint is how little can be done in that way.

'The men breakfast at 7.30 A.M., then clear up the lower-deck. After an hour's work on the ice we muster at divisions, and read daily prayers at a quarter past 10 A.M. The officers breakfast at 8.30, after which there is too little time to settle down to any particular occupation before the general muster on deck about 10 A.M. After prayers, all hands leave the ship, the men for work, and the officers either for exercise or to visit the " Kew " or " Greenwich " observatories. The crew dine at 1 P.M., then out on the ice again until 4 P.M., when their official work is over for the day.

' The officers generally remain on the ice until about 1 P.M. ; between which time and dinner at 2.30 P.M. the time slips away in a surprising manner. After dinner and a smoke the ship is very quiet, so probably many take a siesta ; but there is plenty of noise at tea-time at seven. Then comes school on the lower-deck until 9 P.M., after which one sits down for the first time in the day perfectly ready for study, and with a certainty of not being disturbed. We need not wonder then, if when the regular lamps are put out in the ward-room at 11 P.M. most of the cabins and the ward-room itself remain lit by private candles for some time longer. As this time is really used to a good purpose I do not complain, but naturally, late hours at night lead to uncertain hours in the morning ; so it frequently happens that although all are obliged to attend at the general muster a few have not appeared at breakfast, but choose to call the mid-day meal by that name, making up for the lost meal by a supper at 11 P.M. on whatever is to be had.'

Were the hours misspent, fault might be found with this arrangement, but in our case with a studious set of officers full of resources in themselves it perfectly succeeded, and throughout the winter I never found it necessary to change it.

' An early dinner is necessary on account of the want of fuel obliging us to put out the cooking-fires at 4 P.M. Tea is made on one of the warming-stoves.

' On Sundays, after church on the lower-deck, the general muster is held outside the ship, then all hands scatter over the ice and land ; the distance of their wanderings being dependent on the temperature and the amount of moonlight. On sacrament Sundays, by mustering before church, the service is not interfered with.

' 31*st.*—At noon the ship was clearly visible from the end of the half-mile walk, and we all noticed a decided increase in the duration and intensity of the twilight, or fancied that we did. In a day or two the moon will return, and except during her fortnight's absence towards the end of January, we shall have a fair amount of light daily.

' The old year is dying away calmly. There is perhaps more excuse for us than for many in looking forward anxiously to the next one, for if any can be pardoned for wishing the present time to pass quickly it is those undergoing their term of voluntary banishment in these regions. Not that the time is hanging heavily, for I can confidently say that no former collection of officers or men met their monotonous and lonely Arctic life more cheerfully and contentedly than those under my command are meeting theirs.

' Making due allowance for the difference of time, at 7.55 P.M., it being then midnight in England, we drank a Happy New Year to all absent friends, with earnest wishes for as happy and successful a coming year as the old one has proved.'

The following prologue, written by our chaplain, the Rev. H. W. Pullen, was spoken at the re-opening of the Royal Arctic Theatre, on November 18, 1875 :—

Kind friends, with kindly greetings met to-day,
We bid you welcome to our opening Play;
You, whose indulgent smile forbids the fear
Of scornful wit or captious critic here.
To-day we welcome you, and not To-night,
For all is noon with us—all summer bright;
And though the southern Sun has ceased to pour
His glittering rays upon our ice-bound shore—
Has ceased awhile to touch with drops of gold
The crystal corners of our hummocks bold;
We bear a warm soft light that never fades—
A lustrous light amid these Greenland shades;
All trustful of each other's love, we learn
With steady flame our lamp of Hope to burn:
And suns may set, and twilights disappear—
They shall not rob us of our Christmas cheer;
Nor blinding drift, nor frozen wave, shall chill
Our laughter glad—for laugh, brave boys, we will;
Kindling yet once again the genial glow
Of happy English homes on Arctic floe.

Yet once again; for none would here forget
We are but sons of fathers living yet:
In work and play alike, we but renew
The deeds of men who taught us what to do.
And though, more favoured than the rest, we soar
To loftier flights than theirs who went before;
Though ours the boast, by skilful guidance led,
In virgin climes our shifting scene to spread:
We love to read, on history's faithful page,
Of ancient triumphs on our northern stage,
And boldly for our brave forerunners claim
An Arctic 'cast' already known to fame.

Now let the tell-tale Curtain rise, and say
What we have done to wile your hours away.
Such as we have, we bring you of our best,
And to your kind forbearance leave the rest.
One only grief is ours, and you shall share
With us the burden of that gentle care.
One cherished form we miss—one touch alone—
One glance of love—one tender thrilling tone.
Ah !—in the sweet homes of our native isle,
The dear ones move, and minister, and smile.
We would not wish them here, but this we know—
Their thoughts are with us every step we go ;
Their life sets northward o'er the cold grey sea,
They live in wondering what our life may be ;
And heart draws near to heart, and soul to soul,
Till each has found its true Magnetic Pole.

God bless and keep them in His mighty hand—
Our wives and sweethearts, and the dear old Land!

CHAPTER X.

TIDAL REGISTERS — RETURNING TWILIGHT — SNOW-FLOOR — STARS IN
THE MILKY-WAY — MERCURY FROZEN — CONTRACTION OF CABLES —
HEALTH OF THE EXPEDITION — MUSKY FLAVOUR OF MEAT — ABSENCE
OF PLANETS — A LEMMING CAPTURED — DOG-SLEDGING — TEMPERA-
TURE OF THE SEA — RETURN OF THE SUN — BANKS RAISED BY ICE
PRESSURE — VEGETATION AT THE POLE.

On the 3rd of January a long continuance of calm weather was followed by a squall from the southward accompanied with a low barometer and a collection of dark cirro-stratus clouds which gathered above Cape Rawson at the entrance of Robeson Channel. The sky in the zenith was unusually clear but of an ominously dark appearance. The weather continued very unsettled until the night of the 10th.

At noon of the 6th and 7th a low misty atmosphere to the northward, beneath the almost full moon, was brightened with a distinct orange tint. On the latter day the temperature fluctuated considerably with every change of the wind.

On the 8th and 9th, and morning of the 10th, stormy weather from the southward and a high temperature were experienced. The squalls were accompanied with a blinding snow-drift, which prevented our leaving the ship except during lulls in the storm; they also effectually stopped the usual magnetic obser-

vations. The direction of the wind on the night of
the 9th could be alone determined by afterwards
observing the direction of the *sastrugi*.

It is noticeable that although the readings of the
barometers at Floeberg Beach and Discovery Bay agree
precisely together, none of these squalls at any time
reached the 'Discovery' in her sheltered position;
neither were the fluctuations in the temperature so
great there as at the more northern station. For thirty-
six hours, on the 8th and 9th, when the temperature
at Discovery Bay was steady at minus 44°, at Floeberg
Beach it was only minus 8°, a difference of thirty-six
degrees in favour of the northern station. I can only
conclude that the ice must have been then in motion
in Robeson Channel, and that there were water-pools
to windward of the 'Alert's' position.

' 10*th*.—During the late gales the drifted snow has
raised a bank about five feet in height on the western
side of the ship which reaches to the embankment
at the bow and stern. In consequence of the increased
weight the floe in the immediate neighbourhood of
the vessel has sunk considerably; the water has oozed
up and now flows over the ice. On the starboard
quarter, near the troublesome floeberg, it is at least two
feet in depth.

' Owing to the weight of the snow bearing down
the ice, the ship tore herself free from the floe last
night, rising suddenly about a foot. This has disturbed
the tidal register considerably; and unfortunately, when
taking down the ship's awning for repair, the registering wire was removed before I obtained the necessary
correction. When held down by the ice the effect

would be to register a lower tide than the true one, the error continually increasing; and although the observations can be corrected for the sudden rise of the ship, it is difficult to regulate them properly for her gradual subsidence. The correct mode of registering the tidal rise and fall would undoubtedly be to observe the actual height of the water itself as it rises and falls on the pole; but owing to the very quick accumulation of ice it is impossible to do this with accuracy.

‘ During the height of the gale the ice grounded at a greater distance from the shore than usual, proving that the pressure of the wind on the pack had caused an extremely low tide, the same as it would have done had the sea not been frozen over.

‘ The strong wind blew down one of the quarters of musk-ox meat which was hanging in the rigging. This was soon discovered by the dogs which had been allowed on board out of the severe weather; and a considerable quantity of the meat, though frozen as hard as a rock, was devoured before the accident was rectified. So greatly did they appreciate their meal that shortly afterwards one dog, in his endeavour to repeat it, was found entangled at a height of several ratlings up the rigging, unable to advance or retreat. Frederick was nothing loath to take advantage of his helpless condition, and from the howls that followed I suspect he was punished for the sins of the many.

‘ When walking a short distance up the hill with Feilden, we thought that we could distinguish a pool of water in the offing; but on repeating my visit during the evening I could see nothing but ice. In such dim light as ours the shadow cast by a line of hummocks may frequently be mistaken for water. At noon the lofty nimbus clouds, which are only seen during a gale—evidently driven up here from warmer regions many hundreds of miles away—were passing quickly from the S.W. to N.E. At 6 P.M., when it was calm in the lower regions, their course changed to S.E., heavy masses collecting about the entrance of Robeson Channel.

'12th.—To-day at noon the sky close to the horizon displayed a decided tint of green, the first we have experienced from the returning sun, although we observed a somewhat similar appearance a week ago caused by the moon. At 9 A.M. the temperature was only minus 3°. It may seem strange that we thus complain of a rise in temperature, but such is the fact. Everyone rejoiced when the temperature fell yesterday to minus 20°. The explanation is that a high temperature indicates unsettled weather with wind, a low temperature means a calm, when the weather, however cold, is bearable.

'Walked up to the top of our look-out hill with Feilden. This was the first visit of the year. The outside floes, lit up by a full moon and the slight midday twilight, look extremely rough and hummocky. About a mile north of Cape Sheridan was a streak of water-smoke, rising evidently from a tidal crack. My companion, forgetting the cold temperature, longed to be there with a dredge.

'Owing to the comparatively slight snow-fall during the last few months, there is now far less on the hill-tops than there was last autumn. In fact, on the look-out hill the snow, which had then collected to a depth of two feet, and which had resisted the September and October winds, has since disappeared, leaving the ground quite bare, and exposing to view an ample supply of stones for cairn-building. The snow blown from the uplands has accumulated on the lower grounds and on the ice. It can now, however, scarcely be called snow, for it has lost all resemblance to its original feathery composition. Rounded off and reduced in size by attrition while being drifted along by the wind, it would be more appropriate to designate it snow-dust.

'All hands are employed in digging out the entrances to " Greenwich " and " Kew." Fortunately the snow-houses were solidly built with blocks of snow two feet thick, for now they are completely buried in the snow slope which covers the land at the foot of the hills. The passage ways between the magnetic houses were roofed with flat slabs of extremely hard snow ; these are now all bending down with their own weight and that of the superincumbent snow, but fortunately when accumulating, the latter solidified sufficiently to form its own support, and we can now remove the original flat roof without danger.

'Since the early part of December we have ceased to be troubled by soft snow ; our walks are therefore only curtailed on account of want of light and the fear of being caught at a distance from home with a sudden fall in temperature or a blinding snow-drift.

'The actual footing is hard enough, but that does not necessarily mean that the snow affords a level road for walking on. Not only are there the *sastrugi* or waves of snow-drift lying in the direction in which the

prevailing wind has been blowing, but on the table-
lands it has furrowed out numerous short, deep, and
irregular ruts from a few inches to two feet and more
in depth, leaving the surface like an agitated sea
suddenly frozen. The ridges which are left were partly
undermined by the recent winds and give way readily
beneath our feet ; they are sufficiently hard to support
snow-shoes, but if used these would snap with the
weight of the wearer when bridging over the troughs.
When proceeding in the direction of the *sastrugi* the
walking is tolerable enough, but otherwise it entails
very severe exertion, how severe may be inferred from
the fact, that when, after a hundred yards of rough
walking, a level patch of snow is met with, the same
amount of exertion that was previously necessary
carries us forward for a short distance at a run ; much
in the same manner as when arriving at the summit of
a hill, on crossing the brow we find ourselves for a
few moments speeding along faster than we naturally
would on the flat. The only extensive level snow-
floors are on the side slopes of the hills and at the
bottom of the valleys lying in the direction of the prevailing wind ; there the snow is so hard that we can
walk at our ordinary speed.

'16th.—The temperature has again fallen to minus
35°, accompanied as usual with calm, clear weather.
The twilight at noon extinguished all the stars in the
Milky-Way, as well as those of less than the second
magnitude within twenty degrees of the horizon. The
tint in the sky has increased from a bright pearly green
to a faint yellow hue. The present small amount of
returning twilight enables us to discern how very dark

it must have been during the latter part of December, although at the time we hardly realised the fact. In comparing the number of days' absence of the sun experienced by different Arctic expeditions it is rather startling to find how much darker it has been with us, but here, owing to the small inclination of the sun's path to our horizon, twilight lasts considerably longer on either side of noon. In fact the actual amount of light and darkness experienced during the year at all places in our hemisphere is precisely the same. Here we have one long day and one long night; in southern latitudes it is far more usefully divided into the ordinary days and nights.

'Owing to the overflowing of the fire-hole another one has been cut farther from the ship. In raising the tide-pole from the bottom, a quantity of hard grey mud was found sticking to the end of the pole where it had been pressed with great force into the ground. This appears to indicate that the ground at the bottom is not frozen. At a short distance from the beach, for as far as the fresh water can by any means percolate down through the ground with the temperature of the sea at 28·5, the bottom is probably frozen.

'During the afternoon we experienced squally weather from the southward; the temperature at minus 40°, rising twenty degrees in as many minutes, and falling again fourteen degrees in ten minutes.'

It is remarkable that this warm wind passed the sheltered position of Discovery Bay without affecting the temperature there. The thermometer at that place ranged between minus 49° and minus 52°.

'18th.—While walking at some distance from the

ship a "bear scare" is not uncommon; but when we consider how difficult it would be for these animals to see or capture their prey in the darkness which envelopes us, that there is no open water, and therefore very few seals in our vicinity, we conclude that it is almost beyond the range of probability that these animals should wander in winter to our latitude. Still there is no certainty in these matters, and few of us are exempt from a momentary feeling of nervousness as the returning light now and again discloses suddenly some previously unnoticed object.

'The ship is now heeling over from two to three degrees to port. As the tide rises and falls she is pressed over by the tidal motion exerted on the thick ice-hinge lying between us and the floeberg on the starboard side, and by the weight of the snow bearing down the ice on the port or inshore side.

'The smokers complain greatly about their tobacco pipes freezing. Unless the stem is very short it soon becomes clogged with frozen tobacco juice which defies all attempts to remove it by wires.

'When travelling a satisfactory smoke could only be obtained in the morning, after the pipe had been thawed near the body during the night. If lighted on board the ship where the temperature keeps it thawed, and then taken into the air, it becomes solidly frozen before it is smoked out; consequently very little smoking goes on outside the ship. In addition to this difficulty, the few who persevere in smoking with shortened pipes, well covered, complain of shortness of breath and a choking feeling.

'20th.—Mercury has been frozen all day. That

in the thermometers contracted gradually after freezing, and by so doing registered the actual temperature tolerably correctly, until it fell to about minus 47°·5 ; below that degree the contraction was irregular and increased considerably.

'The appetites of all are returning in a most marvellous manner ; so much so that instead of the allowance of meat not being all used as in the fall of the year, there is now scarcely sufficient. It is difficult to account for our loss of appetite in November. Sir Edward Belcher remarks the same fact as having occurred on board the "Assistance" in 1852–53.

'While working in a snow-house on shore Dr. Moss observes that any small quantity of snow left on the gravel floor of the house has evaporated before his return on the following day ; the moisture set free rising and collecting on the inside of the dome of the house as rime. This probably explains the nature of the decay which takes place on the under surface of the whole extent of the snow covering the ground ; by which means a clear space is produced some one or two inches high, giving ample room for the lemmings to run about, and free space above the dwarf Arctic plants, with an uniform temperature many degrees higher than the atmosphere. If the same decay takes place below ice it must greatly assist in producing the downward movement of a glacier.

'24th.—A very low barometer, 29·02 inches, with dark clouds hanging above Cape Rawson, but the weather continues calm with a temperature down to minus 58°. Though many noses were frost-bitten we all " did " the " ladies' mile " as usual, with heads well wrapped up. Hoods on the sealskin dresses afford valuable protection, but the edges collect a large amount of frozen vapour which it is difficult to remove. A comforter covering the lower part of the face freezes to the beard and from its hiding the chin is dangerous. One officer was frost-bitten in this way for some time, without his companion being able to observe it and warn him. He is now suffering in consequence.

'The twilight at noon is increasing very rapidly. Looking in a southerly direction we can now just distinguish a man at a distance of one hundred and twenty-five yards; looking in a northerly direction with our backs to the light we can see an individual at a distance of one hundred and seventy five yards, but this applies only to mid-day.

'With the cold weather the ice has contracted and cracked near the shore: the temperature in each crack is minus 2°, which may be taken as the maximum temperature of the vapour ascending from the water. I therefore conclude that unless there is some open water in our neighbourhood it is impossible for us to experience a warmer temperature than this before the return of spring. The amount of contraction is well marked by the opening of two parallel cracks between the land and the floebergs; these fissures, which are two and-a-half inches across, being on an average about three hundred feet apart. A cask, situated on the intermediate ice, supporting the chain cable which connects the ship with the shore, has rolled back one inch. Unless we suppose the ship and the mass of floebergs, resting on a base of at least one hundred and fifty yards broad, to have moved off shore, the cables one hundred and eighty yards in length must also have contracted very considerably, for in the autumn they were merely stretched fairly tight ; now they are so much strained that it has been necessary to slack them eight feet.

'During the evening the southerly wind foretold by the low barometer reached us ; with as usual a very fluctuating temperature. At 9 P.M., while it was almost calm on deck, a sharp squall, force 5, lasting fifteen minutes, was heard as it passed through the rigging aloft. The temperature rose from minus 52° to minus 30° in fifty-five minutes, and on a sudden change of wind to the northward it fell twenty-one degrees in half an hour.

'The frequent fluctuations of temperature which we have experienced during the winter show how fallacious are comparisons of the temperatures experienced at different positions in the Arctic regions when adopted as the sole guide towards ascertaining the position of greatest cold. A local wind from the southward, blowing up Smith Sound and Robeson Channel, produces a rise in temperature which would certainly not be experienced at a more sheltered station fifty miles to the westward of our position. Our yearly mean temperature is therefore entirely dependent on the number of southerly disturbing gales which we may experience.

'Owing to the limited quantity of mist hanging above Robeson Channel, I infer that this last gale was not sufficiently severe to move the ice there, and that the channel must now be frozen over completely. With a difference in temperature of eighty degrees between that of the water and the air, the atmosphere must necessarily be misty near a water-pool.'

Afterwards we found that neither the southerly wind nor the rise in temperature were experienced at Discovery Bay, the temperature there ranging between minus 56° and minus 63°.

'The manner in which wind rebounds from a steep cliff, leaving it calm at the base, or, in nautical parlance, "does not blow home against the weather shore," is well indicated here by the collections of snow-drift. As the wind encounters an obstruction it divides, passing on either side and above with increased strength ; but so great is the reflux in front, that the snow-drift falls and settles there, forming a bank inclining upwards according to the height of the obstacle.

' 31st.—Temperature minus 40°. Except for a short time on the 24th, and again on the 28th, the mercury in the thermometers has been frozen for the last eleven days. To-day the barometer is falling and the *stratus* clouds, the usual precursors of a southerly wind, are collecting above Cape Rawson.

' During the recent cold weather the lower-deck was damper than usual, rendering it necessary to increase the supply of coal ; at the same time some of the ventilating tubes which were " uptakes " in ordinary weather, when the difference of temperature between the inside and outside of the ship was only about eighty degrees, became " downtakes " whenever the difference increased to above one hundred degrees. When left open too much cold air comes down, which necessitates extra coal being used to dry it and prevent it condensing on the beams overhead.

'Throughout the winter the frozen condensation which collects as ice in the upper part of each entrance hatchway has had to be removed weekly with sharp scrapers. Although my cabin is perfectly dry, and the temperature ranges between 40° and 60°, an iron bolt which extends through the ship's side conducts the cold so readily that moisture has collected on the end of it, forming a projecting round head of solid ice, like the head of a boiler rivet upwards of an inch in depth. Spero Capato, my steward, removed it daily for several weeks, but he has now become reconciled to its presence.

'Owing to misty weather the occultation of Mars was lost.

'Our nearest friendly, or perhaps unfriendly, floe-berg has rolled over towards the ship, proving that the inshore ice is still contracting with the colder weather, and that there is no offshore motion in the floebergs. The cracks in the floe are also more open than before. In consequence of the movement of our neighbour, the snow embankment has fallen away from the starboard side of the ship and will require a considerable amount of labour to repair it.

'The moon will be above both horizons to-morrow, so although the sun will not return for another month, we consider our dark period at an end. On the moon leaving us in a fortnight's time we shall have sufficient twilight to enable us to read small print for upwards of three hours daily when outside of the ship. During the last few days we have each been straining our eyes to try and read ordinary print. The near-sighted men have a great advantage over the others.

We fancy that our eyesight is stronger than before the winter commenced, but the presence of the moon will prevent our deciding the question.

'The beams and ceiling of the mess-deck are becoming rather black from the lamps so constantly burning.

'*February* 1st.—At the monthly medical inspection to-day, with the exception of two of the crew, all are reported to me as being in the best of health. The two men who sleep nearest to the entrance hatchway complain of the drip from the beams damping their hammocks during the late cold weather. The remedy was simply to change their sleeping-places.

'To-day the ice formed this season measured fifty-one inches in thickness. Since the freezing of the sodden floe on the 22nd of October no increase or decrease has taken place on the surface. I certainly expected to have found the surface of the floe lowered by evaporation, but such is not the case.'

On the morning of the 2nd, at Floeberg Beach we experienced a breeze from the N.N.W., force 6, which lasted twenty-four hours. It was accompanied as usual by a rising barometer, but strangely enough also by a heavy fall of snow, and a rise in temperature up to minus 7° instead of the usual fall. On the 3rd a return S.S.W. wind blew for eight hours, the barometer still rising, with a high thermometer. At Discovery Bay a somewhat similar rise in temperature was experienced, with a heavy fall of snow, but as usual in that locality, with very little wind.

After a short calm, on the morning of the 4th, a very heavy gale from the northward set in, lasting at its full strength until 8 A.M. of the 5th. The ' Discovery' then experienced light airs, but at Floeberg Beach the wind did not lull until the evening. Owing to the peculiar position of the ' Discovery,' hemmed in by lofty mountains, the squalls were very heavy and frequently blew from the southward.

In the log book it was entered, that in consequence of the weather, prayers were read on the upper deck instead of on the ice, the first time that it had been necessary to do so during the winter; also that snow-pillars two feet by one, when broadside to the wind, were blown down and carried about two feet in a southerly direction. After the gale was over, high cirro-cumulus clouds were observed moving from the north-west, a very unusual phenomenon.

It is deserving of notice that on this occasion the temperature was much higher under the lee of the land at Discovery Bay than at the position of the ' Alert ' on the weather shore. At the former place the maximum temperature registered was plus 2° and at the latter minus 10°.

' 3rd.—The " Thursday Pops," as they are called, are as much appreciated as ever ; they command full audiences and show no signs of falling off. The songs in character are admirably got up, and " the ladies " have now become perfectly at home in their dresses. Dr. Colan this evening gave us an interesting lecture on the composition of the food supplied to us. He was very happy in making such a dry subject amusing as well as instructive.

' 6th.—Sacrament Sunday. Mustered on the ice by sledge crews for the first time ; but in consequence of misty weather we could not clearly distinguish each other's faces. Calm weather with a temperature at minus 20° permitted us all to lengthen our usual daily walk.

'The late gale from the northward having raised a new set of snow ridges at right angles to the usual line of the *sastrugi*, which lies in an east and west direction, has rendered walking more laborious than it was before. The "ladies' mile" has now many ridges crossing it; fortunately the quickly returning light will soon enable us to leave that well-worn track. Feilden and I reached the valley under Cape Rawson, but owing to the deceptive light and want of shadow we experienced many a slip over the rough places, being unable to distinguish the raised from the depressed irregularities in the snow.

'The last of the patients that were frost-bitten in the autumn got on deck to-day, after spending nearly four months on the lower-deck and the greater part of the time in bed.'

It is to be remarked that three out of the four frost-bitten men, who obtained so little exercise during the winter, proved themselves in the spring to be in an excellent state of health, and although they were not employed on the most extended sledging service, they were absent from the ship as long and performed as hard work as any of the other men.

'8th.—Since the late gales we have enjoyed magnificent weather with a temperature just below the freezing point of mercury.

'I walked towards Cape Rawson with Mr. Pullen. The rocky sides of the valley near Cape Rawson, swept clear of snow by the wind, once again gladdened our eyes with their dark brown colours. Inhabitants of southern climes, suddenly transported to such a scene, would doubtless have pronounced it the very acme of desolation; but to our eyes, wearied with ever-present whiteness, these sad-coloured rocks and dingy precipices seemed to reflect hues of extraordinary beauty.

'We obtained a very fine view of the pack for a distance of six miles from the land. The southern side of each purely white snow-covered hummock was brilliantly lighted by the orange-tinted twilight. The stranded floebergs lining the shore extended from half to three-quarters of a mile off the land. Outside were old floes with undulating upper surfaces separated from each other by Sherard Osborn's "hedge rows of Arctic landscape" or barriers of pressed up ice of various height and breadth. It will be as difficult to drag a sledge over such ice as to transport a carriage directly across country in England.

'When looking down on this icy sea, one of my companions remarked how impossible it was to realize that water would ever exist there again.'

During the following spring I arranged with Captain Stephenson that the three ice-quartermasters belonging to the 'Discovery,' men experienced in the ice navigation of Baffin's Bay, should visit the 'Alert,' to see for themselves the Polar ice. So completely was the ship entrapped and surrounded by an apparently massive wall of floebergs and the heavy Polar pack, that they exclaimed—'She'll ne'er get out of that.' With such a view before them the expression

was far from being an unnatural one; and, indeed, if
the removal of the ice, formed during the nine winter
months, between September and May, while the temperature of the air is below the freezing point of salt
water, were dependent alone on the decay caused by
the heat of the sun during the three months of summer,
the ice in the Polar sea would certainly accumulate
and effectually prevent any navigation

The due balance in the quantity of ice in the North
Polar sea is preserved, and navigation rendered possible,
by the drifting southward of the pack to a more temperate region, there to dissolve, leaving navigable water
spaces in its rear.   There is also a considerable amount
of decay produced by the warmth transported northwards by the oceanic currents.

It is only in narrow channels, where, in consequence
of the contraction in the breadth of the stream, the
tidal currents run at a maximum rate, that the ice
dissolves *in situ* during the summer.   In such places as
Robeson and Kennedy Channels and Bellot Straits,
the ice forms late in the season, and owing to its
weakness, is more readily broken up during heavy
gales; consequently polynias or water-pools are met
with on rare occasions throughout the winter, and
during the early summer the thin ice decays before
the surrounding ice has broken up.

'Yesterday we experienced a decided musky taste
in the musk-ox meat.   Up to the present time,
although there have been a few complaints, the meat
has been excellent.   I heard through my steward that
the ship's company's allowance was tainted.   Thinking
that there might be a prejudice against the meat, I

waited to see what would happen at the wardroom table ; but it was soon evident that there was no bias on the mess-deck, one and all exclaiming about the musky flavour, but not wishing to lose a fresh meat meal we all persisted in eating it. The after consequences were far from agreeable, for several of us had the musky flavour in our mouths all night and this morning ; in fact last night it was an excuse for an extra pipe and glass of grog which, however, did not mend matters. This morning many, even of those who did not try the corrective, complain of headache. It is impossible to ascertain with any certainty why this piece of meat was pervaded with such a strong musky flavour ; it is supposed not to have been skinned for four or five hours after it was killed. In nearly all cases where the carcase was skinned and cleaned immediately after the animal was killed the flesh was free from taint ; but whether the skinning or cleaning is the more important operation is an undecided matter amongst us. With tainted meat the part nearest the outside has a more musky flavour than that near the bone.'

So many musk-oxen were shot by the crew of the ' Discovery ' at a distance from the ship, during the autumn, that they were obliged to be left on the ground unskinned and uncleaned for several hours, before being carried on board. Nearly all the meat, thus left for a time unprepared, proved to be unfit for food owing to its musky flavour.

' 9th.—Temperature minus 50°. The calm weather of the autumn seems to have returned to us, but the severe cold prevents our wandering far from the ship.

So long as it remains calm we can regulate the heat of our bodies very readily by walking faster or slower, but the slightest breeze conquers us at once. Although we all carry an additional comforter ready to tie round our faces, yet we are wearing no extra clothing.

'Only three days ago the sun was the same distance below our horizon as it was on the shortest day in Lancaster Sound, where I passed the winters between 1852 and 1854 on board the "Resolute;" but to make up for its longer absence in this latitude the sun is now returning at the rate of one degree in every three days. To-day at noon, when there was a clear sky overhead, stars of the second magnitude could be distinguished, but only in the northern heavens. The southern sky was clear of all stars except the planet Venus shining as a brilliant white light close above the southern uplands, sometimes hiding herself behind a ridge, then appearing again as she passed a hollow. Ten degrees higher Mars could just be distinguished by those who knew where to look. Unfortunately these are the only planets that have visited us during the winter, and they have but lately appeared.

'The light enabling us to extend our walks in other directions, the "ladies' mile" is nearly deserted. Returning to the ship when we arrive at the end of this well-known road, it feels like approaching one's home, and however tired, once on the well-beaten track we forget that we are weary. Everyone without exception is complaining of shortness of breath. I certainly do not remember experiencing the same at Melville Island, but it was probably the case; we suppose it due to the excessively cold temperature. In more than one instance severe running has been followed by blood-spitting from otherwise healthy men.

'I walked a short distance out to the northward among the hummocks with Mr. Wootton. Although the snow-banks are hard, yet it is certainly as rough a road for sledges as can be imagined.

'Egerton reports having found the track of a hare on the land. It will not be long before Dr. Moss, our most persevering hunter, shoots the poor creature.

'A few pieces of musk-ox meat, left from yesterday, were again cooked by accident to-day ; detection was immediate. The musky flavour apparently increases the more the meat is cooked.

'12th.—Preparations are being made for the spring travelling campaign. To-day all the tents were spread on the ice to ascertain whether further alteration was necessary. In the autumn we found that none of them quite reached the full measurement ; they have now been altered, allowing sixteen and a half inches to each man, or rather thirty-three inches between two men sleeping head to foot as they are obliged to do when sledging. Less space may be conducive to warmth, but probably also to cramp.

'While walking yesterday with Parr, we found a hare's burrow in the snow, and to-day Markham has found another. It is difficult to say how these hares can protect themselves from the foxes, whose footmarks we have seen lately, but it would appear that there are very few in the neighbourhood. Lemmings are also making their appearance ; we find their holes in the

snow everywhere. These holes are apparently made
for the purpose of ventilation or for the little creatures
to look at the returning twilight, for they do not often
appear on the surface of the snow at this season ; still
their tracks which are very pretty, reminding one
of a strip of finely traced embroidery, are to be seen
here and there. They appear to be usually contented
with the exercise they get in the hollow space under
the snow, where the temperature is very little below
zero ; their nests must be considerably warmer. I
have tried to find these, but they are never situated
near to the bottom of the passage by which the lemmings come to the surface.

' On examining a plant of *Saxifraga oppositifolia*,
which has not been protected by any snow, and therefore has been exposed to the severest temperature,
green buds were distinctly visible. In 1853 we killed
a ptarmigan at Melville Island in February with green
buds of willow in its crop.

' To-day, at noon, we could distinguish the outline
of a man at half a mile distant and faint blue and green
tints were observable in the ice-hummocks ; since the
1st of November up to this date the ice has been perfectly white and colourless.

' 13*th*.—All the frost-bitten people have at last
been put out of the sick list. The temperature remains
remarkably steady at about minus 48° with calm
weather. A few of us walked to the southward beyond
the " Gap of Dunloe." The snow is soft in places, but
nowhere is the walking very bad ; the uncertainty in
the footing is, however, most annoying. When an
apparently hard surface turns out to be soft the severe

shake is much more trying than when walking through snow of the same depth known to be soft. On our return, when about a mile distant from the ship, we experienced a light breeze for about ten minutes; with so low a temperature the sensation of stinging cold in the exposed parts of our faces, was intensely painful.

'Markham's dog "Nelly," that is permitted to live on the lower-deck, enjoys herself wonderfully when taken out on the ice, and appears only to feel the severe cold in her paws, which become clogged with ice-balls between the toes; she does not complain much unless her walk is extended beyond a distance of four or five miles, when the ice having time to accumulate cuts into the flesh. The similar troubles of our poor Eskimo dogs are now close at hand; they will commence exercising during the coming week.

'To-day the United States Mountains to the north-west were visible; the Greenland hills in the opposite direction have been very distinct for several days.

'The double doors over the entry hatchways having been more carefully closed, and the leaks repaired in the porches, the lower-deck has been much drier lately, notwithstanding the cold weather.

'The spring-tides continue to split and force up the ice between the ship and the neighbouring floeberg. The cold weather has not only cracked the floe in many places but several of the floebergs have split through the middle, the cracks opening and the pieces separating from each other.

'17th.—Still the same calm, cold weather with a light mist hanging within about a hundred feet of the ice; above that the atmosphere is remarkably clear.

From the look-out cairn the Greenland hills are to be seen rising above the mist, the upper surface of which is perfectly level.

'I have experienced trouble in obtaining the accurate temperature of the sea, in consequence of the thermometer becoming coated with ice immediately it was taken out of the water and exposed to the air. The first time the thermometer was lowered, it registered a temperature of 28°·5, but each time subsequently, when it was coated with ice, it ranged between 28° and 28°·2. To-day the thermometer was placed in warm water between each observation, to insure all the ice being removed, and not lowered before it registered a temperature of about 40°. The mean of seven observations then gave the temperature at the bottom in forty-two feet of water as 28°·54. At a depth of two feet below the surface it was the same, and with the bulb of the thermometer placed in the freezing sludge, it marked 28°; which may be taken as the temperature at which the sea-water was changing into ice. The instant that any part of the glass bulb was exposed above the sludge the temperature fell considerably. The ice which collected on the lowering rope when out of the water, became thawed and fell off when put back into the water at a temperature of 28°·5.

'During the winter several weakly dogs have died from fits, or have been shot, leaving one strong team of nine dogs, as many as we can possibly feed on the ship's ration. Yesterday they commenced exercising, preparatory to a trip to Discovery Bay early in March. Rawson and Egerton with Frederick took them beyond

Cape Rawson; only one fit occurred during the six miles' journey over rough ground : this we consider a satisfactory result. The road round the Cape is reported to have improved, the long slopes of snow at the base of the cliffs being less abrupt than they were during the autumn. To-day the journey was extended to ten miles, the time occupied being about three hours. Two dogs had fits; the temperature during the time they were exercising was minus 55°. Each of these animals is now receiving two pounds of preserved meat daily.

'At noon when the sun was only five degrees below the horizon there were no stars visible and the blue tints in the ice were very decided.

'19th.—After three days' hunting in the twilight Dr. Moss has shot a hare; it is in excellent condition, and has been feeding on the leaves of the purple saxifrage, willow and lichens. It is extraordinary how these animals find sufficient food with which to support life during the dark season, or how the buds of the plants can withstand such a low temperature; even when protected by the snow, they must endure and survive a normal temperature slightly below zero. The track of an ermine has been traced some distance, but no hole or place of abode was discovered. The lemmings are evidently feeding under the snow, for the few tracks they leave on the surface do not point towards the patches of vegetation left uncovered.

'Yesterday when obtaining a comparison of all the spirit thermometers, at a mean temperature of minus 56°, the standard was only 0°·2 different from the mean of ten instruments, only two of which varied more than one degree and a half. Afterwards the temperature was observed at different heights from the floe, with the following results:

60 feet above the surface .		. minus 52·1
11¾ ,,	,,	. . ,,	56·9
3¾ ,,	,,	. . ,,	57·9
0¾ ,,	,,	. . ,,	57·7
0¼ ,,	,,	. . ,,	55·8
On the ice .	. . .	. ,,	48·9

The first observation, recorded as taken at a height of sixty feet, was above the stratum of mist that clung to the floe.

'21st.—To-day the dogs reached the snow-hut built by Rawson last autumn; all the provisions left in the hut not packed in tin cases had been eaten by a fox, which appears to have taken up his abode there. The dogs are getting on very well; there have been no fits since the second day's exercise, and their regular allowance of food keeps them farther away from the dirt-heap than formerly.

'Yesterday, from the summit of Cape Rawson, after a difficult climb up the steep snow slope, we obtained a fine view of Robeson Channel. The floes although old are of large size, and will afford a fair travelling road for at least half way across the channel.

'22nd.—Markham and I scrambled out, over the half-mile of rough ice which borders the shore, and arrived at one of the old floes in the offing, the age of which—whether it be fifty or five hundred years—we have no means of determining. The one we reached, evidently a fair sample of the rest, was about one mile square, separated from its neighbouring floes by broad ridges of pressed up ice, rising in many places thirty feet in height and extending to a hundred yards in width. Here and there, however, the rough parts continued for a mile or more in the same direction. The surface of the floe was above our line of sight when standing on a narrow ridge of young ice, which itself was about half a foot above the level of the water. The height of this old floe above water may therefore be taken at about eight feet; gaining its surface we found it covered with slippery ice-knolls of a dark blue colour from twenty to one hundred feet in diameter, and rising from ten to twenty feet above the general level of the drifted snow which covered the floe. These knolls generally lay in disconnected ranges and were evidently the remains of heavy lines of hummocks pressed up years ago, when the floe was in course of formation, and since melted down into their present rounded form by repeated summer thaws. We congratulated ourselves that if a succession of such floes were met with in the contemplated journey to the northward the travelling would not be very bad.

'Between the shore hummocks and the floes outside we found a crack in the ice, parallel with the coastline and eight feet broad, recently frozen over. When we returned on board we learnt that some of the crew when wandering about the ice the previous Sunday, found this crack recently formed, and that one of the men in trying to jump across had fallen into the unfrozen water.'

On the return of Captain Markham from his northern journey over the pack later in the season, he reported as follows concerning the age of the Polar floes.

'It is impossible for us to estimate, or even to hazard an opinion, regarding the thickness of what we term the palæocrystic floes, having no foundation to form any conjecture upon. On one occasion, at the edge of a large floe, bounded by young ice, the perpendicular height, from the top of the floe to the surface of the young ice, was measured and found to be from five feet six inches to six feet ten inches, but we had no opportunity of measuring the height of the heavier and larger sized floes. On the heavier floes were high hillocks, apparently formed by snow-drift, the accumulation probably of years, resembling diminutive snow mountains, and varying from twenty to over fifty feet in height.' . . . .

' This afternoon the cold weather broke up with squalls from the S.S.W., lasting six hours; the temperature rising immediately from minus 50° to within a few degrees of zero. At midnight a northerly wind again lowered the temperature to minus 40°. During the previous sixteen days the mercury has remained thawed only for forty-eight hours.'

Neither this wind nor the rise in temperature were experienced at Discovery Bay. After a short calm a southerly squall raised the temperature both at Floeberg Beach and Discovery Bay; but at the latter place, although the snow was observed to be drifting from the southward off the high land, it did not reach the ship. At noon the temperature at both stations was minus 14°.

' 25th.—A beautiful clear day. Walked to Cape Rawson with Mr. Pullen; Rawson, Egerton, and Frederick, following us with the dog-sledge. The weather

being very clear we
could distinguish
that three or four
miles to the south-
ward a very exten-
sive old floe occu-
pied at least half
the breadth of the
channel; it was evi-
dently so good a
roadway for the
sledges that it was
at once named the
" Crossing Floe."
The north shore of
Greenland was seen
extending to the
eastward for an
unknown distance
until lost in the
mirage.

' When descend-
ing the hard snow-
slope on the hill,
off which the softer
snow had been
carried by the late
gale, Rawson slipped
and slid down the
steep incline head
first for at least
a hundred yards.

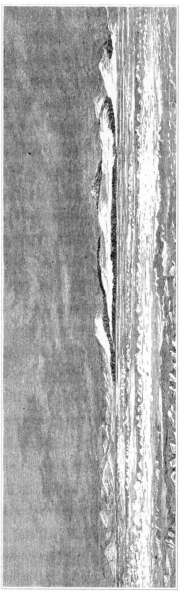

MOUNT HALL—NORTH COAST OF GREENLAND.

Fortunately he had the ability and presence of mind to steer himself and so landed in a soft place. I at first thought it a bit of his usual fun, and a quick method of getting down a slope of snow, but as the rapidity increased, it was evidently an accident and no laughing one either.

'A lemming was caught in its winter coat; when it saw that escape was hopeless it backed into a hollow in the snow and attempted to defend itself by striking vigorously with its fore-feet, uttering a shrill squeak. Except by quickly retreating to their burrows these animals have little protection from their enemies the snowy owls and skua gulls. If caught at a distance from their retreats a dog or fox can readily run them down.

'When returning to the ship Mr. Pullen and I followed in the track of the dogs and sledge which had preceded us. At one spot the sledge had fallen over a perpendicular snow-bank eight feet in height on to hard pieces of ice at the bottom—a very awkward place for an accident. Our anxiety for the drivers was much relieved by seeing the sledge moving along some half a mile ahead of us as if nothing had happened. It appears that the weather being too misty to permit shadows forming, the edge of the pit was not seen until the dogs disappeared into it. Egerton and Frederick rolled off in time, but Rawson found himself amongst the dogs with the sledge turned over on top of all. Most fortunately neither sledge, animals, or human beings suffered in the least.

'During the calm weather which preceded the late gale the bare patches on the hill-tops had gradually become whitened with the invisible precipi-

tation of fine snow which is constantly taking place.
Now there are again many parts left completely bare.
The fresh deposit of snow-drift which has collected near
the ship gives quite a clean appearance to the floe.

'At a distance of half a mile inland, we lately
found a raised sea-bed, 150 feet above the present level,
off which the snow had been swept by the wind. It
was strewed over with marine shells, some so well preserved that the hinges of the valves were still joined.
We also found two small pieces of wood about five
inches long, which appeared as if they might have
been cut artificially, but shortly afterwards two logs of
drift timber were found, from which they had evidently
become detached.'

The rapid elevation of the shores of Grinnell Land
illustrates in a remarkable degree how powerful is the
agency of the heavy Polar ice in raising banks of mud
and gravel in lines parallel with the coast. Wherever
points of land stretch seaward into water of moderate
depth, lines of grounded floebergs mark very distinctly
where they and their predecessors have pushed up
ridges on the bottom as they were forced on shore.
Where two points are near neighbours the banks
continue to increase with the elevation of the land,
and eventually produce a bar, which extends from
point to point and forms a sheltered bay, into which
the heavy Polar ice can no longer be forced. Year
after year the mountain torrents, charged with mud
and _débris_. continue to fill up this protected bay,
which, from the continuous elevation of the land,
becomes at last converted into a lake. In course of
time, after the lake has become silted up, the ancient

bar is cut through, and the torrents again scoop out the accumulated material, depositing it afresh in a similar manner at a lower level.

Thus in Grinnell Land we found at various elevations, to heights of 1,000 feet above the sea-shore, convincing proofs that during the period which represents this great elevation of the land, the same fauna flourished as now exists in the Polar Sea, and that the deposits alluded to were created under the same physical conditions as are now present.

' 27th.—The crew have lately been employed in transporting the coal which was stacked on shore in the autumn, on to the ice near the ship, ready for it to be put on board during the summer.

' Although the sun is still absent, so bright is the light at mid-day that on first descending to the lamp-lit deck it is some time before the retina has accommodated itself to the change and enables us to see our way.

' At the usual Sunday's muster on the ice we all remarked how quickly the pale complexions have disappeared; one or two, however, are still rather white.

' 28th.—A beautiful day; temperature minus 48° with a low mist, but a clear sky overhead. As the sun would appear above the southern horizon by refraction, a general holiday was given to enable all hands to enjoy the sight. The mist, however, prevented anyone being gratified. The crimson and orange colours in the northern sky, resting above the blue and purple tints near the horizon, were very fine and almost made up for our loss. As usual with sailors, three men walked beyond the prescribed distance, and caused a temporary anxiety by not returning for several hours after the main party.

' Giffard and Egerton, with Simmons, had a long and cold journey to-day with the dogs. They reached Cape Union, and ascertained that the despatches which Rawson left there last October have not been disturbed by any party travelling north from the " Discovery." This proves that they, like us, were unable to journey along the shores of Robeson Channel.

' Experience teaches us in these regions never to run with a dog-sledge during severe weather, for although the weather may be perfectly calm, the fast journeying through the air at a temperature below minus 50° has naturally the same effect as if a light breeze were blowing. To-day Simmons became greatly heated while running behind the sledge to guide it; afterwards when sitting down to take his turn to drive his right arm became uncovered and exposed to the cold, and before being aware of it he was severely frost-bitten, so much so that he is now under Doctor Colan's care.

' 29th.—Rawson and Egerton having taken the dogs to the hill-top, from thence saw the upper limb of the sun returning to awake nature from its long repose.

' At the ship we experienced a light breeze from the north-west, but on the hills the wind was from the south-west sufficiently strong at times to create a light snow-drift. The temperature, curiously enough, was only minus 51°, whereas that in the neighbourhood of the ship was minus 60°.'

This was explained afterwards by our learning
that at Discovery Bay, from which direction the wind
was blowing, the ' Discovery' experienced a similar
temperature of minus 51°.

' The vaporisation of our breath in the cold air
presents precisely the same appearance as if we were
smoking tobacco ; and when severe work causes
extreme perspiration, the worker becomes surrounded
by a cloud. To-day, when the dogs were approaching with a light favourable wind, they and the sledge
were as completely hidden as a ship is after firing
a salute. In fact, with misty weather and a snowy
background we did not perceive them coming until
they were close alongside.

' The great difficulty that cold air finds in rising,
and warm air in descending, is well exemplified in the
snow-built observatory on shore, where the temperature
without any fire is always above zero. In consequence
of the entrance passage leading up-hill the cold outer
air cannot ascend, and that inside the chamber, warmed
by the candles used when making observations, cannot
force its way down-hill.

' In a similar manner we have experienced a considerable advantage in consequence of the ship floating
in water throughout the winter. By carefully covering
the engine-room hatchway, and preventing the cold air
descending to the ship's holds, the temperature has been
very seldom below 28°·5, the same as that of the
water beneath the ship.

' In this we are far more fortunate than Lieutenant Weyprecht and his companions on board the
" Tegetthoff." Completely cradled in ice as that ship

was during two winters—between 1872 and 1874—
the temperature of the holds became so lowered that
most of the provisions froze.

' Now that the midday twilight enables us to extend
our walks to the uplands, which have been wholly or
partially denuded of snow, we find few traces of
flowering plants, though the lichens attain a better
development there than they do nearer to the sea.
The valleys and the coast slopes with a northern
aspect show traces of far more vegetation than might
have been expected.

' This is evidently due to the great power of the
midsummer sun, which remains at an altitude of sixteen
degrees above the horizon for several hours while on a
northern bearing. As the altitude and heat-giving
power would be still further increased nearer to and at
the Pole, and as the amount of light—the other necessary for the production of life—is precisely the same,
we may safely reason that if land exists at the North
Pole it is as richly vegetated as the neighbourhood
of Floeberg Beach.'

CHAPTER XI.

GEOGRAPHICAL DISCOVERIES — ABSENCE OF LAND TO THE NORTH—
DECIDE ON THREE LINES OF EXPLORATION—BOATS FOR NORTHERN
PARTY— ADOPT THE PLAN OF SIR EDWARD PARRY — SCURVY—
DIETARIES OF SLEDGE CREWS — EGERTON LEAVES FOR DISCOVERY
BAY—PETERSEN'S ILLNESS—DOG-SLEDGING — SPRING VISITANTS—
WOLVES AND MUSK-OXEN.

In arranging my plans for the sledge travelling during
the spring, I naturally took into consideration the result
of our previous geographical discoveries. We had
ascertained that the land to the westward of Cape
Joseph Henry trended in a north-westerly direction for
a distance of not less than eighty miles from our
position; there was no saying whether it might then
stretch towards the north, or turn off to the southward.
The coast of Greenland was in sight trending to the
north-east for about eighty miles; beyond that distance
its direction was doubtful. Immediately to the northward was a very heavy pack, decidedly impenetrable
for a ship, and of a description which former Arctic
travellers had considered impassable for sledges.

In my orders it was impressed on me that the
primary object was ' *to attain the highest northern
latitude, and, if possible, to reach the North Pole.*' The
more I considered the character of the ice in our
neighbourhood, the more convinced I became that the

only way to carry out my instructions was by advancing along a coast-line; and that unless we discovered land trending to the north, neither the ship nor our sledges would be able to advance far in that direction. Our great object therefore was to discover land leading towards the north.

I accordingly decided to explore the shores that were in sight, in order to ascertain if either coast turned in the desired direction, and at the same time to send a secondary party over the ice to the northward; to discover whether or not the pack was in motion in the offing, and if stationary, whether, in the event of our not finding land towards the north, it would be feasible to journey over it the following year with the combined strength of the crews of the two ships.

When organizing the party to proceed directly to the north across the pack, little or nothing was known with certainty regarding the nature or movements of the ice, but the experience of the 'Polaris' expedition led us to expect that if the pack were not already in motion it would certainly break up early in the season. Accordingly, in order to insure the return of the party in the event of the ice breaking up in its rear, and endangering the retreat, it had to be supplied with boats suitable for navigation. But such a boat weighs within a few pounds as much as the total amount usually dragged by a sledge crew, and at once completely disarranges the plans usually adopted in Arctic travelling along a coast-line.

When a boat is added to the necessary equipment of the sledge the 'constant weights' become raised to about 200 lbs. for each man, and therefore only allow provisions for two or three days to be added. To advance fifteen or twenty days the maximum weight of 240 lbs. a man must be transported. It is thus evident that if the crew of each sledge is to be provided with a boat, the usual mode cannot be adopted of pushing forward one sledge to an extreme distance by provisioning it through a system of relays and supporting parties, which return to the ship one at a time.

After calculating the weights most carefully, I finally decided to follow the plan of Sir Edward Parry, namely, for the travellers to advance the requisite weights each day by stages ; first dragging forward the boat, then to return and transport a second sledge laden with provisions. From my former experience I well knew, as is stated in the fifteenth paragraph of my orders, that ' *in the absence of continuous land, sledge travelling has never yet been found practicable over any considerable extent of unenclosed frozen sea.*' Nevertheless, I trusted that we might advance such a distance from the land as would enable us to ascertain the nature of the pack-ice in the offing, and learn whether it could ever be travelled over for a reasonable distance, on a future occasion, with or without boats. There was also the chance of a northern land being sighted.

Knowing well how extremely irksome such a journey would prove to all concerned in it, I determined to despatch two sledge crews to mutually support each other.

As the north-western exploration promised to be the most important, I offered the command of it to Commander Markham ; but he considering that the land would probably not be found to stretch in the desired direction, elected to take command of the party whose duty it was to ascertain the nature of the pack-ice to the northward.

I then arranged for Lieutenants Aldrich and Giffard, with fourteen men, to explore the coast of Grant Land, whilst Commander Markham, with Lieutenant Parr and fifteen men, supported by two additional sledges until they left the land, were to advance directly towards the north over the ice. Captain Stephenson and the officers and crew of the 'Discovery' were to explore the northern coast of Greenland, endeavour to ascertain whether Petermann Fiord was a channel leading to an eastern sea, and to examine Lady Franklin Sound, which was reported to be a channel.

The 'Discovery' being upwards of two hundred miles north of the arranged rendezvous at Cape Isabella, I considered that sending a party there would be so much strength thrown away; for in the event of a ship from England visiting Cape Isabella during the summer of 1876, and finding that we had not com-municated with the post at the southern entrance of Smith Sound, it would be at once understood that our two ships had advanced far to the northward, and were well placed for exploration. Sir Allen Young on visiting Cape Isabella in August at once drew this inference.

In order to communicate my intentions to Captain Stephenson, Sub-lieutenant Egerton was prepared to proceed with the dog-sledge to Discovery Bay, as soon as the sun returned, carrying the necessary instructions. As Lieutenant Rawson would be employed in the exploration of the coast of North Greenland, it was desirable that he should confer with Captain Stephenson, under whose directions the Greenland party would be organized; accordingly Rawson was to accompany Mr. Egerton.

As the Expedition subsequently experienced a severe attack of scurvy, which has been attributed in some quarters to errors in the sledge dietaries, I may here conveniently refer to the subject, and give my reasons for adopting the scale of diet used by the travellers from the 'Alert' and 'Discovery.' In doing this, I fear that I shall leave the actual cause of the outbreak of scurvy in as undefined a state as others who have endeavoured to explain it.

On the return of the Expedition to England a committee, consisting of three admirals and two medical men, was appointed to enquire into the causes of the outbreak of scurvy. On the 7th of May, 1877, they reported, 'We attribute the *early* outbreak of scurvy in the spring sledging parties of the Expedition to the absence of lime-juice from the sledge dietaries.' The italics are my own.

Soon after the publication of this report Admirals Sir George H. Richards and Sir Leopold M'Clintock, the two surviving members of the Arctic Committee of 1875, and whose experiences in Arctic sledge-travelling are certainly greater than those of any other living men, thus expressed their views in the public press. Sir George Richards wrote under date of the 20th of May, 1877 :—

' This can be no more than an opinion, as it is positively unsusceptible of proof; but it is entirely opposed to all former experience on similar service. It appears in the evidence taken before the Committee that Sir Leopold M'Clintock in all his varied Arctic journeys, extending over some thousands of miles, never carried lime-juice or considered it necessary. Certainly the evidence of Dr. Rae in regard to his own remarkable journeys and his long experience as an officer of the Hudson's Bay Company in Arctic America does not justify the conclusions arrived at by the Committee.

'For myself I must say that, during some seven months passed on the ice at different times, and with, perhaps, larger parties than any one person ever had the charge of, my crews never used lime-juice. The same may be said of the early and extended sledging parties of all previous expeditions. Lime-juice was undoubtedly used by some of the parties which made short excursions in moderate temperatures; but there remains the fact that many previous parties exposed to the same temperatures and pretty much the same hardships as those experienced by the late Expedition, and for considerably longer periods, did not use lime-juice, and were practically exempt from scurvy, or the cases which did occur were so few in number, and of so mild a character, that opinion actually differs at the present time among medical men as to whether they were cases of scurvy or not.

'The fact is that it has always been regarded as unnecessary and impossible to administer frozen lime-juice to sledge crews, and in the Arctic regions it is always frozen during the month of April and the greater part of May; at any rate the expedient has never been tried.

' I state, moreover, without fear of contradiction, that there is not one experienced Arctic officer living who would not have followed precisely the course Captain Nares did in regard to his sledge diet.'

Sir Leopold M'Clintock wrote :—

' I think it due to Sir George Nares and his officers that former Arctic experience should not be lost sight of. If Sir George Nares erred in not having supplied his sledge parties with lime-juice, then we Arctic travellers have all likewise erred.

' I have myself made several sledging journeys, varying in length from 20 to 105 days each, without either lime juice or scurvy in any of my parties ; and the experience of my brother officers in the Franklin Search agreed with my own. Briefly, we lived upon pemmican, and enjoyed sound health. Therefore, acting as I have always done upon experience when obtainable in preference to any number of suggestions, however valuable they may appear, had I been in Sir George Nares' place I also would have left the lime-juice behind.'

As two of the members of the Committee appointed to enquire into the outbreak of scurvy had personal experience in Arctic travelling, it is to be regretted that in their report they did not draw conclusions from the knowledge gained during the numerous sledge journeys which have been successfully undertaken in the Arctic regions, on practically similar dietaries and without any lime-juice whatever ; such as those of Baron von Wrangell, Parry, Franklin, Richardson, Back, Richards, M'Clintock, Sherard Osborn, M'Clure, Collinson, Kellett, Rae, Hamilton, Mecham, Hayes, and many others.

On the other hand, parties commanded by Sir James Ross, Allen Young, Mr. Kennedy, and Mons. Bellot suffered from scurvy.

Sir James Ross, starting from Port Leopold in 1849 on the 15th of May, when the weather was warm, was able to issue a daily ration of one ounce of lime-juice to his sledge crews; but nevertheless, at the end of thirty-seven days, his men returned to their ships as completely prostrated by what is said to have been debility as the sledge crews of the 'Alert' and 'Discovery' were from scurvy.

When I had to arrange a diet scale for a crew of healthy men, most of whom had the previous autumn performed successful journeys of twenty days' duration without any sign of disease, I based my arrangements on those which had proved efficient in the numerous previous sledge journeys in the Arctic regions. A copy of the official reports of these journeys had been supplied for my information by the Admiralty; at the same time was forwarded a memorandum of recommendations and suggestions drawn up by the Medical Director-General, one paragraph of which recommended the use of lime-juice during sledge journeys; but inasmuch as the few sledge parties which had been supplied with lime-juice during the months of April and early May—viz. those of Sir Horatio Austin in 1852 and of Sir Edward Belcher in 1854—had utterly failed to use it as a ration during the cold weather, owing to its rock-like condition when frozen; and moreover, as every one of the many sledge crews who had not been so supplied had, after performing journeys, some of them 100 days in duration, returned safely to their ships, thereby proving that the diet was fairly suitable, I decided to follow the former custom, and only to send lime-juice for use during weather when it could readily be melted. Accordingly, arrangements were made for it to be forwarded to the most distant depôts for the use of the advanced sledge crews when returning in May or June, which was as early a date as any sledge party travelling in the Arctic regions had ever consumed such a ration.

I take the report of the Committee to mean that in their opinion had lime-juice been supplied the disease would nevertheless have broken out at a later period. If this be a correct reading of the words ' early outbreak,' then all future Arctic explorers are warned that they must, sooner or later, expect an attack of scurvy unless a decided change can be made in the usual Arctic rations, and some plan devised of keeping the ship as dry and comfortable as if she were in a temperate climate.

I fully concur that a change of dietary for the crews of both ship and sledge is advisable. I am further of opinion that the numerous successful sledge journeys performed during the Franklin Search had induced a dangerous confidence in arctic men, and that former travellers, without being aware of it, were in reality on the verge of the same dire disease which attacked ourselves.

It is possible that the painful experience gained by us may render Arctic exploration by sledges safer than it has hitherto been ; but unless for the purpose of saving life I consider that no one should be called upon to undergo the fearful privation of an Arctic sledge journey during March or the early part of April, when a temperature of more than sixty degrees below freezing-point is certain to be experienced.

After a careful consideration of all the circumstances of the case, the chief difference that I can find between the experiences of our travellers who suffered, and those of former expeditions who did not, is the greater or rather different labour undergone in consequence of the heavy nature of the snow and pack-ice met with by the parties from the 'Alert' and 'Discovery,' and also the almost total absence of fresh meat; whereas most of the former expeditions obtained an occasional meal of fresh game of one sort or another, and some were fortunate enough to shoot as much as they could possibly consume.

I now continue the extracts from my journal relating to the proceedings on board the 'Alert.'

'1st.—The temperature is down to minus 64°, with a light breeze from the north-west. It is far too cold for human beings and, judging from the movements of the dogs, for animals also; although they refuse to go into an enclosure they are glad enough of any shelter obtainable between them and the wind. The weather prevented any work being undertaken outside the ship except what was absolutely necessary, and the walking parties were contented with shorter exercise than usual; every possible kind of face protector being tried.

'The preserved meat for the use of the dogs while travelling has been taken out of the tins and broken up into pieces of about two pounds in weight; exposed to the cold this has become frozen as hard as marble, and in that state has been stored ready for use in a canvas bag. As it is impossible to thaw the food when travelling, the poor creatures will have to swallow these lumps of food at a temperature sixty and seventy degrees below freezing-point; it is therefore not surprising that fits occur but rather that any dogs are left alive.

'In consequence of the saving of lime-juice which will occur during the absence of the travellers in April, the ration has now been doubled. The evening issue is not compulsory, but I am sure that very few will neglect to take it.

'The mean temperature for February was minus 38°. I am fully certain that at a position a few miles farther to the westward, out of the range of the warm southerly winds blowing through Robeson Channel, which invariably raise the temperature considerably, the mean temperature for the month would have been much lower.

'Owing to the gradual accumulation of newly formed ice on the starboard side of the ship, caused by the freezing of the water which overruns the surface when depressed by the tide, she is now forced over to port, heeling four and a half degrees; a very decided incline. It is quite impossible to remedy matters before the thaw commences. We must be thankful that the rise and fall of the tide is not greater; otherwise we should be as badly placed as the "Polaris" was under similar circumstances at Thank God Harbour.

'2nd.—The sledge preparations occupying the whole of each evening, to-day was the last of the

Thursday evening gatherings for lectures and other entertainments. These have been kept up throughout the winter with unflagging interest, everyone attending without exception.

' 4th.—The sun was seen clearly above the southern hills at 11.30 A.M. To-day had been fixed for the departure of the dog-sledge for Discovery Bay, but the cold weather prevented the start. The mean temperature for the last two days has been minus 69°·6 ; yesterday two reliable thermometers registered below minus 73°, the mean being minus 73°·75, or more than one hundred and five degrees below the freezing point of fresh water. At noon on the summit of the look-out hill 480 feet high, the temperature was minus 62°·5, six degrees warmer than the temperature at the ship. A breeze from the south-west was blowing at the time on the hill, and a light northerly air near the ship.

' The appearance of the southern slopes of the Greenland hills which were to-day tinted a warm crimson afforded a rich treat to all of us, and the feeling of intense cold was greatly modified by feasting our eyes on the glorious shades of colour.

' Parr and May when observing occultations of stars found it extremely cold work, and the spirit in the levelling tubes was so thickened by the cold that it became useless. In order to compare all the spirit thermometers together, Rawson, Egerton, and I were obliged to remain exposed on the ice for about an hour. Unfortunately, while so employed a light breeze sprang up, and as the thermometers could not be safely handled except with hands covered only with the finest mits, we were obliged to relieve each other con-

stantly, running about for at least ten minutes before
our hands recovered their warmth sufficiently to obtain
another observation.   Whisky placed on the floe for a
few minutes froze hard ; so a few of us had the rare
opportunity of eating it in a solid state.

'5th.—When falling in for muster on the ice,
although the men were permitted to keep moving
until the last moment, several were frost-bitten about
the face.   It is amusing to notice how angry anyone
becomes when informed that his nose is frost-bitten ;
being uncertain whether he is the victim of a joke, or
whether it is really the case.   The frozen breath collects so quickly, and the ice is so excellent a conductor
of cold that those who cover their noses and mouths
with a comforter are certain to suffer.   Masks for the
face are not to be recommended, it is better to wear
nothing when walking near the ship.   Travellers who
are obliged to face the cold know that they must suffer,
and a projecting hood or blinker worn on the weather-
side of the face is perhaps the safest protector.   There
is a widespread popular notion concerning the treatment of a frost-bite by applying snow, but our snow is
far too cold for such a purpose.   When frost-bitten
the object is to restore the circulation gradually.
With a superficial frost-bite the best remedy is the
gentle application of the hand to the affected part ; the
slightest friction would certainly remove the skin.

'6th.—The temperature has risen to minus 58° ;
it is the same on the top of the hill as on the floe.   A
thermometer exposed to the sun which was not quite
two degrees above the horizon registered minus 52°.
Frost-bites are very frequent, but now no one moves

anywhere without a companion at his side ready to warn him of danger. Fortunately these extremely low temperatures never occur with a high wind, or no human being could possibly endure the weather.

'A parhelion with prismatic colours on each side of the sun was observed to-day. Very light snow-flakes, or more properly speaking snow-motes, were falling, so fine that they were only visible as they passed across the lighted arc, after which they were invisible until they crossed the corresponding arc on the opposite side of the sun, showing that each particle of snow between the eye of the observer and the extreme distance assists in forming the parhelion. The ray rising perpendicularly from the sun was not prismatic.

'A puppy born three days ago has mysteriously disappeared; it has doubtless been eaten, as usual, but in this case the mother herself is suspected of being the culprit.

'9th.—Yesterday on the temperature rising to minus 45° the dog-sledge was made ready to start, but to-day it has fallen again to minus 58°, so I have countermanded the order for its departure. When on the top of the look-out hill this morning the air was so perfectly calm, that, notwithstanding the excessive cold, after becoming thoroughly warm by the exertion of climbing, I was able to keep my hands bare for ten minutes whilst sketching; but that was only during a very quiet interval, for shortly afterwards, although the weather was nominally calm, it would have been impossible to have uncovered the hands for two minutes. At noon a thermometer backed with a piece of black cloth, when exposed to the sun, which was three degrees above the horizon, registered twenty-two degrees higher than when in the shade. The black-bulb thermometers supplied for measuring solar radiation are all mercury thermometers and are consequently useless at present. No one expected that when the heat from the sun was sufficient to raise the temperature so considerably the mercury would be frozen and the instrument perfectly useless.

'The men are employed daily in cutting a ditch in the ice on the starboard side of the ship, in the hope of reducing the pressure, and keeping her from heeling over any farther to port. The ice has again sunk suddenly away from the ship at the stern, or rather the ship has suddenly jumped up one foot, tearing her stern clear of the ice.

'12th.—A misty morning with a falling barometer, and a temperature risen to minus 30°, gave notice that the extremely cold weather was at an end. Accordingly Mr. Egerton and Lieutenant Rawson, accompanied by Petersen and nine dogs, started for the "Discovery," the sledge being weighted to 51 lbs. per dog.

'When walking with Aldrich we crossed the tracks made by the dogs when exercising yesterday, and noticed the numerous frozen pellets of blood lying on the floe which always form between the toes of these animals when working during severely cold weather. The heat of the foot causes the snow to ball, this soon changes into ice, and, collecting between the toes, cuts into the flesh. On board the "Resolute" in 1853, we endeavoured to fit our dogs with blanket pads on their feet, but these were found to increase the mischief by first becoming damp and then freezing, when the hardened blanket cut into the sinews at the back of the leg.

' A piece of heavy ice lying aground, not far from the ship's bows, was turned completely over last autumn, leaving the part which had rested on the ground exposed to view; it shows distinct groovings or furrows on its surface and some imbedded ice-scratched pebbles, proving that floebergs or stranded ice grinding along the bottom of the sea with the tidal motion or pressure from the pack produce scratchings on stone or rock similar to those produced by glaciers. The long thermometer which was let into a floeberg with the object of measuring the conduction of ice has unfortunately become broken in consequence of the upper portion of the mercury freezing in a defective part of the tube, while that below remained in a liquid state and was unable to expand.

' 13th.—We commenced to-day taking down the upper-deck covering, in order to let in as much light as possible. The cold will prevent the hatchways or skylights being uncovered of snow for some time. Dr. Moss being desirous of seeing the true tints of colour when painting, has uncovered the skylight in his cabin, but the frozen condensation accumulates so rapidly on the inside of the glass that the ice has to be cleared off constantly, if any benefit is to be derived.

' 14th.—Blowing in squalls from the south-west with a force of 8, which will be sure to keep the travellers in their tent; but as the temperature has risen to minus 18° their hardships will not be greater than those of the many Arctic voyagers who have preceded them. The grounded ice around us denotes an unusually low tide, evidently caused by the pressure exerted by the gale forcing the water, although covered with ice, towards the north-east. The ice on the starboard quarter is unable to rise again, consequently with the return of the flood the water has overrun it and risen two feet above the level of the floe.

'To-day I published the programme of the spring sledging parties. It is eminently satisfactory to find how every officer and man, after a long and severe experience during the autumn of what Arctic sledging really is, has been anxiously pushing his claims for employment with the advanced parties; those bound north over the ice, a journey thoroughly well known to entail the most trying and tedious work, being esteemed the most favoured.

'15th.—This evening I was astonished at the return of Mr. Egerton's party, and much distressed to learn that it was occasioned by the severe illness of Petersen. He was taken ill on the second march with cramp, and afterwards, being unable to retain any food whatever, nothing could keep him warm, and he became badly frost-bitten. By depriving themselves of their own warm clothing and at great personal risk the two officers, his only companions, succeeded in restoring circulation. The following day, Petersen being no better, they wisely determined to return with him to the ship. But the gale of the 14th rendering it impossible to travel and the tent being very cold—temperature minus 24°—they burrowed out a hole in a snowbank, and with the aid of a spirit lamp raised the temperature inside it to 7°. With a noble disregard of themselves they succeeded in retaining some slight heat in the man's body by alternately lying one at a time alongside of him while the other was recovering his warmth by' exercise. On the morning of the 15th the patient being slightly better, and the weather permitting, they started to return to the ship with the sledge lightened to the utmost.

' During the journey of sixteen miles over a very rough ground, although frequently very seriously frost-bitten themselves, they succeeded in keeping life in the invalid until they arrived on board. He was badly frost-bitten in the face and feet '

Notwithstanding the professional ability and incessant care of Dr. Colan, Petersen never recovered from the severe shock which he had received, and eventually expired from exhaustion three months afterwards.

During severe weather Arctic travelling of any sort, at a distance from all other human help, is only just bearable for strong men when all goes well. The slightest mishap is sure to entail serious consequences, and a severe sickness, which providentially has seldom occurred amongst the hundreds of travelling parties, is almost certain to terminate fatally.

Mr. Egerton, whose own conduct was beyond all praise, thus speaks in his official report of Lieut. Rawson's behaviour on this occasion :—

' It is with great diffidence that I presume to say anything regarding the very valuable assistance that I received from Lieutenant Rawson, but I feel I should fail in my duty if I omitted to bring to your notice the great aid I derived from his advice and help ; without his unremitting exertions and cheerful spirit my own efforts would have been unavailing to return with my patient alive to the ship.'

The popular supposition that sledge travelling with dogs in the Arctic regions is a comfortable, expeditious, and exciting method of locomotion is very far from the truth. With a light sledge, perfectly smooth ice, and a good team of dogs, rapid journeys may be made over great distances where supplies of food for only a few days have to be carried on the sledge. Dog-sledging as practised by naval expeditions in districts where food cannot be obtained on the road, is necessarily of a different nature. The object frequently being to prolong the journey to the utmost extent, or, in other words, to enable the sledgers to be absent from their ship the greatest number of days, the sledge at starting is loaded to the full amount of provisions and gear that the dogs can draw with the aid of the men. The driver walks or runs at the side of the sledge, guiding the animals with his whip, while another of the party runs ahead, choosing the best path through the piled-up hummocks or rough ice, the rest of the crew pushing the sledge from behind, but very frequently they have to use their drag-belts. Owing to the repeated delays among rough ice, where the dogs stubbornly refuse to do any work whatever, and the men facing the sledge have to drag it three or four feet at a time by standing pulls, the rate of advance is seldom over two or three miles an hour. In fact, the crew of a dog-sledge have even more laborious work to undergo than those who drag a man-sledge.

The dogs should never be permitted to advance faster than the travellers can walk themselves with comfort and without losing breath.

During Egerton's return journey with the lightly-laden sledge, there was great difficulty in preventing the dogs running away when they knew that they were homeward-bound. In passing the deep snow slope at Cape Rawson, the invalid being fortunately off the sledge at the time, they could not be restrained, and the sledge rolled over the side of the bank, a depth of thirty feet. After the sledge was righted, and while Egerton was employed clearing the entangled harness, the dogs suddenly broke away, dragging him more than a hundred yards, and bruising him severely, before they were stopped by his body becoming jammed in between two pieces of ice.

He reports :—

' During the journey all the dogs except " Bruin " worked very well, and no fits occurred I picketed them each night, and they remained quiet, only one dog, " Flo," breaking adrift. I found no difficulty in giving them their food—two pounds of preserved meat each, daily—which had been frozen and broken into pieces before leaving the ship. Though it was as hard as the ice itself, they appeared to enjoy it thoroughly.'

' 16th.—To-day the skylights above the lower-deck and my cabin were freed from snow, and daylight introduced, an inestimable blessing; but with it the cold also finds its way in. The difference in temperature between the inside and outside of the glass was sufficient to crack one pane before the quickly accumulating frozen vapour on the inside formed in sufficient thickness to protect the glass. Previous to this taking place, owing to the quick conduction of cold through the unprotected glass, snow-flakes formed and an actual fall of snow took place in my cabin.

'17th.—A bright sun, but a cold nipping wind, with squalls from the south-west, atmosphere very clear. I walked to Cape Rawson with Parr and George Bryant, the captain of the "Discovery's" sledge crew, to show him the "Crossing Floe," stretching for a distance of six or seven miles across Robeson Channel.

'In the ravine north of the cape, on the same plot of sparsely vegetated ground where foot-prints of ptarmigan were last seen in the autumn, we found their fresh traces. On the 10th three small birds were reported to have been seen by one of the crew; it is now probable that they were ptarmigan, our first visitors from the south. The "Polaris" did not observe any before the 25th of this month.

'At noon, when the temperature in the shade was minus 20°, the black bulb thermometer in the sun registered plus 40°. Some snow on a cask, well saturated with salt, melted when exposed to the sun, the staves being quite wet. At the same time the snow on the black ship's side was merely evaporating without wetting the woodwork.

'We have had great trouble in finding the snow-house containing the powder which was landed for greater security in the autumn. During the winter the house has become covered by snowdrifts, and in the darkness the pole marking its position has been lost.

'20th.—A magnificent day; calm, with a bright sun and a light violet-tinted mist hanging above the Greenland hills, a certain indication of fine weather.

'Mr. Egerton, with Lieutenant Rawson, accompanied by John Simmons, and Michael Regan one of the crew of the " Discovery," started with a sledge drawn by seven dogs for Discovery Bay ; the dogs dragging seventy-eight pounds each.

' The sledge crews have commenced exercising for their long journeys. In order to utilise their labours I intend to form a large depôt of provisions near the " Crossing Floe," ready for Beaumont's use.

' During a walk of about twelve miles the only tracks of animals met with were those of a fox and an ermine. The fox, like our Eskimo dogs, had melted the snow in its lair, leaving an icy surface.

' The weather was so calm, and the sun so powerful that, when standing still and facing it, although the temperature was actually minus 30°, it felt appreciably warm ; and yet ice formed on our eye-lashes thick enough to impede our sight considerably. After a six hours' exposure the cold had penetrated so far into our dresses that a woollen waistcoat, worn inside a thick box cloth coat and a duck outer covering, had ice on it thick enough to brush off. This may enable people to realise the condition of a traveller's clothes after eleven hours' hard work and how quickly his garments, which he can never dry, or indeed ever change night or day, become saturated with moisture.

' It is extraordinary how little snow there is left on the uplands, certainly not more than an average thickness of two feet. Had our winter not been specially calm even this measurement must have been lessened.

' The fallen snow drifting before the winds in the form of fine dust is for ever depositing itself in thin strata in the hollows or where an obstruction is encountered, forming snow-banks; the windward side of these drifts is constantly being removed by the wind, while on the lee side the snow is depositing. The bank, therefore, is always changing its position, moving onwards with the wind, its decaying edge forming a steep incline, the other a long slope. With the increasing heat of the sun the snow is evaporating very fast, particularly that on the southern sides of exposed boulders. High clouds coming from the southward this afternoon are a new feature, and indicate that the atmosphere is again becoming moist. We may accordingly soon expect a decided snow-fall, a phenomenon we have very seldom experienced during the winter.

' 24th.—To-day Markham's crews, with their boats lashed on sledges, went out on to the pack for exercise. After much labour with the pickaxes they were enabled to advance one mile and a half in the same number of hours, but that was with the boats alone. If they journey at the rate of three miles a day they will do well; their worst enemy will be the misty weather. We hope that as they advance north the floes will become larger, and hedged with narrower lines of hummocks than those in our neighbourhood.

' The drifted snow which lies upon the land just above the sea-level is hard, and will form a fair road for travelling on; but we can hope for no level ice-floes like those met with by former expeditions.

' Yesterday, when walking with Feilden and May, we endeavoured to reach Mount Pullen, only seven miles distant from the ship in a direct line. After three hours' hard walking, and when only one mile

from the mount, the ravine up which we had journeyed,
over hard snow, opened out into a shallow basin half a
mile across; there the snow had collected under the
shelter of the hill, and was so deep and soft that we
were obliged to give up the attempt to cross it, and to
content ourselves with ascending a nearer and smaller
hill which is called the Dean. This hill, which rises
to a height of 1,400 feet above the sea-level, is separated from Mount Pullen by a deep ravine which has
all the appearance of a gigantic railway cutting. The
impression left on our minds was that a glacier must
have been the agent that had carved out the gap. The
summit of the Dean hill is strewed with granitic
boulders and erratics of various kinds, the mountain
itself being composed of dark indurated slates, thrown
up at an almost vertical angle, the strike being east and
west. The view from its summit was very fine; the
pyramid-shaped hills of the United States Range to the
north-west having every slope sharply defined against
a back-ground of clear sky.

' 25*th*.—Temperature minus 37°, and calm weather.
The sun is only ten degrees high at noon, and yet the
glare was intense when walking towards it over the
snow. It afforded much relief to our eyes to occasionally face about and gaze at one's own shadow, the
only dark object to be seen. The accumulation of ice
about our eye-lashes and on the fur caps acts as a
number of prisms, refracting the light into the eyes.

' There are now many ptarmigan tracks in those
parts of the ravines where the scanty vegetation has
been here and there exposed by the winds; we meet
with tracks of hares occasionally, but it is evident that

few are left in our neighbourhood; three only have been killed since the return of light. The heat of the sun is very powerful; the exposed surface of each dark boulder is to-day free from snow, which has evaporated or thawed away without any melting being apparent.

'The white painted boats being objectionable for snow-blind travellers to gaze on, Dr. Moss has been painting those belonging to Markham's party with diversified colours, but the paint does not appear inclined to dry. The backs of the travellers' white-duck jumpers have also been marked with appropriate designs, in order that when pulling at the sledge-ropes each man may have some colour to rest his eyes on. As every individual has been left free to choose his own crest, the variety and originality displayed is somewhat quaint.

'In consequence of the ice having become thick enough to reach down to the mouth of the discharge-pipe, we are at last unable to use the ship's pumps, The fire-engine suction-pipe being lower will remain free so long as the temperature inside the ship is above 28°·5.

'While walking to-day with Mr. Pullen near Cape Rawson, we observed that the sea-face of the cape, up to a height of 200 feet above the present sea-level, had been ground smooth by the pressure of the floebergs or of the ice-foot. The rock remaining so distinctly scored for such a lengthened period as must have elapsed while the land was rising to the height mentioned, is remarkable.

'We measured a stranded floeberg, forced up on

its side. It was 120 feet long by 105 feet broad, and 80 feet in depth, the highest part being 63 feet above the water-line. It was consequently about 25,000 tons in weight, a cubic foot of ice weighing 55·5 lbs. Although this floeberg was the highest out of the water, it was by no means the largest in our neighbourhood. When ascending its side, so long as the slope was at an angle of 30° from the horizon, and covered with hard snow, we could climb up with the help of an alpenstock, but it was slippery work descending. When the angle increased to 35°, we were obliged to kick steps with our boots; at 40°, steps had to be cut with an axe; and at 50°, although we could have ascended by means of steps cut in the ice, I doubt if we could have descended without the help of a rope.

'For several days past there has been an animated scene on the cleared part of the lower-deck. One or other of the officers, and the leader amongst the crew of his sledge—styled "captain of the sledge"—have been alternately in possession of the weights and scales, preparing the provisions for the spring journeys. As Arctic sledge travellers are entirely dependent for subsistence on what they drag, the preparation of the provisions is a serious undertaking. Once started from the ship on a journey lasting from eighty to upwards of a hundred days, there is no means of rectifying a mistake or neglect, for nothing can be obtained from the ice but water, and to get that, fuel has to be carried for melting it. Carrying too much entails more weight being added to the already heavily-laden sledge; I need not mention the consequences of taking

too little. In a matter of such vital importance the
commander of each party must rely only on himself.
Every article has to be weighed with the greatest nicety,
and the lightest material procurable used for wrapping
up the parcels ; for this purpose a raid has been made
on all the private linen. After three days' work in
weighing out groceries, which were tied up in some
yellow calico, Dr. Moss discovered that the dye used
to colour it contained arsenic, and this wrapping had
to be discarded.

'It is only a month to-day since the sun reappeared,
and yet it is now so light at midnight that stars are
no longer visible.

'29th.—Lieutenant Parr reports having seen a
snowy owl; it was very wild, and though pursued
for a long distance would not allow him to get within
gunshot range.

'A south-west gale last night, force 8, with a
high temperature, was followed with cirro-stratus
clouds, the first decided ones seen this season. To-day
the Fox instrument was taken on shore in order to
obtain base observations ; but the parts froze so solidly
together that the instrument could not be used.

'No traces of Eskimo have yet been discovered
in our neighbourhood, and as it would be quite impossible for them to sustain life here during winter we can
scarcely expect to find any. Probably at Polaris Bay,
and other favoured places in Smith Sound pools of
water remain open, and seals may be procured ; but
here, since November, and for at least another month
—making half a year altogether—they certainly could
not be obtained.'

At Discovery Bay a seal was seen in the fire-hole several times, during January and February, proving that a few remained in the neighbourhood throughout the winter.

'The quicksilver on the reflecting glasses of the sextants is much affected by the extreme cold Even at a temperature of minus 30° the film on the back of one glass has split and requires to be re-silvered.

'30th.—A very strong mirage over the Greenland coast enabled me to obtain the bearing of a mountain apparently to the northward of the land seen before, but whether it is so or not will depend on its distance. In these high latitudes distant land may actually be to the southward of our position, although bearing to the northward of east. Land bearing due east must necessarily be farther from the Pole than our position.

'31st.—To-day, with a temperature of minus 30° in the shade, but the black bulb thermometer registering plus 40°, we observed that the sun, for the first time this year, had a visible effect on the surface of the snow, rendering it glazed and slippery. The mocassins, soled with the thin upper-leather cut from our long fisherman's boots are serviceable, so long as we walk only on snow, but the sharp slaty shingle on the bare patches of land cuts them sadly.

'The sledges are now drawn up alongside of the ship, all ready packed for a start on Monday, the 3rd of April, should the weather be favourable.

'*April 1st.*—On being called this morning I was informed that a wolf had been seen near the ship. Dr. Moss at once started in pursuit, but returning without having seen the animal, he was naturally greeted with doubts as to whether advantage had not been taken of the day to hoax us. However, when walking to Black Cape we observed the unmistakable footprints of a wolf, which considerably exceeded in size those of the largest of our Eskimo dogs. Later in the day more than one of these animals were seen in the vicinity of the ship, and in the afternoon Frederick came across the recent traces of three musk-oxen. A party from

FROZEN BEARD.

the ship at once started in pursuit of them, but were unsuccessful; evidently the wolves are following the musk-oxen.

'The pemmican biscuits, prepared at the recommendation of Mr. Thomas Grant are much liked; the sledge crews are supplied with a quantity of them instead of the ordinary ship's biscuit.

'During the last few days officers and men have clipped all the hair off their faces ready for travelling, and it is now difficult to recognise individuals by a casual glance.'

If the beard and moustaches are worn the moisture from the breath settles on them and quickly forms into a fringe of icicles, which after two hours' exposure have grown large enough to effectually prevent anything being drank out of a tumbler until it has been thawed off. The comforter worn round the neck also freezes to the beard, and after returning on board has to be thawed off before a fire. When such a circumstance happens in a tent, with the temperature many degrees below zero, nothing can be done except to cut the beard away close to the skin. As the eyelashes if removed may not grow again, Arctic travellers have to put up with the annoyance of ice forming on them; if not removed this gradually unites at the corners of the eye and eventually seals up the eyelids. The usual remedy is to thaw it away every now and then by the application of the ungloved hand. In very severe weather when the hands of the travellers cannot be thus exposed, instances have occurred of men being temporarily blinded in this manner, and unable to see their way.

CHAPTER XII.

DEPARTURE OF THE SLEDGE PARTIES—NEWS FROM THE 'DISCOVERY'
—ACCOUNT OF EGERTON'S JOURNEY—TRIP TO GREENLAND—DR.
MOSS AND MR. WHITE RETURN—ARRIVAL OF SLEDGES FROM THE
'DISCOVERY'—ARCHER VISITS POLARIS BAY—CAPTAIN STEPHEN-
SON'S ARRIVAL—GIFFARD'S RETURN — HIS PARTY ATTACKED BY
SCURVY—EGERTON AND FEILDEN RETURN—EXCURSION TO CAPE
JOSEPH HENRY—MOUNT JULIA—RETURN TO THE 'ALERT.'

On the morning of the 3rd, the day fixed for the departure of the sledge travellers, general disappointment
was felt at the non-arrival of Rawson and Egerton with
news from the 'Discovery.' We had hoped that the
dog-sledge would have returned by that date, and that
our parties might have left the ship with the gratifying
knowledge that our friends on board the 'Discovery'
had passed a comfortable winter.

The weather, however, being settled and favourable,
with the temperature ranging between minus twenty-
five and minus thirty degrees below zero, the temperature usually experienced by Arctic travellers early in
April, I gave the order for departure. The party consisted of fifty-three officers and men, all apparently in
robust health ; those remaining on board the 'Alert'
numbered six officers and six men. All hands assem-
bled for prayers on the ice alongside of the laden
sledges, which were drawn up in line, their silk banners

lightly fluttering in the breeze. Every man of our company was present, the ship being tenanted only by poor Petersen, who was bearing his sufferings and trials most patiently. Mr. Pullen ended the usual daily prayers with the doxology, in which everyone joined. It was a most impressive scene ; each heart being inspired with enthusiasm, and with a feeling of confidence that the labours, privations, and hardships that the travellers were about to undergo would be manfully battled with.

They started at 11 A.M., each man in the northern division dragging 230 lbs., and those of the western division 242 lbs. The programme was as follows : Lieutenant Aldrich, assisted by a sledge crew under the command of Lieutenant Giffard, was to explore the shores of Grant Land towards the north and west, along the coast-line he had discovered in the previous autumn. Commander Markham, seconded by Lieutenant Parr, with two boats, and equipped for an absence of seventy days, was to force his way to the northward over the ice, starting off from the land near Cape Joseph Henry : three sledge crews under the commands of Dr. Moss and Mr. George White, accompanying them as far as their provisions would allow.

' 4th.—A calm day with a temperature at minus 30°. During last night it fell to minus 45°, which is far too low a temperature for tent-life, but such risks have to be run when travelling in these regions. At 8 P.M. Egerton and Rawson, with their two men and seven dogs, returned from Discovery Bay, after an extremely rough and severe journey with a temperature ranging between minus 44° and minus 15°. They are all in excellent health and spirits, and beyond sore faces and frost-bitten fingers not much the worse for their exposure. The news received from Captain Stephenson is most cheering ; with the exception of one man who has suffered from scurvy all our friends are well and have passed a happy and comfortable winter. Over thirty musk-oxen had been shot during last autumn, and frequent rations of fresh meat have been issued to the crew throughout the winter. There was naturally much excitement at Discovery Bay on the receipt of our news, and great rejoicing on the parts of both officers and men on learning that they were to join in the exploration of the northern coasts. Preparations for sledging were hastened, and Captain Stephenson immediately despatched a party across Hall Basin to visit the depôt of the " Polaris " at Thank God Harbour, to ascertain whether the provisions left there by the Americans would be fit for use by our travelling parties.

'The sledge crews of the " Discovery " have been told off as follows : Lieutenants Beaumont and Rawson and Dr. Coppinger, with three sledges and twenty-one men, are to explore the north shores of Greenland. Lieutenant Archer and Mr. Conybeare, with two sledges and eighteen men, to explore Lady Franklin Sound. On Conybeare's return to the " Discovery," after completing Lieutenant Archer's sledge with provisions, he and his men are to transport a boat across Hall Basin, to enable Beaumont to return later in the season to Discovery Bay, should the ice have broken up. Captain Stephenson, after seeing the Lady Franklin Sound party well on their way, intends to visit Floeberg Beach to confer with me, and to see his Greenland division of sledges fairly started.'

The following extracts from Mr. Egerton's official report of his journey describe the nature of the travelling met with in Robeson Channel:—

'*March* 20*th.*—Left the ship at 9.45 A.M.; by 10.40 we had got over the difficulties at Cape Rawson, and by 11.15 those at the Black Cape, without unpacking the sledge.

'Intending to make our first day a short one, encamped at 4 P.M., having reached the beginning of the steep cliffs where the bad travelling commences, for up to this point, with the exception of rounding Cape Rawson and the Black Cape, the travelling was very good.

'By 6 o'clock we were all in our bags, with the exception of the cook, but as we brought spirits of wine we are able to cook inside the tent; this raises the temperature slightly and is much more comfortable for the cook, the only objection to it, a very slight one, being that it makes the air in the tent rather thick; between this and four smokers the atmosphere becomes much like a London fog; of course we tied up the ventilating holes, as we had no intention of letting any warmth inside escape into the cold air without.

'Temperature in the tent minus 7°, in the air minus 42°.

'21*st.*—Under weigh by 9 A.M. What we considered difficulties before when returning to the ship with Petersen, were now comparatively easy, having two good working hands with us, and by 10 o'clock we had arrived at the snow-hut, or rather hole, where we were detained an hour clearing the snow off the sail over the hole; and repacking the sledge. The travelling now became worse; we were keeping to the land, and the whole of the drift between the slope of the cliff and the hummocks was at a considerable angle, sometimes very steep, up and down hill always; the latter we did not object to, though the sledge capsized frequently, but the former gave us much trouble, and unless there had been four of us our progress would have been very slow, for the dogs are of little or no use in this kind of travelling; one man walks ahead to lead them, while the other three, having cut a footing with a pickaxe, sit down and with " One, two, three, haul ! " drag together, until the sledge is up, when the dogs, finding the strain eased, start off at a full swing down the hill the other side ; the sledge slides down a short way sideways and then capsizes, sometimes turning over three or four times ; this style of thing went on incessantly until we became rather more knowing, and found it better for one to walk down the hill very slowly in front of the dogs with the whip in his hand ; by so doing we sometimes avoided the usual capsize, being able to ease the sledge down gradually.

' After half a mile of such work we came to the conclusion that, although the pack beneath us was nothing but what is commonly called ' rubble,' it could not be much worse than what we were then having, and determined to try it. To get the sledge down from our position, which was about twenty feet above the pack, we untoggled the dogs, secured the drag-ropes and tent guys to the back of the sledge, and then, all having obtained as firm a footing as

possible, we lowered the sledge over; unfortunately
our backing ropes were not long enough, but there
was nothing for it but to let go, trusting to Providence
for the rest; the sledge being uncommonly strong

SLEDGE LOWERED OVER HUMMOCKS.

stood the blow it received at the bottom splendidly.
After getting the sledge over a short distance of the
boulder ice we came to a lane of perfectly smooth ice
running along just underneath the cliffy wall of ice
formed by the grounded hummocks and floebergs, the

outer sides of which were cut as straight, and polished as smooth as a piece of marble, with parallel lines scored out by the pack grinding against them when in motion.

'The travelling over the smooth ice was excellent, but we seldom came to more than a hundred yards or so of it without hummocks intervening, which generally had to be cleared away with pickaxes. As we got farther on, we found water on the top of this lane of ice, which appeared to be continuous; and the pack being too hummocky to attempt, we were compelled to take to the land again just opposite the third ravine from the cairn on Cape Union. Half a mile farther on the slopes became too much for us, so we lowered the sledge on to the floe once more, preferring the " one, two, three, haul!" and getting something, to the same with no result.

' When we came to any good travelling, Lieutenant Rawson and I walked on ahead, the dogs keeping close to our heels, while the men took it in turns to sit on the sledge and to steer. At 6.15 we reached the depôt at Lincoln Bay, and encamped beneath it, men and dogs pretty tired.

'Temperature of the air, minus 37°; tent, minus 3°.

' 22nd.—Across Lincoln Bay the travelling was very fair, the line of sastrugi running exactly in our course. Here we had a slight misfortune; the toe of the sledge runner caught under a ridge and sprung. As we approached Cape Frederick VII., getting under the land, the travelling became more hummocky, and the snow was just hard enough *not* to bear.

' Off the point it was far too hummocky to hold out any hopes of getting round on the ice, so we took to the land, but found it as bad as the worst part yesterday, the dogs being seldom able to do their share

HELPING DOG-SLEDGE DOWN A HUMMOCK.

of the work. Once, when the sledge capsized, the uprights forming the back caught against a hummock and both were carried away, causing a short delay.

' Temperature of the air minus 24°.

' 23rd.—We all suffered considerably from cramps in the legs last night, more so than usual.

' By ten o'clock we were under weigh. For the first mile and a half we kept to the land, travelling on the snow-slopes inside the hummocks; but this becoming steeper, we tried the floes again. The travelling was very rough, and we had continually to assist the dogs and sledge over the hummocks, but occasionally we got a smooth piece without any water. The point at the southern extremity of Wrangel Bay gave us great trouble to round; we tried the land, but found it perfectly impassable, even on foot; the cliffs were very steep, coming down to the water level at an angle of, I should say, 35°; the hummocks were forced well up on the land, showing considerable pressure has taken place here. We lowered the sledge on to the floe, a height of twenty-five feet, after clearing a way with pickaxes. There being too much water on the crack, which still continued outside the hummocks, we struck out more from the land, and came to one or two very good floes, and, by mounting hummocks continually, were able to pick a very fair road.

At 6.45 encamped on the floe. Each night we picketed the dogs, and found it acted very well, none of them breaking adrift except " Flo," who managed to get out of her harness, and any other lashings we put round her, every night, but she always lay down quietly and gave us no trouble. Though the tempera-ture was not very low, we all felt very cold, and could not get warm, do what we would; the tips of my fingers, which were frostbitten during my last trip when clearing harness, have become blistered and are rather uncomfortable.

' 24*th.*—Under weigh by 9.15 A.M. Found a floe which would take us into the land. Got to Cape Beechey at 11.10, having come through about half a mile of very hummocky stuff just off the point. A glorious day, and the prospect of good travelling before us. All very thirsty, so halted for a quarter of an hour to melt some snow.

' All along Shift Rudder Bay we had excellent travelling on the snow-foot, then came another bay, deeper than the last and about three miles wide. As there appeared to be a good even floe in it we struck across, but found the snow just hard enough not to bear ; it appears to be getting softer as we get more to the southward. At 6.15 we pitched at the northern side of St. Patrick's Harbour.

' Temperature of the air minus 30°.

' 25*th.* — At 9.15 A.M. started. Crossed St. Patrick's Harbour on a large blue-topped floe, extending nearly the whole way across, the snow upon it soft. Saw a Dutch ensign flying on a small island, which we recognised as the place where the " Alert " touched the ground last year. Took to the land here, and found a well-beaten track, so we stepped out at a brisk pace, the dogs getting very excited. After rounding numerous small points, which shut out the ship from view, we at length sighted the " Discovery," and gave three cheers as loud as ever we could. We were all in very high spirits at the thoughts of seeing our friends on board, and the prospect of a comfortable night instead of the usual cold and cramps. We were

about half a mile from the ship when we cheered, and
we could see one or two figures alongside the ship stop
and look in our direction; we gave another cheer, and
presently we saw all hands running out to meet us, and
shortly afterwards there was shaking of hands and
answering questions by the hundreds. When we could
get a word in we were very glad to hear that they
were all well, and had spent a very pleasant winter.
At five o'clock we were on board.

'30th.—At noon left the "Discovery," accompanied
by Lieutenant Rawson. The snow was considerably
harder than on our journey down, which is due to a
westerly gale which has been blowing for the last two
days. Crossed the floe in St. Patrick's Harbour, and
encamped at the north side of it, as there was a sharp
cutting wind, with a good deal of drift, and we were
being frost-bitten frequently.

'Temperature of the air minus 37°.

'31st.—A splendid morning, without wind. Instead of crossing the bay to the south of Shift Rudder
Bay, we kept to the land and had very good travelling
as far as Cape Beechey. A mile farther on we made
straight out for the floes, through half a mile of hummocks, when we came to a small floe, but saw a large
one farther on, so pushed straight out from the land,
and reached a good large floe, snow tolerably hard,
and the line of sastrugi running in the direction we
were travelling. Temperature of the air minus 44°.

'April 1st.—A clear morning, but blowing a little
from the north-east. When getting under weigh it suddenly came on to blow much harder. The wind right

in our teeth, and a great deal of drift; could not see more than a few yards before us, so decided to wait until the wind went down a little. There being no signs of the wind abating, resecured the tent and prepared for a day of misery, for the best part of the day is when we are on the march; to be cramped up in one's bag, or get miserably cold if you get out of it, is not a pleasant prospect to look forward to. However, we determined to make the best of it, and having one book—"The Ingoldsby Legends"—with us, we read, smoked, sang, and slept all day; and, excepting the pains in one's shoulders and legs from cramp, it was not so bad as we had expected.

'The highest temperature we could raise in the tent was $10°$ above zero; that was while we had the lamps lighted; the temperature outside was only minus $19°$.

'*2nd.*—The wind has gone, and it is a fine day. One of the dogs was very unwell to-day; he refused to eat anything, and was not able to pull. Slipped him from the drag-ropes, but as he would not keep up with us, were obliged to lead him. By keeping well out from the land we got on very well for the first two hours, but after that we came to a regular stop. No more floes in sight, so there was nothing for it but to make for the land. Between us and the shore there was nothing but hummocks. After an hour or so at it we picked up one or two "wrinkles;" instead of cutting a broad path for the sledge we simply made a way for one runner, and then canted the sledge up, one hand preventing it from capsizing; by one of us walking ahead to lead the dogs and pick the way, two

walking, one on either side in front of the sledge to
guide it, and give it a heave over to right or left as
required, and to clear the lines, which frequently catch
in pieces of ice, and the fourth man steering at the
back of the sledge, we got on at a very fair pace, and
reached the land at the north point of Wrangel Bay.
We then travelled on the crack underneath the ice-
wall until we came to an obstruction, when seeing a very

DOG-SLEDGE DRIVING OVER HUMMOCKS.

nice-looking floe not more than a couple of hundred
yards off, we unfortunately were tempted to try it,
finding very good hard snow; but it led us gradually
away from the land, and by the time we had got to
the end of it we found we were a mile from the shore
hummocks, and with a rough road between. Having
picked out the best route, set to work with pickaxes to make a way for the sledge, but it was not

until 5.30 that we got to the land again. Travelled on the slope between the land and grounded bergs to about a mile from Cape Frederick VII., where we camped.

'Temperature of the air minus 40°.

'3rd.—A fine day, but very misty. Simmons' ankles a little swollen, and when walking he feels his "tendon Achilles" a good deal. We knew what to expect in the way of travelling, so were not disappointed at having an hour's work to get round Cape Frederick VII. The travelling across the bay was much the same as we had before. After reaching the land at the northern side of Lincoln Bay, we had a very good road as far as the ravine, where we took to the ice, and kept on the crack as much as possible, but occasionally we were obliged to leave it, as it was too narrow to pass. These places were generally caused by pieces of very heavy floes having grounded outside the regular line of hummocks, and, having relieved the latter of the pressure, became piled up with the débris of the pack as it crushed up against it. When abreast of Arthur's Seat, we found great difficulty in getting the sledge over the hummocks on to the land, the lowest and best place we could find for the purpose being a straight wall of ice ten feet high, which was so steep that we had to cut a footing in it to climb up at all. Then we cut away at the edge, and placed boulders underneath, slipped the dogs, and hauled the sledge over. We found the interior of the snow-hut just as we had left it, hardly any snow having found its way in. Placed all our gear inside, and then pitched the tent over the hole. There was ample room inside for four of us, and for the cooking apparatus, and though the temperature of the air outside was minus 42°, we got it up to plus 15° inside while cooking. We were very much warmer and more comfortable in this snow-pit than we should have been in the tent.

' 4th.—A beautiful day ; travelling bad for the first two hours, the sledge capsized a great many times down the slopes, being rather top-heavy. Had a very heavy drag up the slope at the Black Cape ; and the dogs, evidently knowing they were not very far from home, were so eager to get on, that we could not prevent them from tearing down the other side of the slope at full speed, the sledge overtaking them before they reached the bottom ; but they contrived to keep clear of it in the most remarkable way. Just before reaching Cape Rawson we met Lieutenant May and Mr. Pullen, who very kindly assisted us round, and we arrived on board at 8 P.M., very disappointed at finding the main sledging parties had started, but very thankful for returning to the ship all well.'

On the 6th I walked with Feilden to Black Cape to choose the best spot for cutting a road through the barrier of shore hummocks, in order that a path might be prepared for the Greenland division. We found the ice heaped up to a height of from fifteen to twenty feet above the level of the floe, forming a barrier a quarter of a mile in width, without one level spot large enough for a sledge to rest on in an even position. Simmons brought the dogs along with us as far as the barrier ; he was now an experienced dog-driver, and being a stronger man than an Eskimo was more useful when amongst heavy ice, but where manual force is not the chief requisite, the patience and judgment of the Eskimo, with their dexterity in handling the long-lashed whip, places them far beyond the European in the art of dog-driving.

I again quote from my journal.

' 6th.—Passing the Cape Rawson snow-slope we came upon the marks of Egerton's sledge and saw traces of the last of its numerous capsizes. At this spot the dogs, knowing that they were near home, could not be restrained and ran away with the nearly empty sledge although the four men got on it to increase its weight. After crossing the brow, sledge, dogs, and tra-vellers rolled down the steep descent, a depth of at least twenty feet ; wonderful to relate, not the slightest damage was incurred by the sledge, men, or animals. Certainly dog-sledge travelling is not for those who wear fur coats and mufflers.

' 7th.—At midnight the upper limb of the sun was above the north horizon, giving a refraction of more than thirty minutes. Thus we are experiencing the anomaly of a sun remaining continually above the horizon day and night yet with a temperature ranging from 20° to minus 46°. We must hope for the sake of the travellers that this severe weather will not continue. I am also anxious about the silvered glasses in their sextants.'

Although the mercury back-ground split across during the cold weather the glasses remained fairly serviceable.

' 8th.—George Bryant with the sledge " Blood-hound " returned to-day from the main party of travellers, having accompanied them to Cape Richardson, where they had arrived on the 6th.

'Captain Markham reports that, as usual on first starting, a few of the men were suffering from the severe and unaccustomed work, and the want of sleep occasioned by the extremely cold weather; and, also as usual, that a great deal of double manning had been necessary with the heavy sledges. One of Bryant's sledge crew returned slightly frost-bitten.

'The ship is dryer but colder between decks since the departure of the travellers.

'10th.—The temperature rose to minus 11° in the middle of the day.

'Lieutenant Rawson and Mr. Egerton started this evening, with two light sledges, four men, and seven dogs, to search for an available road across Robeson Channel, in readiness for the heavier exploring sledges under Lieutenant Beaumont, expected shortly from the "Discovery." This party is to travel by night in order to escape the glare of the mid-day sun which is now considerable and liable to cause snow-blindness; and also for the great advantage of sleeping during the warmest part of the twenty-four hours. They started after an afternoon's sleep and a good supper, which to them was in reality a breakfast. Although many of those remaining on board were drinking a glass of spirits and water before going to bed, the voyagers, both officers and men, preferred tea or coffee, knowing from experience that spirits are bad to travel on.

'Parties starting as these did, with dearly bought experience, carry neither more nor less weight than is actually necessary. The men fully know the value of taking care of themselves, and of the sledge on which their lives depend. The most minute attention is given, therefore, to every article of dress, equipment, and provisions. The horn spoons occasion many jokes; they melt in the hot mess and become nearly flat, having to be bent into shape again before getting cold, so that literally each man has to fit his spoon to his mouth, and when it is spread out nearly flat his mouth must be stretched to fit his spoon. Metal spoons are now carried, each man keeping his own as warm as he can in his bag.

'The sun rising fifteen degrees above the horizon the glare during the day is becoming very decided, and owing to the extreme cold it is difficult to protect our eyes. When wearing neutral-tinted spectacles the evaporation from the eye condenses so quickly on the glasses that they have to be taken off and wiped every few minutes. A gauze veil, from which the condensation cannot be removed, is even more useless.

'Previous to the sun attaining an altitude of about fourteen degrees little annoyance is experienced from its glare and cases of snow-blindness are rare. This is in consequence of the sun's rays being only refracted by the snow at and beyond a radius of about twenty-two degrees from it. At that distance during clear weather, the most brilliant prismatic colours are displayed by each minute snow-prism, and in combination form a sparkling arc on the snow-covered ground, the bright light from which is too powerful for the unprotected eye. The "diamond dust," as we term it, becomes more open as the length of the radius is increased.

Consequently when the sun is between fourteen and twenty-three degrees in altitude, the refraction of its rays is set forth with the greatest effect, and snow-blindness has to be guarded against. In the bright arc, while each tiny prism displays its complete set of colours, the red tint is the most prominent nearest to the sun, the purple lying on the outside indistinctly defined.

DIAMOND DUST.

'The iridescent hues illuminating the high cirro-cumulus clouds or mackerel sky, which occasionally favour us, present even a more wondrous effect of colouring. Each minute crystal component of the clouds, within a radius of about twenty-two degrees around the sun, displays all the tints of the spectrum; the vast quantity of colouring, blending softly and har-moniously together, is so intermixed that it is difficult to determine which hue predominates at any one point or which shines most gloriously in the fairy scene. After a careful inspection I think that purple is the most prominent colour near the sun, red is decidedly the principal colour fringing the outer border of each cloudlet.

' 11*th.*—A calm day with the temperature at noon at last above zero. Clothes hung up in the sun dry quickly. This is the perfection of weather for the travellers, and very different to what they must have experienced during the first week. We were able to work outside on the ice without adding to the clothes usually worn on board the ship, merely putting on a cap without ear-laps. The snow on the land, particularly on the southern slopes, is greatly hardened and glazed by the sun. The estimated fall during the last six weeks is only one inch, which is certainly not equal to the quantity that has evaporated.

' Petersen is progressing favourably; we look anxiously at our best vegetated spots for game, hoping to obtain a ptarmigan for him as they pass us journeying towards the N.W., but we can find nothing.

' A fine circular prismatic halo was seen round the sun with a distinct prismatic parhelion at the usual distance on each side and above it, with a second circle curving upwards through the upper mock sun. The wardroom skylights have been uncovered and the sunlight permitted to take the place of the spluttering lamps. How changed everything appears, but how dirty !

' 14*th.*—Doctor Moss and Mr. White with their sledge crews returned to-day, having accompanied Commander Markham to the depôt at Cape Joseph

Henry and helped him for a short distance beyond.
The appearance of the ice within some six miles of the
cape was anything but cheering to the northern party,
but they hoped that as they got farther from the land
the floes would be larger and less broken up and the
hedges of hummocks narrower.   The ice near the land
afforded such a bad travelling road that Aldrich had
determined to cross the land to the southward of the
cape.   With the exception of one marine (who, it appears, was invalided from the Gold Coast), all the men
were well and in the highest spirits.   The cold weather
had tried them much, and there had been several cases
of frost-bite, which but for the presence of Doctor
Moss might have become serious.   Both Markham
and Parr had suffered from snow-blindness, but had
recovered by changing the hours of travelling from
day to night.   Only one hare had been shot, but the
track of a wolf was noticed at Cape Joseph Henry.
The mid-day tea was very highly spoken of; both
officers and men were unanimous in favour of the
change, and willingly put up with the misery of standing still with cold feet during the long halt needed for
the purpose of boiling the water; and all agreed that
they worked better after the tea and lunch than
during the forenoon.

   ' As usual, the appetites of most of the travellers
had been bad for the first two or three days, but all
were recovered before Doctor Moss left them.

   ' 16th.—Lieutenant Beaumont and Doctor Coppinger, with two sledges and fourteen men, arrived from
the " Discovery " in excellent health and spirits after a
ten days' journey.   A light breeze which we experi-

enced yesterday from the northward, force 2, proved to be a gale in the funnel-shaped Robeson Channel, obliging the travellers to remain in their tents, one of the most trying hardships of an Arctic journey. The party, although dragging only 150 lbs. a man, had experienced great difficulties while travelling amongst the heavy hummocks. A temperature of minus 45° and unaccustomed work had at first tried them severely, but all are now in splendid condition, and after a short rest they will have the advantage, which no former Arctic sledge party has ever enjoyed, of starting on a lengthened journey after ten days' real sledging exercise.

' Captain Stephenson reports that Archer and Coppinger, with two seamen, Hans, and a sledge drawn by twelve dogs pulling fifty-four lbs. each, started on the 28th of March from Discovery Bay to cross Hall Basin direct to Polaris Bay. A few hours after starting the sledge was badly damaged amongst some ice hummocks; after repairing it, they came to a smoother road which enabled them to cross the strait to Cape Lupton without more than ordinary trouble. They arrived at Hall's Rest early on the 31st, and immediately held a survey of the provisions, which were found to be in a serviceable condition, notwithstanding that they had been exposed to the weather by the roof of the observatory in which they were stored having partially fallen in.

' Lieutenant Archer reports that Captain Hall's grave is in a good state of preservation. At the head was a board on which was the following inscription:—

IN MEMORY

OF

CHARLES FRANCIS HALL,

LATE COMMANDER U.S. STEAMER 'POLARIS,' NORTH POLE EXPEDITION.

DIED NOVEMBER 8TH, 1871,

AGED 50 YEARS.

'I am the resurrection and the life; he that believeth in me, though
he were dead, yet shall he live.'

'A small flat piece of upright stone was at the foot, and the willow mentioned by Captain Tyson as having been planted there was alive.

'On the 2nd Archer started from Polaris Bay on his return journey and arrived on board the "Discovery" on the following day. Hans, who had spent the winter on board the "Polaris" and was then always able to hunt for seals in the open water-pools, was much astonished to find firm ice for the whole distance across the strait with no water anywhere.

'18th.—Since the 14th there has been an occasional snow-fall, estimated at two inches, but it has collected deeper in protected places. Covering the hard snow-drift, it hides the inequalities and renders the footing even to the most experienced very uncertain. The temperature of the earth which fell to minus 12° during the winter has now risen gradually to minus 10°·5.

'At noon, when the atmosphere was unusually clear, Lieutenant Beaumont and I thought that we could distinguish cliffs forming the Greenland coast about Cape Stanton, where previously I supposed that the travellers would find a low shore and fair travelling ; but as the land is upwards of thirty miles distant, we hope that we are deceived. In consequence of the drift of the pack towards the east before the prevailing winds which appear to blow continuously from the westward, the coast between Cape Brevoort and Cape Stanton, lying at right angles to the course of the ice, is sure to be an extremely wild one with regard to ice-pressure. Should there be cliffs and the sledges forced to take to the pack, the travelling will necessarily be extremely heavy.

'Lieutenant Rawson and Mr. Egerton returned from Greenland this evening, having succeeded in crossing the strait without more than the usual difficulties amongst the heavy ice hummocks, which they have now become so accustomed to. They landed on the coast near the Repulse Harbour of the chart, and report the land there to be of the same formation as Grant Land and that the floebergs near the shore are, if anything, larger, and denote more pressure from the pack than those on this shore. The ladder sledge is stated to be well fitted for the work it was intended for, namely, travelling over the surface of a glacier. Much to my disappointment no trace of any game was seen, one fox-track only being noticed.

'Lieutenant Beaumont has been busy all day weighing out provisions for his journey, and also some for a more lengthened trip in the spring of 1877. When I can spare men for the duty these will be taken across the channel and formed into a depôt. Three of his crew are too tall for their blanket bags, which therefore have to be lengthened.

' 20*th*.—Temperature, minus 8°, light snow falling
with a breeze from the northward sufficiently strong
to collect it in the sheltered places and so cause very
heavy travelling. After a four days' rest, which has
enabled his crews to recover from their first experience
of Arctic travelling, Lieutenants Beaumont and Rawson, and Doctor Coppinger, with twenty-one men
dragging four sledges weighted to 218 lbs. a man,

CAPE RAWSON SNOW-SLOPE.

started at 7 P.M. for the north coast of Greenland ; picking up their provisions at Cape Rawson, whither they
had been carried by sledge crews of the " Alert " while
exercising preparatory to starting on their journeys.

' 22*nd*.—Rawson returned unexpectedly from Lieutenant Beaumont's party for a new five-man sledge,
one having hopelessly broken down while crossing the
barrier hummocks, although a roadway had been made

through them. The heavy eight-man sledges stood the great strain in what would be a surprising manner even to the carpenters who made them. The sailors are even beginning to think that now with the pliable uprights it is impossible to break them. They are certainly a great triumph of ingenious workmanship, but the small sledges are far too slight for our work; indeed, they were never intended for it; even Sir Leopold M'Clintock never expected that we should have to travel over such heavy ice. They are broken by sliding too quickly down an inclined hummock or sastrugi, and striking the front horns against the next ridges, the weight of the cargo acting like a battering ram. The drag ropes reversed would of course enable the sledge to be eased down; but in misty weather the snow-road is so deceptive that the crew do not become aware of the declivity until they have floundered to the bottom of it themselves, it is as much as they can do to escape out of the way of the descending sledge; fortunately at the bottom of most of the inclines there is usually soft snow in which it buries itself and so generally escapes. The eight-man sledges being longer and stronger are better fitted for the rough work than the smaller ones.

'The sledge which has been to the " Discovery " and also to Greenland and back this season, after all the perils and numerous capsizes it has gone through without being much damaged, is naturally a favourite one with both Egerton and Lieut. Rawson. Many jokes are made that the latter broke his own before starting on his long journey on purpose to obtain Egerton's well-tried one. If so, he was successful, for while Egerton was out of the way Rawson obtained possession of the coveted article, with which he quickly disappeared to rejoin his party.

' 23rd.—Captain Stephenson and Mr. Mitchell, Hans the Eskimo, with William Dougall ice quartermaster, and Henry Petty a marine, arrived with twelve dogs from the " Discovery," having left that ship on the 18th. They have experienced strong northerly winds during the journey, and, like the other travellers, a very rough road; but, with the exception of the leader who is severely attacked with snow-blindness, all are in excellent health.

' Over rough ice a large team of twelve dogs is too many for one sledge. If their traces are all of equal length the dogs become collected too close together, and those who keep on the outside of the crush are forced to drag with their trace at a considerable angle, while several of the weak dogs being unable to push their way into the crowd cannot tighten their rope at all.

' A large party of dogs should certainly have traces of different lengths; but then in rough ground those in advance would turn the corners too sharply, and get out of sight of the driver. Amongst hummocks, the frequent sharp turns require the dogs to be as close to the sledge as possible.

' Dr. Moss, adopting night travelling, started late in the evening for Cape Joseph Henry with a depôt of provisions for the return of the main party of travellers, his crew dragging 207 lbs. a man.

' Captain Stephenson accompanied Lieutenant Archer for twenty miles on his way up Lady Franklin

Sound, and saw his men through the first difficulties which inexperienced travellers must always expect in these regions. Owing to the sheltered coast-line along which they journeyed, the snow was found to be very soft, which rendered the travelling more than usually laborious. The steel runners of the large eleven-man sledge had given way, and necessitated a change being made for the more serviceable eight-man sledge.'

Captain Stephenson states in his report :—

' On the 14th, I went on with them till luncheon time, when bidding them farewell, accompanied by Mr. Miller, I retraced my steps over their tracks to the ship, arriving on board at 4.30 P.M. of the 15th ; just taking me a day and a half to walk the distance the heavy sledges had occupied six whole days to accomplish.'

The travellers from the ' Discovery ' had improved upon the plan of painting a badge on the back of each man's duck-jumper, in the hope of protecting the eyesight of the man pulling behind him, by each sledge crew adopting a well-executed special badge, which appeared more orderly than the individual taste in design permitted among the sledge crews of the ' Alert.' Captain Stephenson's badge was the Prince of Wales' feathers.

The details of the winter passed on board the ' Discovery,' as learnt from Captain Stephenson, so closely resemble those of the ' Alert ' that it would entail a great amount of repetition were I to record them here. A full report by Captain Stephenson will be found in the Parl. Papers, c. 1636, of 1876, and further observations will shortly be printed. The

Meteorological Abstract and the Game List are published with those of the ' Alert ' in the Appendices.

' 24*th* — As the road near the base of the cliffs in
Robeson Channel will be impracticable for sledges after
the thaw has set in, I have sent Lieutenant May, who
has now quite recovered from the effects of the frost-
bite he received in the autumn, with the dog-sledge to
Lincoln Bay to look for a road overland. Feilden
accompanies him, and Mr. Wootton has joined the
party as a volunteer worker.

' 28*th*.—The temperature has risen to 5° and the
black bulb thermometer in the sun's rays registers 79°;
consequently on the black surface of the ship's side,
and on the exposed faces of the snow-capped rocky
cliffs, long icicles have formed. On the southern side
of the floebergs the hitherto transparent ice has become
cloudy, and is covered with a beautiful coating of
efflorescence, consisting of elegant feathery crystals.

' Where the stratification of the snow-covered floe
has become exposed at a newly-formed crack, the
lower part of the snow is observed to have granulated,
the grains appearing inclined to collect together perpendicularly, and to increase in size by amalgamating,
leaving intermediate air-spaces. The snow near the
ship's side granulates in a similar manner, leaving a
space at the back or underneath, proving that the greater
portion of the work is performed by reflected heat.
To-day I noticed a marked evidence of this power:
a piece of wood was coated with a layer four inches in
thickness of clear transparent ice, which when in the
shade could not be removed from it without bringing
away pieces of the wood ; after being exposed to the

sun for a few minutes when the temperature was only 5° the ice became separated from the wood, the heat apparently passing through it and melting the ice only where it touched the wood.

'The sun being so powerful, articles dry readily in the open air. On the return of any sledge party the damp blanket bags and tent robes are hung up on the south side of the ship. They at once become coated with numerous minute feathery crystals, which appear to be ever evaporating and ever forming. The oftener they are brushed off the better.

'The snow has been cleared off from above all the skylights and bull's-eyes, but still the lower-deck is perfectly dark. This is a very great disadvantage; besides rendering it necessary to expend candles and oil, it is gloomy work living in the dark, while the sun is so bright during the whole twenty-four hours that when on deck we are obliged to wear coloured spectacles.

'The invalids who are unfit to join the sledges have a great press of work to perform in the necessary duties on board the ship. They have far too little outdoor exercise. The officers are obliged to help in many ways, and anyone who will turn a hand to manual labour can readily find useful employment.

'Where dampness was prevalent during the winter mildew is now collecting, and would do so to a very prejudicial extent if left undisturbed. This mildew grows rapidly on the beams, clothes, books, papers, etc.

'Since the 18th I estimate that two more inches of light snow have fallen, making five inches altogether since the 1st of March. As the evaporation is now exceeding the precipitation this does not represent the total fall. The tops and brows of the hills, which were quite bare in February and March, are now hidden under the thin but universal covering of snow. Any stone projecting through, and against which the sun has full play, is, however, kept clear by the quick evaporation; the snow apparently changing first into ice and then disappearing without wetting the dark background.

'The ptarmigan passing the neighbourhood are evidently seeking better feeding-grounds. There are no willow-plants uncovered by snow near us. All the tracks we see are those of birds proceeding towards the north-west, generally in pairs. They light near any uncovered patch of ground likely to be vegetated, run across it, winding their way through the snow furrows in search of the willow or other food. On gaining the western edge of the cleared ground the trail is lost by their flying to the next uncovered patch, where it is sure to be found again.

'30th.—After a week's stay, Captain Stephenson, with his crew of Hans and two men, with eleven dogs —one very fine one having died during a fit—started on his return to the "Discovery," leaving Mr. Mitchell on board the "Alert."

'In the evening Lieutenant May returned with his party from Lincoln Bay, having travelled overland to Cape Union, but from thence he was obliged to follow the coast-line.

'At the head of Lincoln Bay vegetation was rather abundant, with numerous traces of hares and ptarmigan, but no musk-oxen as we had hoped. One hare was shot by May and Feilden, after a walk of over twenty miles in search of game; it was brought back for Petersen.

'At midnight Dr. Moss returned from Cape Joseph Henry, having established the depôt of provisions and secured it from the depredations of animals; a duty which, as men's lives depend upon it, requires the utmost care and forethought. Three of his men are complaining of their legs being stiff after their quick travelling; but there is nothing alarming in this, as the journal of every Arctic traveller relates similar troubles.

' *May* 1*st.*—George Emmerson, captain of one of Beaumont's auxiliary parties, returned from Repulse Bay for a second load of provisions. While crossing Robeson Channel Beaumont had severe work. Both the small sledges were damaged and one man had injured his side by being jammed between the laden sledge and an ice hummock; otherwise the journey had been fairly successful.

' *2nd.*—Mr. Egerton, taking charge of the "Discovery's" auxiliary sledge, started for Greenland, the crew dragging 161 lbs. a man. He carries orders to Dr. Coppinger to proceed to Polaris Bay, visiting on his way all the cairns erected by Captain Hall and the other members of the "Polaris" expedition. Mr. Egerton also carries over one of Mr. Berthon's canvas boats for Beaumont's use later in the season.'

Up to this period all had gone well with the Expedition. We had advanced to the extreme limit of navigation at the northern end of Smith Sound; the ship was admirably placed for exploration and other purposes, and the sledge crews, formed of men apparently in full health and strength, had obtained a fair start on their journeys under as favourable circumstances as possible considering the heavy nature of the ice. But on the 3rd Doctor Colan informed me that five of the crew had undoubted scorbutic symptoms. However, as each case had some predisposing cause I was not then seriously alarmed for the general health of the Expedition.

'3rd.—This evening Lieutenant Giffard returned, having left Aldrich thirty miles beyond Cape Joseph Henry; he reports all the party well and in the highest spirits. Owing to the soft snow the travelling had been very slow. No game had been seen except one ptarmigan and four hares at Cape Joseph Henry, which were shot.

'4th.—Lieutenant May started with the dog-sledge, weighted to 68 lbs. per dog, for Greenland; to bring back Mr. Egerton who is conducting the "Discovery's" auxiliary sledge across Robeson Channel. Simmons being ill, Joseph Self has now taken his place as dog-driver.

'To-day the ice was $79\frac{1}{4}$ inches thick.'

This proved to be the maximum thickness it attained throughout the season.

'Last night we experienced a strong breeze from the northward, with a heavy snow-drift and a fall in temperature to minus 10° combined with a damp mist; the hoar-frost collecting on the rigging for the first time this season. This damp wind is peculiar; we trust for Markham's sake that it is not caused by the ice breaking up.

'We must now expect a long continuance of foggy weather. When the tops of the snow-clad hills blend with the misty sky without any line of demarcation, and nothing but ice in sight, it is anything but inspiriting to weary travellers. Few can realize what the northern party are undergoing struggling along their monotonous road of rugged ice, unable to see far enough ahead to choose the most level route through the hummocks.'

This fog was experienced by each of the travellers. Captain Markham remarks:—

'After advancing for about half-a-mile, which distance took us nearly four hours to accomplish, we arrived at such a confused heap of hummocks that in the present thick state of the weather rendered a farther advance impossible; we were therefore compelled to halt and pitch the tents' . . . .

'7th.—Dr. Colan is becoming very anxious about poor Petersen, who bears his trials cheerfully and patiently, but is very weak.

'Lieutenant Giffard started with a sledge crew, dragging 173 lbs. a man, to complete the depôts of provisions for Lieutenant Aldrich's return. He also took some provisions to Cape Joseph Henry for Commander Markham, and one of Berthon's collapsable boats.

'Along the borders of the old lake-bottoms the mud, which was frozen as hard as any rock during the winter, is now pulverized; where a month ago it was difficult to dig out stones and shells with a metal instrument, a stick or the finger can now easily be forced an inch deep into the softened earth; this must be entirely due to evaporation. The hoar-frost collected on the rigging three days ago has disappeared again, the hair-hygrometer registering ten degrees' difference of tension.

'9th.—May and Egerton returned from the Greenland coast; this will be the last trip across the north end of the channel this season. The same road having now been travelled over by so many sledges, each party helping to improve it, it is in fair order and enables a rapid journey to be made. Egerton had met Dr. Coppinger, returning from Beaumont's advanced party, at the Repulse Harbour depôt, just in time to stop him crossing the channel to the "Alert."

'Dr. Coppinger reports that Beaumont's sledges have experienced even greater difficulties and worse travelling than we expected. From their place of crossing the Straits, they found that the coast-line for nearly the entire distance to Cape Stanton, was formed either by very steep snow-slopes or precipitous cliffs, the bases of which receive the direct and unchecked pressure of the northern pack as it drifts from the north-westward and strikes against that part of the coast nearly at right angles. The chaos amongst the floebergs near the shore was something indescribable, and the travelling the worst that could possibly be imagined, seven days being occupied in moving forward only twenty miles.

'It was difficult to say which was the better road— through the wilderness of pressed-up ice or along the steeply inclined snow-slopes, where a roadway had to be cut for the entire distance travelled. The party was, however, persevering with light hearts and determined spirits; looking forward to the travelling becoming better after they rounded Cape Stanton, then only two miles from them.

'Lieutenant May had followed up the M'Cormick valley lying to the eastward of Cape Brevoort and leading towards Newman Bay. He discovered a fair road, with a hard snow-floor and a gentle incline some two or three miles long, leading up to a dividing plateau about 400 feet above the sea-level. From the summit of the cape, 2,000 feet high, he obtained a magnificent view; but the heavy climb having necessitated his taking off his outer coat, he was almost frozen before he could do more than obtain the most important bearings.

'The first snow-bunting was seen to-day. Many are the speculations whether they also will pass us for more favoured quarters.

'At noon, water was seen for the first time trickling down a cliff with a southern aspect, but on reaching the colder ground at the foot it again froze into ice. The temperature in the shade during the afternoon rose to 17°.

'11th.—Mr. Wootton, commanding a sledge crew with the remainder of Commander Markham's provisions, left to-day for Cape Joseph Henry. On the completion of this duty all our travellers will be provided for. I have, therefore, started off Captain Feilden with Mr. Egerton, Frederick and James Self and six dogs, for an excursion amongst the United States Range of hills. Mr. Mitchell accompanies them with a few dry photographic plates. We trust that they will discover the musk-oxen haunts, for we are sadly in want of fresh meat for our invalids. Strict orders are given to each sledge party to bring back for the use of the sick all game shot, even a single ptarmigan. To-day there are nine men recommended to have a change of diet in consequence of showing scorbutic symptoms. Three of these are the ice-quartermasters, three are cooks and stewards, and three seamen, one of whom has, however, been employed as ship's cook on board the " Discovery " during the winter. One of the seamen has been ailing for a considerable time ; he is a most inveterate smoker, and it turns out that he prefers salt to preserved meat, and has eaten very little of the latter during the winter.

' 14*th*.—Poor Petersen died this evening, passing away quietly without pain. Dr. Colan has been incessant in his attendance, not only in a medical capacity but as a nurse ; so perfectly self-sacrificing is he that I am seriously alarmed for his own health.

' Yesterday the snow on the upper-deck above the cooking-galley melted, the water running out through the scuppers. It is high time that it was entirely removed, but our few workmen can only be spared to work occasionally. Owing to the weight of that which has already been thrown overboard the water has overflowed the ice in such quantities that we cannot now approach the ship on the inshore side without getting wet feet. In the clods of frozen snow and gravel exposed to the effect of the sun the snow evaporates quickly without melting or trickling down.

' The temperature of the earth at a depth of eighteen inches has risen to minus 5° ; the mean temperature of the air is therefore now warmer than that of the earth.

The snow-fall since the 28th of April is estimated at one and-a-half inches, making six and a half since the 1st of March.

'17th.—Doctor Moss shot a snow-bunting to-day. Although the temperature of the air is only 15°, near the sunny sides of the floebergs it is above 32°, consequently each is decorated with a hanging necklace of short graceful icicles.

' The snow on the hill-tops is disappearing very fast by evaporation. The hair-hygrometer continues to work in an unsatisfactory manner; after being cleaned it acts correctly for two or three days, but then remains fixed in one position.

' 19th.—Niels Christian Petersen was buried to-day on the brow of a hill a quarter of a mile from the ship where the snow never collects; the grave will therefore always remain conspicuous. No documents are buried near it, so it need never be disturbed.

' To-day the gravel exposed to the sun ate its way down into the snow for the first time, but the ice is not affected yet. The large flakes of snow that fall now are conspicuously different from the fine particles which fell during the cold weather.

' We are all unanimous in favour of a snow-shoe brigade for journeying overland, but they would be of no use when sledging over the hard ice such as the Franklin Search Expeditions met with.

' 21st.—Mr. Wootton returned this evening from Cape Joseph Henry with his party in good health. He brings us two ptarmigan for the invalids, who appear to make no progress whatever towards recovery, and evidently require a fresh meat diet.

'Snow-buntings in their summer plumage and a lemming with his summer dark fur were obtained to-day.

'23rd.—The temperature of the sea-water has risen to 29°, both at the surface and at a depth of five fathoms. This is a rise of half a degree since the winter and before the temperature of the air has risen to anything like the same degree. It is an interesting problem whence comes the warmth unless by an ocean current.

'In digging a hole in the ice in order to measure its thickness it was found to be saturated with water, which drained into the hole as it does through the earth into a well. During the cold weather the ice was perfectly dry.

'When the temperature of the air was 16° a thermometer buried 18 inches in a floeberg registered 11°; a lower temperature than that of the air for the last three or four days. From this we may reason that while an ordinary piece of ice seven or eight feet thick becomes saturated with water and readily melts, a floe eighty feet thick retains its cold temperature and remains free from water for a long time. I very much regret the long glacier thermometer having been broken through the freezing of the mercury during the cold season, otherwise an important series of observations might have been obtained.

'24th.—Her Majesty's birth-day : dressed the ship with flags, but I trust we shall be forgiven for putting off the general holiday for a more opportune season.

'Lieutenant Giffard and his sledge crew returned on board from placing Lieutenant Aldrich's return depôt. They have done their work well and expeditiously, but unfortunately two of his men have broken down, with scorbutic symptoms.

'This trip is another instance of how dependent Arctic travellers are on all the sledging arrangements being carried out to the letter, and how the failure of one supporting sledge may entail disaster on the chief party. Mr. Giffard was obliged to establish the depôt of provisions at the point agreed upon previous to the return of the advance party under Lieutenant Aldrich. On his journey to perform this duty two men hopelessly broke down; not having sufficient time to return with them to the ship before the main party would arrive at the pre-arranged depôt, he was necessarily obliged to leave the invalids for five days in a snow-hut, made as comfortable, or rather as free from discomfort, as circumstances permitted. The following extract from Lieutenant Giffard's journal refers to this incident :

' On the 12th of May I came to the conclusion that I must leave Lorrimer behind in a snow-house whilst we went on to Cape Colan with the depôt. He has been gradually getting worse ever since we left the ship, and there is not much chance of getting him off the sledge again now for some time. On the 13th, whilst luncheon was getting ready, the sledge with a half load, advanced to James Ross Bay, and I looked about for a suitable place to build a snow-house. Both on the land and bay the snow was too soft; however, close to the shore of the bay, was a large old hummock, which looked promising; we went up to it, and found a capital place.

'The following things were left for the use of the two
men who remained :—For the sleeping place, besides
the bags, the lower robe, the sail, and the two duffle
mats ; for cooking, the stewpan and a pannikin for a
lamp, which answers very well, as I knew from having
had it tried during the morning.   Amusements : a
book, " Peveril of the Peak," and the two small packs
of cards supplied to each sledge, presented to the Expedition by the Empress Eugénie.   For telling the
time, a compass belonging to one of the men, and a
copy of the true bearings for the month.   The rifle,
ammunition, saw, and snow-knife were also left.

'Woolley, not knowing that I intended him to
remain on account of his own stiffness, volunteered to
stay behind to take care of the patient.   Lorrimer was
assisted down to the snow-house and put in his bag.
Having said good-bye to the two men, we started across
James Ross Bay.'

Five days afterwards, on the return journey,
Giffard relates : ' On the 18th Woolley was seen coming
to meet us from the hospital.   He told us that
Lorrimer was no better, and would certainly have to
go back to the ship on the sledge ; he took a little
exercise daily, but it has not taken away the stiffness.
The snow all about the hospital and neighbouring
land was too deep and soft to allow of any extended
walk being taken.   No living thing was seen during our
absence ; once Woolley thought he heard the scream of
a gull.   The hospital was never too cold, nor did the
wind trouble them at all ; the great discomfort was the
damp from the snow melting inside whilst the men were
asleep.   The time had passed very slowly, and would

have been very dull had it not been for the Empress's cards, which afforded great amusement to the men, who are delighted with them. On reaching the hospital we all went in to see Lorrimer, who was very glad to see us again; he was very weak and low-spirited, quite unable to walk, or do anything almost, without help.'

During the homeward journey Woolley was obliged to fall out from the drag-ropes, and finally had to be carried on the sledge. The day following their arrival at Floeberg Beach a third man was taken ill with scurvy, while the remaining four appeared in good health. One, however, was attacked twenty-four days afterwards; and another, Stuckberry, forty-four days after having been placed on the regular ship's ration.

To the westward of Cape Joseph Henry, the snow in the sheltered hollows had proved to be even softer than it was earlier in the season; the sledge was frequently buried, and the men sank knee-deep at every step. Under such circumstances a flat sledge would be better than the high-runner sledge; but for general service, and more especially for travelling over ice, the latter is to be preferred. No traveller can afford to take both.

Mr. Egerton and Captain Feilden returned on the 24th from their exploration in the United States Range. Like Giffard they found all the plains and valleys which were sheltered by mountains from the westerly winds, to be simply impassable from the quantity of soft snow collected in them. Selecting a wide valley that opened up from the coast in lat. 82° 40′ N., and which stretched in a westerly direction into the interior, they followed it up for about twenty miles, but were finally brought to a standstill by soft snow-drifts which stretched continuously across it. About four miles beyond the extreme point they reached a wall of snow or ice, rising perpendicularly to a height of forty or fifty feet extended across the valley and sloped upwards to the westwards, until at a distance of thirty miles the tops of the mountains, at least two thousand feet high, just appeared above the enormous snow-slope.

Though the travellers used every effort to reach this barrier, they failed, owing to the softness of the snow-drifts, and were unable to determine with certainty whether it concealed the edge of a glacier or was a stupendous collection of soft snow. It seems, however, impossible that such an enormous quantity of snow, over a thousand feet in thickness, could accumulate without turning into ice through pressure, so that although we cannot definitely state that we met with glaciers in Grinnell Land between the eighty-second and eighty-third parallels of latitude, yet there is good reason to believe that they do exist in the interior of the country. Each of the large valleys on the southern slopes of the United States Range also, apparently, contains a glacier; and a snow-cap was observed on the most northern land sighted on the Greenland coast. Recent traces of musk-oxen were seen, but none of the animals met with. Four hares and four ptarmigan were shot; and a snowy-owl and several snow-buntings seen. Frederick the Greenlander returned from this journey attacked with scurvy, though he had taken his lime-juice regularly both on board ship and when travelling.

As all the depôts of provisions for the use of the travellers on their return journeys had been deposited, I decided to go to Cape Joseph Henry, to obtain a view of the northern ice from the lofty mountains in that locality. Lieutenant May and Captain Feilden accompanying me, we started from the ship on the 25th.

Following the coast-line as much as possible, we reached our destination on the 29th. The weather being remarkably clear, the opportunity was taken to ascend Mount Julia, the highest peak near the sea, which rises to an elevation of not less than 2,000 feet. The climb through the snow was very laborious, and we were more than five hours reaching the summit of the hill, its base being four miles from our tent.

The view from the top was superb ; the atmosphere was surpassingly clear, not a cloud appeared in the sky from the horizon to the zenith ; in some of the valleys and along parts of the shore directly below us, a low mist hung, but a few miles to seaward this entirely disappeared. Tier upon tier of pyramid-shaped hills stretched seventy or eighty miles to the westward, averaging from 2,000 to 5,000 feet high. The two highest peaks of this range were named Mounts Rawlinson and Bartle-Frere. To the eastward, distant not less than a hundred and twenty miles, the hills of Greenland about Cape Britannia were plainly seen, but to the northward no land or the faintest appearance of land was visible.

The interminable pack appeared from our lofty station to consist of small floes hedged round by broad barriers of rough ice, until in the extreme distance it blended with the horizon ; not a pool of water or the faintest appearance of water-cloud was to be distinguished within the range of our vision, which embraced an arc of a hundred and sixty degrees. We were perfectly satisfied that no land of a great elevation exists within a distance of eighty miles north of Cape Joseph Henry, and none at all within fifty miles, which from our look-out bounded the visible horizon. We may rest assured therefore that from the coast of Grinnell Land in latitude 83°, to the eighty-fourth parallel of latitude, stretches the same formidable pack which was encountered by Markham and his companions. Whether or not land exists within the three hundred and sixty miles which stretch from the limit of our view to the northern axis of the globe, is, so far as sledge travelling is concerned, immaterial. Sixty miles of such pack as we now know to extend north of Cape Joseph Henry is an insuperable obstacle to travelling in that direction with our present appliances; and I unhesitatingly affirm that it is impracticable to reach the North Pole by the Smith Sound route.

To our great disappointment we observed that the extensive plains, with numerous deep and broad watercourses leading from the mountains into James Ross Bay, were covered with deep snow; not a solitary rock or boulder was showing above the continuous white surface. Perhaps in August, when the snow has melted, there may be good feeding-grounds for musk-oxen, but the state of the country when we saw it precluded any hope of meeting with those animals.

After passing more than an hour on the top of the mountain, taking bearings with a theodolite, we became so intensely cold that we were obliged to desist.

We then built a cairn of sufficient size to be visible from the shore, and returned to the camp ; though we descended the hill with great reluctance, for I would gladly have obtained a fuller series of observations. Mount Julia is composed of grey mountain limestone ; and it was a curious reflection to make, as we built the cairn in the midst of as glacial a scene as can be imagined, that the shells and corals which were embedded in the rocks we handled, had in the far-off past inhabited a tropical sea.

During the next two days we were partially confined to the tent by a strong westerly gale, with a continuous heavy fall of snow ; in the midst of our discomfort it made us realize how exceptionally fortunate we had been in obtaining the view we did from the top of Mount Julia.   During the lulls in the gale, which sometimes lasted for a couple of hours, we employed ourselves by quarrying in a neighbouring ravine, where the exposed strata on either side were replete with fossil forms belonging to the mountain limestone or sub-carboniferous period.   I need scarcely mention that we loaded up our sledge with these precious relics, regardless of all consequences, wrapping up the more delicate specimens in our spare change of clothing, our only regret being that we had to abandon a quantity of the original collection.   As it was, our return journey to the ship could only be accomplished by advancing with half-loads at a time, and so heavy in many places was the sodden floe that we were frequently obliged to turn round and face the lightened sledge, and advance a few feet at a time with repeated ' one, two, three, hauls.'

On Feilden Peninsula there appeared to be a considerable amount of vegetation, judging from the remains of former seasons, and we came across more than one skeleton of musk-oxen, so that I have no doubt that later in the year it is a favourite resort of these animals.

On the 3rd of June we started on our return to the ship, burying three hares, the only game that we had been fortunate enough to procure, in a crack in a floe-berg, for Markham and his men. Little did we think at the time that they were actually encamped on the ice only two miles distant from us, though completely hidden from our view by a thick mist, which, shrouding their outward track, had landed them in a wilderness of heavy ice in a truly deplorable state.

Out of a party of two officers and fifteen once powerful men, five were lying helpless on the sledges dragged by the two officers and six men, all of whom were themselves considerably crippled; whilst four others, unable to lend a hand at the drag-ropes, just managed to crawl along, keeping pace with the slow advance. The boats, and every article of provisions or clothing which could possibly be spared, had been cast aside in order to lighten to the utmost the sledges weighted with the invalids.

In all probability, had we known of their being in our neighbourhood, the life of poor George Porter, who died six days afterwards, would have been spared.

On the 4th, we encamped on a gravel spit forming the south point of the second bay south of Cape Richardson, greatly enjoying the dry ground after a long journey over the sludgy floe. Snow-buntings in considerable numbers now enlivened us with their sweet happy song, and several knots (*Tringa canutus*) with small parties of turnstones (*Strepsilas interpres*) and sanderlings (*Calidris arenaria*) were feeding on a patch of well-advanced purple saxifrage.

The bay where we encamped, which I named Knot Harbour, is the most northern sheltered position on the coast. It is open to the north-east, but owing to its narrow entrance, which is not more than a quarter of a mile wide, no large floe could enter. Its neighbourhood appears to support more game than any other position north of Discovery Bay.

On the 6th we crossed the land behind Cape Belknap, and encamped on the projecting spit between the Dumbell Lakes, where we were disappointed to find both hill and plain completely covered with snow. In fact, the late snowfall had buried the land deeper than at any time since the previous autumn.

The ice in Dumbell Lake, which had not yet begun to thaw, was $91\frac{1}{2}$ inches thick, and the water from below, when reached, rose to within $8\frac{1}{2}$ inches of the surface of the ice. All the water in this lake had certainly not been frozen during the past winter, and afterwards we found that it was well stocked with a small species of charr, *Salmo arcturus*, Günther; indeed, we did not ascertain that any of the lakes that contained fish froze to the bottom; the evidence tended to the contrary.

On the morning of the 7th, Feilden and I started to walk to the ship, twelve miles distant, where we arrived in the afternoon. The snow from the last storm was very soft, wet, and heavy, and rendered the travelling extremely laborious.

During my absence Mr. Egerton obtained a temperature-sounding half-a-mile distant from the land off Black Cape, in thirty-two fathoms of water. The temperature at a depth of two fathoms was 28°·5; at five, 29°·2; at twenty, 29°; and at thirty, 29°·4. The thickness of the ice, which was a small patch frozen during the past winter, was 49½ inches.

At this date, with a mean temperature of the air at about 30°, a pool of water, which rose and fell with the tide, encircled each grounded floeberg, causing the ice in the neighbourhood to decay rapidly. Although my visit to Cape Joseph Henry was made during the neap-tides, it was noticeable that there the rise and fall of the tide was decidedly less than at Floeberg Beach.

CHAPTER XIII.

INCREASE OF SCURVY—CONYBEARE ARRIVES FROM DISCOVERY BAY—
PROCEEDINGS OF PARTIES FROM ' DISCOVERY '—LADY FRANKLIN
SOUND—BOATS TAKEN TO GREENLAND—POLARIS BAY—CAPTAIN
HALL'S GRAVE—HIS LAST RECORD—CHRONOMETER—VITALITY OF
WHEAT—COPPINGER'S JOURNEY.

EARLY in the month of June three more of the crew
were placed under medical treatment with scorbutic
symptoms ; each of these men had been employed with
the sledges, but two had been receiving the regulated
ship's diet with lime-juice for three weeks prior to the
appearance of the disease.

On my return to the ' Alert' on the 7th there were
fourteen men belonging to that ship, and two belonging to the ' Discovery ' who had been under treatment
for scurvy. Of these only one, a very mild case, had
recovered ; the others did not appear to improve
rapidly, although they were given the most complete
change of diet at our disposal ; with the exception of
fresh meat, it was as good as could be desired.

Although one or two men of the sledge crews
employed on former Arctic expeditions had been
attacked·by this disease, the generality had entirely
escaped ; therefore, considering the carefully selected
provisions with which we were provided, the outbreak

was most inexplicable and unlooked-for. It was, however, encouraging to learn from the reports of our predecessors how transient the attacks had usually proved, and how quickly the patients recovered with rest, the advance of summer, and a change to a more generous diet. Nevertheless, so serious an outbreak naturally made me anxious for the health and safety of the numerous travellers absent from the ship; but as they were the strongest men out of two crews specially selected for Arctic service, I certainly never contemplated such a complete breakdown as actually occurred.

Mr. Conybeare arrived on board the 'Alert' on the 31st of May, after a journey of nine days from Discovery Bay. Owing to the water having forced its way up through the tidal-cracks and overflowed the ice in many places, he had experienced even greater difficulty in travelling up Robeson Channel than any of his predecessors. Off Cape Frederick VII. he met with three pools of water, the largest of which was over three hundred yards in length.

Mr. Conybeare was the bearer of despatches from Captain Stephenson, which informed me that Lieutenant Archer had returned to the 'Discovery' on the 2nd of May, after having explored Lady Franklin Sound to a distance of sixty-seven miles in a southwest direction from Discovery Bay, where it terminated in two fiords. Mr. Archer reported that—

'The inlet originally called Lady Franklin Strait may be described as a deep sound or fiord, which extends for a distance of sixty-five miles into Grinnell Land. It is nine miles broad at the mouth, and at a distance of twenty miles from Distant Cape separates into two arms. Conybeare Bay, the most northerly of the two, does not seem to extend more than ten miles to the west of the Keppel's Head; it has not, however, been thoroughly explored. The southern arm is between four and five miles broad at the mouth, and forty miles long, trending to the south-west, till at Record Point it divides into the two small bays in which the sound terminates. For the whole of its length it is surrounded by steep precipitous cliffs, which at the farther end are very high, being in one place over 3,000 feet sheer. A considerable quantity of the heavy Polar ice was met with till within a few miles of the head of the bay. The remainder of the ice was of a small lumpy description, with but few young floes amongst it.'

In the most southern of the two fiords at the head of the sound a large glacier was observed in a valley descending from the Victoria and Albert Mountains, estimated to be 5,000 feet in height. The glacier ended at a distance of about ten miles from the shore ; its end was therefore considerably above the sea-level.

In the northern fiord, Lieutenant Archer, after a severe climb, which occupied him seven hours, reached the summit of Mount Neville, 3,800 feet above the sea. From that elevated point the United States Range was sighted to the W.N.W., and a glacier was discovered in one of the valleys, but ending at a considerable height above the sea-level; an extensive plain led from Beatrix Bay some twenty miles inland to the foot of the United States Range. To the westward the mountainous land was lower, estimated to be about 2,000 feet high, and extending for an unknown distance. Mr. Archer remarked that, considering the height to which he ascended, it was somewhat remarkable that no high mountains were visible at any great distance to the westward.

Two small glaciers were observed on the southern shore of the sound in valleys descending from the mountains on Judge Daly Peninsula. In both cases the glaciers ended at a distance of about a mile from the sea.

A herd of eleven musk-oxen were seen, but none were procured. The tracks of hares were numerous in the neighbourhood of Ella Bay and other places; two of these animals were shot.

After an absence of twenty-four days the party under the command of Lieutenant Archer returned in good health to Discovery Bay.

Mr. Conybeare, who commanded the auxiliary sledge in the expedition to Lady Franklin Sound, had returned to the 'Discovery' on the 20th of April, after an absence of twelve days from the ship. His crew of eleven men were in excellent health with the exception of one, who was slightly frost-bitten in the foot. The only fresh meat obtained by this party was a single hare, which was killed on the southern side of Bellot Island.

On the 2nd of May Mr. Conybeare left the 'Discovery' with a crew of eleven men to transport a fifteen-foot ice-boat across Hall's Basin to Polaris Bay. On the 5th of the same month, Lieutenant Archer's return having placed a greater number of men at his disposal, Captain Stephenson decided to send two boats across the channel to the Greenland shore. A dog-sledge despatched to recall Mr. Conybeare and his men overtook them on the 5th, when about six miles from land.

On the 7th of May Lieutenant Fulford and Mr. Conybeare finally started from the ' Discovery ' with eighteen men, dragging a twenty-foot ice-boat on a twelve-man sledge. On the following day they reached the spot where the boat had been left ; the party was then divided, eleven men dragging the larger boat and seven the smaller one. On the 12th, after five days' travelling, the boats were safely deposited near the depôt at Polaris Bay, and the same evening Captain Stephenson accompanied by Mr. Hart likewise arrived there.

While crossing the channel the weather was thick and gloomy with a strong breeze from the southward, which made the journey very unpleasant, but the ice was the best they had yet travelled over. Some large floes of young smooth ice were met with in Hall's Basin, but on both sides of the channel, near the shores, hummocks and pressed-up ice formed considerable barriers ; the greatest obstacles being met with on the Greenland coast.

On the 13th of May, in the presence of twenty-four officers and men, Captain Stephenson hoisted the American flag over the grave of Captain Hall, and at the foot erected a brass tablet brought from England. The inscription read as follows :—

SACRED TO THE MEMORY OF

CAPTAIN C. F. HALL,

of the U.S. Ship 'Polaris,'

Who sacrificed his Life in the Advancement of Science
on November 8th, 1871.

This Tablet has been erected by the British Polar Expedition of 1875,
Who, following in his footsteps, have profited by his experience.

GRAVE OF CAPTAIN HALL.

On the 15th, Doctor Coppinger arrived from Refuge
Harbour. His party had found Captain Hall's cairn on
the north side of Newman Bay, and brought away
the record, leaving a copy in its stead. They then
crossed the bay and visited the boat-camp on its
southern shore, where a party from the 'Polaris,' under
the command of Mr. Chester, endeavouring to proceed
to the north, spent part of the summer of 1872. The
following extract from Doctor Coppinger's Report gives

an account of his finding the cairn erected by Hall on his last journey, and refers to the condition of the boats and stores left at the boat-camp.

'The point of Newman Bay which I had reached, after crossing the land from Repulse Harbour, proved to be about five miles to the eastward of Cape Brevoort ; therefore, after coasting about two miles to the westward, I came to the position of Captain Hall's cairn. Here I found the record in a good state of preservation, buried ten feet east (true) of a stone at the margin of the cairn on which was cut " 10 FEET E." Having taken the original document and deposited in its stead an accurate copy, accompanied by a brief account of my past and projected movements, I proceeded across the mouth of Newman Bay towards the boat-camp. The latter I found situated, as expected, about one and-a-half miles from Cape Sumner, but only five and-a-half miles from Hall's cairn. We camped on the floe about a quarter-of-a-mile from the site of the tent and boats. Although our stay extended over forty hours, we were most of the time confined to our tents by a gale from the southward, and consequently unable to make a very complete examination of the American stores. One tent we found near the mouth of a ravine, collapsed, frozen to the ground, and partially covered with snow. The whale-boat lay bottom upwards on a flat piece of land about a hundred yards from the beach, lashed down to heavy stones and frozen in by mud ; while the canvas boat was with difficulty discovered, buried in snow, and lying about eighty yards from the whale-boat and two hundred from the tent. The whale-boat was stove in on the starboard bow, for which defects the materials necessary for repairs were at hand; in other respects she was serviceable.

'The stores found under the boat seemed to have been but little affected by the weather; for instance, some biscuit, of which there was about twenty pounds, lying loose in the lockers, was in good condition. Great difficulty was experienced in getting at some of the gear, the bags, for instance, being frozen so stiffly that it was impossible to examine their contents without tearing them in pieces.

'Expecting to find two tents to correspond with the two boats, I searched in various directions for a second, but in vain. Therefore having made a rough list of such stores as circumstances would admit of our examining, having packed upon the sledges the instruments and documents which I could transfer to Polaris Bay, and having erected a conspicuous cairn and attached thereto a record of proceedings, we struck tents, packed up, and proceeded to the eastward.'

Captain Stephenson during his stay at Thank God Harbour, took the precaution of placing a depôt of provisions on the shore of Newman Bay, in order to insure relief to the party under the command of Lieutenant Beaumont, in case the heavy snow lying on the neck of land between that bay and Hall's Rest delayed the travellers on their return journey from the north. This duty was carried out by Lieutenant Fulford and Doctor Coppinger.

From the 12th to the 15th of May the travellers at Hall's Rest experienced a gale from the northward. On the 16th the barometer fell, accompanied by a second gale from the same direction, with a great deal of snow-drift, which confined them all to their tents. The drift was so thick that, notwithstanding the five tents were pitched close together, it was at times impossible to communicate between them.

On the 17th, Captain Stephenson and his party of thirty officers and men recrossed the channel in seventeen marching hours, leaving Lieutenant Fulford, Doctor Coppinger, with two men and eight dogs, to explore Petermann Fiord ; with orders to return to Polaris Bay before the 15th of June, on which date it was expected they would meet Lieutenants Beaumont and Rawson and their men, returning from the exploration of North Greenland.

The rock in the vicinity of Polaris Bay was found to be a hard limestone containing no fossils, though over the entire country fossiliferous drifted limestone was scattered. Evidences of the recent elevation of the land, in mud-beds rising to 500 feet and containing marine shells, were abundant. Traces of fox, lemming, hare, ptarmigan and snow-bunting were observed. Eight flowering plants, the remains of last season's growth, and some mosses and lichens, were collected.

The ice-foot north of Cape Lupton was observed by Captain Stephenson to be of a more massive construction, and the pack generally of a heavier description than that on the western side of the channel.

All the records, and articles brought from Polaris Bay and the boat-camp in Newman Bay, together with the American ensign which was hoisted over the grave of Captain Hall, during the stay of our men in the neighbourhood, were, on the return of the Expedition

to England, forwarded by the British Admiralty to the
United States Government. The chronometer found
at the boat-camp, after four years' exposure to the
vicissitudes of Arctic temperature, kept excellent time
from the period of its arrival on board the 'Discovery,' until that ship returned to England during
November 1876.

A bag of wheat was found at Polaris Bay, which
was, I understand, sent to the Arctic Regions from the
Smithsonian Institute of Washington, for the purpose of
ascertaining the power of cereals to resist the extremes
of cold ; after an exposure for at least four successive
winters and three summers at Polaris Bay, out of a
small sample tried at Kew by Sir Joseph Hooker,
sixty-two per cent. germinated ; the rest of this grain
was returned to the Smithsonian Institute.

In order to avoid the heavy pack outside of Cape
Brevoort all the North Greenland division of sledges
crossed the land at the back of the cape, through the
M'Cormick pass, on their return journeys. During
the month of May when the snow-floor, cemented
by the frequent gales, presented a hard road for
sledging, Dr. Coppinger was only a day and a half in
crossing. Between the 21st and 24th of May, Rawson,
with an invalid on his sledge and himself snow-blind,
was a little more than three days in performing the
journey ; and between the 14th and 19th of June,
when most of the snow had melted, and water was
rushing down the southern ravine, Lieutenant Beaumont returning with his crippled party crossed in five
days.

I append the following extract from Dr. Coppinger's

account of his journey through the Pass; the estimated height of which is about 400 feet.

'Having completed our work at the Repulse Bay depôt, we started on the 8th of May, and proceeded along an excellent ice-foot towards the mouth of M'Cormick Valley. The cliffs of this coast, under which we passed, present a bold, unweathered surface of dark limestone, apparently devoid of fossils, but containing some yellow ore, probably iron pyrites. On reaching the mouth of the valley we camped on a low flat piece of land bordered by old raised beaches. After three hours on the march we made good four miles, temperature 5°.

'At 10 P.M. started and proceeded along M'Cormick Valley, which for the first two miles is a plain half a mile in width, sloping up to the southward by a gentle gradient, and lined on both sides by unmistakable raised beaches. On either side rise cliffs and peaked mountains from 2,000 to 3,000 feet in height; the cliffs on the east side being formed of vertical, slightly contorted layers of a clayey barren limestone. All about this reach of the valley we found numerous fragments of shells, which mark the area of the old sea-bed. Some of the raised beaches present clearly cut sections twenty feet high, showing well-defined alternate layers a half to two inches thick of stratified mud and sand.

'As the land loses its marine character, we entered a narrow winding valley, nearly level, and bordered by rounded hills of about two hundred feet in height. While prospecting from the summit of one of these I picked up a drift fossil, apparently a worn

cup-coral. Frequently in the sides of the gully we
passed rock *in situ*, not covered by snow, and consisting
in some places of a calcareous slate ; in others of a
confused mass of clayey limestone in the form of
rectangular sticks one to two feet in length.

' Following the sinuosities of the valley, the travelling was excellent, and the general direction S. by W.
In about three hours it led us by a gentle rise to an
elevated plateau covered with hard crusted snow.
Having traversed this plateau for about half a mile,
the floe of Newman Bay came into view for the
first time, appearing to be about two miles off. We
now found, right in the course which we had been
pursuing, a ravine leading down towards Newman Bay ;
and expecting to find in it better snow-travelling than
on the land on either side, we determined on following
it. At 7.45 A.M. of the 9th we camped in the ravine.

' At 9.30 P.M. we started and proceeded down the
ravine, which soon degenerates into a narrow tortuous
gully, whose precipitous sides of clay slate approach
so closely in places as only just to give passage to
the eight-man sledge. The bottom is, however, well
packed with snow-drift, and being sheltered from the
sun by vertical cliffs, probably remains a good road for
sledging until the spring is far advanced. This ravine,
from its commencement in the high plateau, slopes
rapidly to the southward, *i.e.* towards Newman's Bay.
We spent a great deal of time road-making along the
sides of snow-slopes, cutting down opposing snow-banks,
and with drag-ropes reversed, easing the sledges down
steep inclines. In one place we lowered the sledge down
a little snow-precipice sixteen feet deep. At 12.40 A.M.

of the 10th we reached the shore of the bay and halted for lunch, having made good two miles.'

Dr. Coppinger found a smooth floe of one season's ice extending across the mouth of Newman Bay, between the position of Hall's Cairn and the boat-camp; both old and young floes were met with inside the bay. The entrance must, therefore, have been free from pack-ice when the frost set in the previous autumn.

The fresh tracks of a bear were observed in the bay, it is therefore probable that it managed to exist in the neighbourhood during the previous winter.

On the plains between Polaris Bay and Newman Bay, estimated to be 300 feet above the sea, the soft snow rendered the travelling bad, but being favoured by a strong easterly wind Dr. Coppinger's party crossed in two days. He states in his report, ' Our road is still the same undulating plain, covered everywhere with soft snow, without a track of bird or beast, and presenting to the eye as dreary and monotonous an aspect as can well be imagined.'

CHAPTER XIV.

LIEUTENANT PARR ARRIVES ON BOARD 'ALERT'—DISTRESSING CONDI-
TION OF NORTHERN DIVISION OF SLEDGES—RELIEF PARTY START
—DEATH OF GEORGE PORTER—MARKHAM'S JOURNEY.

ON the evening of the 8th, Lieutenant Parr made his
appearance on board the 'Alert.' As he crossed the
quarter-deck, silently nodding to the one or two who
chanced to meet him, his grave and weary expression was unmistakable, and in a very few
moments the certainty that some sore calamity had
occurred had spread throughout the ship. So travel-
stained was he on entering my cabin that I mistook
him for his more swarthy friend Beaumont, then on the
Greenland coast, and therefore anxiously questioned
him concerning the disaster which had occasioned his
totally unexpected return.

I then received the distressing intelligence that
nearly the whole of Commander Markham's men were
attacked with scurvy and in want of immediate assistance. Markham and the few men who were able to
work had succeeded in conveying the invalids to the
neighbourhood of Cape Joseph Henry, twenty-seven
miles distant from the ship, and were still advancing
slowly ; but each day was rapidly adding to the intensity of the disease and the number of the sick.

Under these circumstances Parr nobly volunteered to bring me the news and so obtain relief for his companions.

Starting with only an alpenstock and a small allowance of provisions, at the end of twenty miles he arrived at a shooting tent in Dumbell Bay, where he hastily made himself a cup of tea; pushing on, he completed his long and solitary walk within twenty-four hours.

Arrangements were at once made to proceed to Commander Markham's assistance, and by midnight two strong parties of officers and men had started; Lieutenant May, and Doctor Moss who wore snow-shoes, pushing on before us, with the dog-sledge laden with appropriate medical stores. By making a forced march they reached Markham's camp within fifty hours of Parr's departure.

Their arrival had naturally a most exhilarating effect on the stricken men; but to our great regret they were unfortunately too late to save the life of George Porter, who only a few hours previously had expired: he was buried in the floe by the wayside.

Early on the following day I joined them with the main relief party, when the hope and trust which had never deserted them was quickened to the utmost; even the prostrate men losing the depression of spirits induced by the disease that had attacked them, and which in their case was much intensified by the recent loss of their comrade.

It is difficult for a stranger to the surrounding circumstances and scenery to realize the condition and appearance of these men, who in spite of their truly pitiable state were yet making slow progress towards the ship.

On my first meeting them Markham and five men were dragging two sledges, three hands at each; each sledge being freighted with two invalids and as much of the tent furniture as was requisite to keep them warm and to form as comfortable a couch as the circumstances and the rough road permitted. Lying on the top of the third sledge, which was laden with the rest of the baggage and the provisions, and left about half a mile in the rear, was a fifth invalid.

Struggling along over the uneven, snow covered, ice as best they could, were four other men whose limbs becoming daily more cramped foretold that they must shortly succumb; they were gallantly holding out to the last in order not to increase by their weight, a moment sooner than could be avoided, the already heavy loads being dragged by their very slightly stronger companions.

These poor fellows were in the habit of starting off each morning before the main party, knowing that if they experienced a bad fall or came to an unusually deep snow-drift they could not recover themselves without help. Frequently the sledge party overtook them lying helpless on the ice; but once raised on their legs, with a smile and some happy cheerful expression, again they would start on their painful and weary journey.

With the exception of Markham, who dragged to the very last, and in addition had to pioneer a way for the sledges before the daily start, the others remaining on the drag-ropes were in a great measure dependent on the leaders, John Radmore and Thomas Jolliffe. Although these two men were the most vigorous of the sledge crews, they were greatly enfeebled; yet rather than resign the post of honour as leaders, which entailed the extra labour of treading down a pathway through the snow, they journeyed along supporting each other arm-in-arm, and by keeping the drag-rope taut afforded a means of support for their more disabled companions in the rear.

The prevailing good-humour and dutiful submission of one and all of these men to the severe labour demanded of them, their manful and determined struggle along the roughest road imaginable, is far beyond all praise. After seeing their condition there is no difficulty in realizing the statement concerning Sir John Franklin's men, as made by the Eskimo to Sir Leopold M'Clintock, ' They fell down and died as they walked along.'

Early on the morning of the 12th the whole party encamped on the shore at Cape Richardson; exchanging the dreary prospect of icy desolation afforded by the confused disarray of ice hummocks, which had so frequently bounded their view for nearly sixty days, for the agreeable sight of the newly-sprouting but sparse vegetation on the sides of the familiar and well-known hills, now becoming partially cleared of snow. Equally inspiriting was the change, from the intense solitude of the inanimate pack, afforded by the frequent sweet song of snow-buntings collected confidingly near the tent, the sharp call of some knots which were flying about in flocks of ten or a dozen, and the occasional deep notes of some geese which had opportunely just arrived from the southward and were looking for a resting-place.

This total change of circumstances, together with the anxious and unremitting care of Dr. Moss, the alteration of diet, and a plentiful supply of fresh game and limejuice arrested the disease, and at once produced a marked improvement in the appearance of all.

The following is an abridged account of this memorable sledge journey which is published in the Parliamentary Blue Book, c. 1636, of 1877.

In addressing the crews of the two sledges previous to their departure I made the following statement:—

' The work before you, although not more perilous than Arctic journeys usually are, will undoubtedly be a very arduous and irksome one, and monotonous in the extreme. The daily advance will necessarily be slow; for you must always journey over the same road twice, and frequently far oftener. You therefore cannot hope for the exhilarating spur accompanying quick progress which others will feel; but are called on to show that we possess the high quality of resolute perseverance to overcome whatever obstacles are before us.

' The only journey to be likened in any way to yours is the similar attempt of Sir Edward Parry to reach a high northern latitude, with much the same equipment, and absent for the same number of days. We all hope that with God's blessing you will at all events be as successful.'

Extracts from my orders to Commander Markham; dated 3rd of April, 1876:—

'Taking command of the sledges "Marco Polo," "Victoria," "Bull-dog," "Alexandra," and "Bloodhound," you will proceed to the neighbourhood of Cape Parry, and from thence force your way to the northward over the ice, with the two boats which have been equipped for that purpose, and provisioned for an absence of about seventy days.

'The object of your journey is to attain the highest northern latitude possible; and to ascertain the possibility of a more fully equipped expedition reaching the North Pole.

'At present we know little or nothing concerning the movement of the ice in the offing. The journey on which you are about to engage is therefore a far more arduous one than Arctic journeys usually are. The heavy nature of the ice across which you have to travel has hitherto baffled all attempts made to cross it, and the formidable obstacles it presents at present, while stationary, must be considerably increased when once it is in motion. Even during the summer, with occasional lanes of navigable water between the floes, Parry and Ross could scarcely average a daily journey of three miles.

'Therefore, while, with full confidence in your ability and discretion, I leave you entirely free as to the carrying out of your journey in all its details, I must direct your most serious consideration—first, to the extreme hazard of attempting an advance beyond the time when half your provisions will be expended; and, secondly, to the danger of separating your party or of leaving depôts of provisions on a road which it is impossible to mark, and which will probably break-up in your rear. It is true that your men on the return journey will be dragging diminished loads; but towards the end of the season the ice will probably be in motion, and one of your chief enemies, the misty weather, will be more continuous. Over stationary ice, however rough, there is a choice of roads; once it is in motion, no choice is left.

' During your absence, should you, contrary to my present expectations, experience a general break-up of the ice, or, arriving at the edge of the firm ice, find the outer pack broken up, you are to consider the position you will then have attained as the limit of your advance; and, after making what observations are practicable, you are to retreat to the ship.'

Extracts from Commander Markham's official journal :—

' 3rd.—Left the ship at 11 A.M. The western division, under the command of Lieutenant Aldrich, in company. The travelling by no means good; snow deep, and the sledges dragging very heavily. This being our first march, and the men showing signs of fatigue, a halt was called at 5.30, and the tents pitched on the eastern side of the neck of land connecting Mushroom Point with the main. Men in capital spirits. Distance made good six miles.

' 4th.—Commenced the march at 7.30 A.M. Double-banked all the sledges over the land, which fortunately for us had a good covering of snow; nevertheless, we found it hard work with our heavy sledges; the travelling round and beyond Harley Spit excessively heavy and laborious. Men getting tired, halted at 4.45, and camped. Everything frozen perfectly hard.

To use Admiral Richards' simile, our sleeping-bags resembled sheet-iron, whilst the currie paste, as our cook observed, was exactly like a piece of brass, and was equally hard. We were all hungry enough to eat our full allowance of pemmican at supper, and enjoyed it. Distance marched ten miles; made good six miles. Temperature minus 35°.

' 5th.—Although the temperature inside our tent last night was minus 25°, we all slept a little more comfortably, or rather a little less uncomfortably, though deprived of all feeling in our feet. Travelling much the same as yesterday, therefore compelled to advance in the same manner—that is, sledges double-banked. The men appear a little stiff, and complain of having suffered a good deal last night from pain in their limbs, and are to-day suffering from great thirst.

' A wolf's track, seen each day since we left the ship, has been the only vestige of animal life observed. Encamped on the floe a short distance from Simmon's Island. The travelling has not improved, and the temperature has been as low as minus 45°. Everything very cold and uncomfortable. Distance marched twelve miles; made good four miles.

' 6th.—Another cold sleepless night over. A beautifully sunny day, but with a temperature at 35° below zero. Everything frozen stiff and hard. Dressing by no means an easy operation. Sledges double-banked as before. Progression slow. Reached a stream of young ice extending to Depôt Point, the travelling on which being good, enabled us to single-bank the crews, and to arrive at Depôt Point at 5.30; off which we camped on the floe.

' 7th.—The sledge " Bloodhound " having fulfilled the duties entrusted to her, she was despatched to the ship at 8 A.M. Gave her three cheers on parting. A beautiful day, but *very* cold. A few slight frostbites were sustained yesterday, but quickly restored. The travelling to-day is a foretaste of what we are to expect; heavy floes fringed with hummocks, through and over which the sledges have to be dragged. Dr. Moss was fortunate enough to shoot a hare on Depôt Point, which is to be reserved as a *bonne bouche* for us when we attain our highest latitude. Land very much distorted by mirage. Camped for the night on a floe off Cape Hercules. Temperature remains extraordinarily low : minus 41°. Distance marched fourteen miles ; made good four and-a-half.

' 8th.—A charming day, although the temperature persists in remaining low. Care has to be taken in selecting the road so as to avoid the hummocks as much as possible ; occasionally we are brought to a standstill by a belt of more than ordinarily large ones, through which we have to cut a road with pickaxes and shovels. Sledges double-banked as before. The large sledge, on which is the twenty-foot ice-boat, drags very heavily. This is caused by the overhanging weight at the two extremities. Glare from the sun has been very oppressive ; the snow in places resembles coarse sand, and appears more crystallised than usual. A few of the party, including Parr and myself, suffering from snow-blindness. Distance marched ten miles. Temperature minus 30°.

' 9th.—Same system of double-banking the sledges continues. Parr's snow-blindness is no better, mine no worse. The snow goggles are worn by all, and certainly afford relief to the eyes. Moss is rendering valuable service by assisting me in the selection of a road—no easy task whilst going through hummocks. Although the temperature is minus 30°, the sun has sufficient influence to dry our blanket wrappers and other gear; the yards of the boats being very convenient for the purpose of tricing up our robes, &c. The snow is still very deep on the floes and between the hummocks, materially retarding our progress. Halted at seven, and encamped on a heavy floe. From its north-western edge the depôt at Cape Joseph Henry was plainly visible; a great relief to our minds, as thoughts of its being buried in deep snow-drift would frequently occur to us. Distance marched thirteen miles; made good four.

' 10th.—Leaving the tents pitched, we started with an empty sledge for the depôt, distant about two miles. We experienced heavy work in cutting a road through the line of shore hummocks that girt the coast, and did not succeed in reaching the depôt until eleven o'clock. Sending the party back to camp, Aldrich, Giffard, Moss, and I ascended View Hill (650 feet), whence we obtained a good look-out. The prospect was anything but cheering. To the northward was an irregular sea of ice, composed of small floes and large hummocks. Our anticipations of slow travelling and heavy work seem about to be realized. The sun was so powerful that the snow was thawing, and the water trickling down on the southern side of the hill. We shall start to-morrow morning with provisions complete for sixty-three days. Thus loaded, the sledges

will drag uncommonly heavy, and over the rough
hummocks we are certain to encounter our only mode
of advancing will be by a system of double-banking,
which simply means one mile made good for every
five actually marched. If we accomplish two miles
a day it will be a fair day's work. On shore we
observed numerous traces of hares and ptarmigan,
but although Dr. Moss followed up the trails of the
former, his attempts to obtain any were not crowned
with success.

'11th.—A dull, overcast day. Snow falling. I was
again greatly indebted to Moss for his efficient aid in
assisting me to choose a road for the sledges, Parr being
still laid up with snow-blindness, and my sight "not
quite the thing." Aldrich has very wisely determined
to return to the land and try his luck through the Snow
valley, instead of rounding Cape Joseph Henry. At one
o'clock, displayed all colours, and parted company
with Aldrich's division and our two supporting sledges
amid much cheering. They were soon lost sight of
amongst the hummocks. Parr in advance with half a
dozen men cutting a road with pickaxes and shovels,
the remainder of the men dragging up the sledges
singly. Got on to a heavy floe and then in amongst
a mass of heavy hummocks, through which appeared
no road or outlet; but the steady and persevering
exertions of Parr and his road-makers performed
wonders, and the sledges were soon travelling over a
road that had before looked impenetrable and impassable. The floes are small, but very heavy. It is
difficult to estimate their thickness, but it must be very
considerable. They appear to have had a terrible

FLOEBERG AND PRESSED-UP RUBBLE ICE.

conflict one with another, the result being what we are now encountering, namely, a great expanse of hummocks varying in height from twenty feet to small round nobbly pieces over which we stagger and fall. Between these hummocks the snow-drifts are very deep, and we are continually floundering up to our waists, but the men struggle bravely on. Possibly when we leave the vicinity of Cape Joseph Henry, and get well clear of the land, we may experience better travelling, larger floes and less snow. One thing is pretty certain, we cannot have much worse, and this is a consolation. Encamped amongst the hummocks, after a very hard and weary day's work. The men appear a good deal done up. The road-making was incessant the whole afternoon. Distance marched ten miles; made good two and-a-quarter.

'12th.—An unexpected but most gratifying change of temperature caused us to pass a comparatively comfortable night; temperature inside our tent as high as 16°, and during supper rose as high as 22°. After breakfast, commenced with half a dozen road-makers cutting a road through the hummocks, leaving the remainder of the party to strike the tents, pack, and bring up the sledges one by one as far as the road was practicable. Being a beautifully bright sunny day, the tent robes and other gear were triced up to the masts and yards to dry. Parr's eyes are improving, and he now works like a slave with pickaxe and shovel, working with and superintending the labours of the road-makers.

'After lunch emerged from the hummocks on to a small floe, and then through another mass of hummocks, having only made about half a mile during the afternoon.

' The surface snow on the floes sparkles and glitters with the most beautiful iridescent colours, the ground on which we walk appearing as if strewn with bright and lustrous gems ; diamonds, rubies, emeralds, and sapphires being the most prominent. At 3 p.m. observed the fresh traces of a lemming. It is strange the little creature should wander so far from the land, the nearest point being quite three miles off. Crossed over some streams of young ice, and through a long fringe of hummocks leading on to a large floe of " ancient lineage " presenting an undulating surface, and having on it diminutive ice mountains, or frozen snow-drifts, from fifteen to twenty feet in height. Halted at the edge of a belt of hummocks, through which a road was cut whilst the tents were being pitched. Camped for the night, the men being rather fatigued, having had a hard day's work. We are all suffering from cracked skin, the combined action of sun and frost, our lips, cheeks, and noses being especially very sore. The temperature all day has been delightful, ranging from minus 8° to minus 20°. Travelling through hummocks is most unsatisfactory work ; it is a succession of standing pulls—one, two, three, haul ! and very little result. Distance marched nine miles ; made good one and-a-half.

' 13th.—Passed through a fringe of hummocks about 200 yards in breadth, then arrived on a fine large floe that afforded us capital travelling for about a mile due north, and then on to another long fringe of large and troublesome hummocks, until we were completely brought up by enormous masses of ice, piled up, piece on piece, to the height of over twenty feet. Through this we resolved to cut a passage, although foreseeing it would be a long and tedious job ; however, there appeared no other alternative, so immediately after lunch the road-makers, always supervised and headed by Parr, who is not only a first-rate engineer but also a most indefatigable labourer, set to work to cut a road. This by 6 P.M.—with such resolution did they work— was completed, the sledges dragged through and on to another old floe, girt by more hummocks which were in their turn attacked by Parr and his gang, and we had the satisfaction of halting and encamping on a fine large floe, which promises to give us a good lead for some way to the north to-morrow.   Parr, I am happy to say, has quite recovered from his snow-blindness.

' 14th.—Crossed an old floe, having a deep incrustation of frozen snow on its surface, rendering the dragging very laborious, then through a belt of small hummocks on to another fair-sized floe.   These belts, or cordons, of hummocks vary in breadth from 50 and 100 yards to as much as a quarter and half-a-mile. As a rule round the larger floes appear the heavier hummocks.   We have been assailed by an unpleasant nipping breeze from the northward, our faces being constantly touched up by Jack Frost.   Temperature minus 28°.   We were employed, during the afternoon, in making a road through a more than ordinary broad hedge of hummocks, and pulling the sledges through, we made in consequence little head-way.   The wind freshening and the weather becoming very thick, we halted earlier than we otherwise would have done.

Many frost-bites about the face. John Shirley complaining of pain in his ankle and knee was duly treated. Distance marched eight miles; made good one and three quarters.

'15*th*.—Blowing a north-westerly gale, with the temperature 35° below zero, and a considerable drift which rendered travelling quite out of the question. Extreme wretchedness and almost abject misery was our lot to-day. We derived no heat from our robes, they were frozen so hard, the temperature inside our tent being minus 22°. It is rather remarkable that we have this day experienced, during a gale of wind, a lower temperature than we have had during any gale the whole winter, which leads one to the conclusion that it is evident there can be no open water existing either to the northward or westward of us.

'16*th*.—The wind this morning was still blowing fresh, though it had moderated considerably; it was, however, so cutting and piercing, and the drift was so dense, making it almost impossible for us to see our way through the hummocks, that it was deemed more prudent and advisable to remain encamped, however unpleasant and disagreeable such a course was to all concerned. We unanimously came to the conclusion that it was the most wretched and miserable Easter Sunday that any one of us had ever passed. Forty-eight hours in a bag, in a gale of wind off Cape Joseph Henry, with a temperature 67° below freezing point, is not a delightful way of passing the time— sleep was almost out of the question. In spite of the cold we did not omit the usual Saturday night's toast last evening; and as it was also the first anniversary of the Ships' commissioning we gave three cheers; this was taken up by the " Victoria," and then we commenced to cheer each other, by way of keeping up our spirits.

' At five struck the tents and commenced the march. Shirley being unable to walk, we were obliged to place him on one of the sledges, keeping him in his sleeping bag, and wrapping him well up in the coverlet and lower robe. This increases our weight to be dragged, besides diminishing our strength. Crossed the floe on which we were encamped, and cut our way through a hedge of hummocks, about one-third of a mile in breadth, on to another floe of apparently great thickness. These floes, although of stupendous size regarding their thickness, are unfortunately for us of no very great superficial extent, varying only from a quarter of a mile to a mile in north and south direction. The recent strong wind, blowing the snow from off the land to the floes, has made the travelling rather heavier than it was before. Between some of the large floes we occasionally meet small patches of young ice along which the sledges run smoothly; but, alas! they are never more than a few yards in extent. Encamped for the night on a large floe. Men appearing more done up, after lying so long idle in their bags, than if they had had a hard day's dragging. Beyond Cape Parry, which is at present the most distant land visible to the westward, can be seen two cloud-like objects that may be Aldrich's " Cooper Key Mountains;" but again they may be clouds or mirage. Distance marched seven miles; made good one and a quarter.

' 17th.—Commenced the march at 11.30 A.M.

Shirley has again to be put on the sledge. Porter is rendered *hors de combat*, and is suffering a good deal of pain. He is just able to hobble after us. Our force is much weakened by the loss of these two men. A beautiful sunny day with the temperature as high as minus 24°. The men are taking kindly to their goggles, rarely taking them off whilst on the march, and quite willing to put up with a little inconvenience rather than be afflicted with snow-blindness. The snow being deep, we found the travelling on the floes very heavy indeed; the large boat comes along very slowly, and it is seldom we can advance many paces without resorting to " standing pulls." Arrived at the edge of a broad belt of hummocks, through which a road had to be cut, then on to a small floe, then through more hummocks, which again had to succumb before the strenuous exertions of Parr and his untiring road-makers; then more small floes and more hummocks, and so it goes on.

'Some of the floes are thicker than others, and it is of no infrequent occurrence that we have to lower the sledges a distance of six or seven feet from the top of one to the surface of another, or *vice versâ*. After lunch, George Porter, being unable to walk any farther, had to be carried on the sledge. This is sad work; it makes our progress very slow and tedious. Distance marched nine miles; made good one and a-quarter.

'18*th*.—Having made a slight alteration in our weights by lessening those on the heavy sledge, we resumed the march at noon. Shirley has slightly improved, and is able to walk slowly in our rear. So hard were our sleeping-bags frozen last night, that the operation of getting into them was positively painful; the night, however, was comparatively warm, and we slept pretty comfortably. Our travelling during the early part of the day was across floes of an uneven surface, and between hummocks, through which, however, there was no necessity of cutting a road; but the deep snow rendered the dragging exceedingly heavy. These floes, or the majority of them, are all massed together, squeezed one against the other, but with few or no hummocks between; vastly different from the huge piled-up masses we had to contend with nearer the shore. After lunch, the description of ice over which we were travelling underwent great change, and it appeared to us that we had at length arrived on the veritable "palæocrystic" floes. We seem to have quite got away from the smooth level floes surrounded by dense hummocks, and have reached those of gigantic thickness with a most uneven surface, and covered with deep snow. The travelling has been rough and heavy. The "Victoria" capsized, but was quickly righted without damage to either sledge or boat, and without even giving the invalid, who was securely wrapped up inside the boat, a shaking. The foremost batten of the "Marco Polo" was also carried away. A south-easterly breeze sprang up at 5 P.M., sending the temperature down sharply to minus 33°, and we had to be cautious about frost-bites. Distance marched ten miles; made good one mile.

'19th.—A fine clear day. Our sleeping-bags last night were rendered a little more habitable from having been exposed during the day to the heat of the sun, which had the effect of extracting from them the greater part of the moisture. The helmet worsted caps so kindly and considerately presented to the Expedition by the Empress, are very warm and comfortable for sleeping in, and are much appreciated by the men, who call them " Eugénies."

' Experienced great difficulty in getting from one floe on to another, some of them being, with the snow on their surface, as much as eight and nine feet above the others. After labouring and toiling for three and a-half hours, " standing pulls " nearly the whole time, during which period we had barely advanced 300 yards, I came to the determination of abandoning the twenty-foot ice-boat. I did not arrive at this decision until after very mature deliberation, and from my own conviction that amongst such ice as we were then encountering, should a disruption occur, the boats would be of little avail to us, except to be used as a ferry from one floe to another. For this purpose the smaller boat will suffice. At 7 P.M. we arrived on some young ice, between the floes and amongst hummocks, that afforded us capital travelling. On this we rattled gaily along, accomplishing half a mile in something like a couple of hours—good work for us. 10.15 P.M. pitched our tents on a regular palæocrystic floe, having rounded hillocks on its surface from twenty-five to thirty feet high. Distance marched eight miles; made good one mile.

' 20th.—In consequence of an impervious fog we were unable to make a start until 2 P.M. Even then the weather was so thick that we experienced great difficulty in making any head-way. Crossing small floes and through hummocks that appear interminable. Snow very deep; prospect anything but cheering, as nothing but hummocks can be seen. At 8 P.M. the weather clearing slightly we succeeded in extricating ourselves from the hummocks, and crossing a large heavy floe got on to a stream of young ice that afforded us good travelling for a short distance. The more we recede from the land, the more young ice do we appear to meet, yet not to such an extent as to be able to derive much advantage from its presence. Distance marched eight miles; made good one and-a-half. Temperature minus 14°.

'21st.—A thick cloudy day, with a cold, piercing breeze from the northward. During the early part of the day our road lay over young ice, on which were some deep snow-drifts, and occasionally ridges of small hummocks; but after marching for about a mile our good ice terminated, and again our troubles commenced, or rather continued. Compelled to deviate to the eastward of our course in order to avoid a mass of heavy hummocks, through which it would take days to cut. Road-makers busily employed. After lunch we were forced to put Shirley on the sledge again in order to prevent him getting frost-bitten, as he was unable to move fast enough to keep himself warm. Although the temperature is only 17° below zero, the wind is so keen and cutting that the cold feels more intense to-day than on any day since we left the ship. It almost cuts one in two. In consequence we halted an hour earlier than we otherwise would have done. Numerous superficial frost-bites among the party.

There appears to be a magnificent level floe ahead, and we predict good travelling for the morrow.

'Some of the greatest enemies that we have to contend with in crossing the large floes are the numerous cracks and fissures that radiate in all directions and are concealed from view by a treacherous covering of snow. Into these we frequently fall, sinking up to our waists. Distance marched nine and-a-half miles ; made good two miles.

'22nd.—Invalids slightly improving. Porter still has to be carried on a sledge, but Shirley, with the assistance of a staff, is able to walk a little. Wind blew in heavy squalls last night, and is blowing fresh from the north-west this morning. Temperature minus 17°. The men are an uncanny lot to look at—very dirty, faces and especially noses scarified and disfigured, lips sore and tips of the fingers senseless from frost-bite—yet they are all cheerful and happy enough. A dull, cloudy day ; a thick mist hanging over the land, entirely obscuring it from view. The floes travelled over to-day are more level than any we have hitherto crossed, and infinitely larger, one being quite one mile and three-quarters in length in a north and south direction and about eight miles in circumference. This, however, is only a rough estimate, as it is difficult to judge. The snow is very deep. These floes appear to have come into contact with each other in a more amicable manner than those we have already passed, few or no hummocks lying between them. At 9 P.M., the weather coming on very thick, accompanied by driving snow, we crossed some hummocks, and camped on a level floe. The wind has been bitterly cold all day, touching up our faces considerably. Distance marched nine miles; made good two and-a-half.

'23rd.—A beautifully sunshiny day, but misty over the land. Latitude 82° 58' 37" N. Crossed a heavy floe with numerous "hillocks" on it, but covered with deep and soft snow, that made it hard work for our sledges. It appears to us that the heavier the floes are, the deeper and softer is the snow on their surface. The temperature inside our tent this morning, before the coverlets were removed, was 20°, a decided improvement.

'Our travelling to-day has been very heavy, and consequently our progress has been slow; much delay was caused by having to cut our way through various belts of hummocks. Distance marched six miles; made good one and-a-quarter. Temperature minus 32° at midnight.

'24th.—On walking to the northern extreme of the floe on which we were encamped, a dismal prospect met our view. Enormous hummocks from twenty to thirty feet high, all squeezed up together with apparently no floes beyond. Foreseeing that time and trouble must necessarily be expended before a road could be cut through these obstacles, a number of road-makers, with Parr at their head, were advanced, whilst the remainder of the party remained in the tents. This course was adopted in consequence of a cold wind that was blowing, in which with the low temperature it would have been unwise to have kept the men standing about waiting for the pioneers to complete their work. The hummocks appeared interminable. From the summit of the loftiest no floe of

any size could be seen—nothing but an uneven range
of shapeless masses of ice. By 4 P.M., with such
energy did our road-makers work, a practicable road,
nearly a mile in length, was completed, and we all
returned to lunch. After this was discussed the tents
were struck, and the march resumed. Although the
keen wind was decidedly unpleasant, by making sail
on the boat, it materially assisted us. Having arrived
at the end of our road, we halted and camped.
Crossed the 83rd parallel of latitude to-day. Porter
was still obliged to be carried, but Shirley was able to
walk after us. Distance marched five miles ; made
good one and-a-half. Temperature minus 26°.

' 25th.—A bright day, but with a low temperature,
and just sufficient wind to keep us fully aware, in a by
no means pleasant manner, that we possess noses, or
rather portions of them. The travelling to-day has
been fairly good, we have been able to make a little
more progress, but the snow remains very deep.
Many of the hummocks passed, although smooth and
rounded on the top and on one side, were precipitous
on the other, resembling in a great measure the
grounded floebergs in the vicinity of the ' Alert's '
winter quarters.

' 26th.—Proceeded at noon. Temperature inside
our tent last night as high as 35°, and outside as high
as minus 2°. This is a change for the better. The
drifts are frequently as much as twelve feet high, and
it is a regular case of travelling up and down hill.
The floes are not of any great extent, but are, notwithstanding, of enormous thickness. They are separated
from each other, apparently having no connection, by

streams of hummocks from ten to fifty yards in breadth. Across these we are compelled to cut a road; our chief difficulty, however, is in getting the sledges from off the floe on to our road, and then up again on to the next floe, so steep and abrupt is the ascent and descent. Our tents were pitched on the northern extreme of one of these ponderous floes, with an apparently impassable sea of hummocks extending north, east, and west as far as the eye could range. It looked like the 'end of all things.' Distance marched six and-a-half miles; made good one and three-quarters. The thermometer when exposed to the sun this afternoon rose to 7°.

'27th. — Parr, with half-a-dozen road-makers, started to make a road through the hummocks, leaving the remainder of the party to strike the tents, pack the sledges, and drag them on one by one. By lunch-time we had advanced a quarter of a mile. At noon the latitude was 83° 6' 41" N. Our invalids exhibit no signs of improvement. Hawkins had to be relieved as much as possible from the drag ropes, and Pearce suffers from stiff ankles, although he makes a show of dragging. Both shovels, from constant use, have come to grief, breaking short off at the handles, but we succeeded in 'fishing' them, thus making them service-able again. At 9.30 halted for the night. Men thoroughly fatigued. Distance marched seven and-a-half miles; made good one and-a-quarter. Tem-perature minus 9°.

'28th. A dull cloudy day and snow falling, but with, for the first time, a temperature above zero. Heavy hummocks, deep snow, and thick weather render our progress slow. Selecting the route is a work of difficulty, it being impossible to see many yards ahead — above, below, and around being all of one uniform colour. Had again the misfortune to capsize the sledge and boat on which was Porter ; but luckily no evil resulted, a slight delay being the only inconvenience. On the surface of a floe crossed during the evening was a crust of ice about an inch thick covering the deep snow. To our great surprise, whilst crossing a fringe of hummocks, we observed the tracks of a hare. They were apparently recent. The little creature was evidently exhausted, the steps being short and close together, and travelling in a southerly direction. These footprints naturally excited our interest, as we were fully seventeen miles from the nearest land. Distance marched six miles ; made good one and-a-half.

'29th.—A fine sunny day, but with a sharp wind from the north-west. Our work to-day has been very distressing, and we advance but slowly ; small floes with huge hummocks, and the snow over our knees. We are often compelled to deviate considerably to the eastward or westward of our course, in order to make progress at all. Occasionally during the latter part of the day we were able to avail ourselves of a few short leads of young ice that we constantly met twining round the heavy floes and between the hummocks, but never to such an extent as to profit greatly by them. Distance marched seven and-a-half miles ; made good one and-a-quarter. Temperature at midnight minus 4°.

'30th.—Shortly after the tents were pitched last night the wind freshened, the clouds thickened, and snow commenced falling heavily, continuing without intermission the entire night and all to-day. So thick is the weather that we are unable to make a move, as we can scarcely see the length of two sledges ahead. Surrounded as we are by hummocks, it would be folly to attempt pushing on. Our patience is sorely tried, enduring this idleness, especially when we consider how little we have hitherto accomplished, and the short period that now remains before we are compelled to retrace our steps. The rest will do no harm to the men.

' *May* 1*st*.—A fine bright morning has ushered in the month of May, to our no small pleasure. Latitude 83° 10′ 30″ N. Invalids much the same. Hawkins totally unfit for duty, and Shirley very weak and faint. Porter's symptoms appear to be scorbutic. After lunch arrived on a large level floe that afforded us a good mile and-a-half travelling in the right direction; the snow less deep on it than on other floes, doubtless on account of its even surface, which prevents the snow from collecting into drifts by the wind. By nine o'clock we were enveloped in a thick fog. Camped amongst hummocks, with apparently nothing but hummocks ahead. Distance marched nine miles; made good two and-three-quarters. Temperature minus 10°.

' *2nd*.—The invalids are not improving, and we are inclined to believe that they are all attacked with scurvy, although we have not been led to suppose that there is any probability of our being so afflicted, and are ignorant of the symptoms.

' Our strength is rapidly decreasing. A fine day,

but with a sharp north-westerly wind blowing; a thick mist hanging over the land entirely concealing it from view. So rough was our road and deep the snow-drifts that we barely advanced half-a-mile before lunch. The travelling was no better during the latter part of the day, and we encamped on a small floe amidst a pile of hummocks, thoroughly fatigued and weary. Towards night the temperature fell as low as minus 17°. Distance marched seven and-a-half miles; made good one and-a-quarter.

' 3rd.—A dull foggy day. The hummocks do not appear to be massed so close together as those we have been lately struggling with, although they are equally large and heavy. The snow-drifts are surprisingly deep, making the dragging very distressing. On one occasion the drift was so deep that the boat-sledge was completely buried in it whilst being pulled through, and we were forced to unload before we succeeded in extricating it.

' A dense fog, but not sufficiently thick to retard our progress altogether, that has persistently hung over us all day, materially increased our labour by adding to the difficulties of selecting a good route through the hummocks. Pitched our tents on the edge of a floe, not of any great extent, but to arrive on which we had to make a considerable *detour* to the eastward. Distance marched seven and-a-half miles; made good one and-a-quarter.

' 4th.—Snow falling thick and fast. Invalids the reverse of improving. Francombe so bad that he is obliged to be put on a sledge. More of the men are complaining of stiffness and pain in their legs, which, we fear, are only the premonitory symptoms. After advancing for about half-a-mile, which distance took us nearly four hours to accomplish, we arrived at such a confused heap of hummocks that in the thick state of the weather rendered a farther advance impossible. We were therefore compelled to halt and pitch the tents. After lunch, the weather clearing slightly, we pushed on with a strong party of labourers, and succeeded in making a very fair road three-quarters of a mile in length. The hummocks appeared interminable; the floes small, not more than fifty to one hundred yards across. A line of discoloured hummocks extended for some distance along the edge of one of the floes; on examination the discolouration was found to be caused by the adherence of mud or clay. It looked as if the side of the floe had been rubbed against, or in some manner come into contact with, the shore. Distance made good a quarter of a mile. Temperature at noon 4°.

'5th.—A dull foggy day, and snow falling. Advanced with one sledge, leaving one tent pitched and the invalids inside. Arriving at the termination of our made road of yesterday, the other tent was pitched, and we returned to bring up another sledge, and so on until the whole camp was advanced. The weather remaining thick, all farther progress was quite out of the question, and, much as we all disliked the forced inactivity, we were compelled to remain in our bags for the remainder of the day. A dreary scene surrounded us; a cold, desolate, and inhospitable-looking scene. Everything of the same uniform colour; nothing to relieve the eye; nothing but one sombrous, uneven, and irregular sea of snow and ice. The temperature has been about zero all day. Distance marched four miles; made good three-quarters of a mile.

' 6th.—A fine bright sunshiny day. Latitude 83° 16′ 36″ N. Our sick men are evidently not improving; three have now to be carried on the sledges. We appear to have arrived at a perfect barrier of hummocks and portions of floes, all broken and squeezed up, and covered with deep snow. It is possible we may be able to penetrate these obstacles, eventually reaching larger and more level floes, on which we may be able to make more rapid progress. We ascended one large hummock, from the summit of which the prospect was anything but encouraging—nothing but one vast illimitable sea of hummocks. The height of this hummock was ascertained by means of a lead line, and was found to be from its summit to the surface of the snow at its base forty-three feet three inches. It did not appear to be a floeberg, but a mass of hummocks squeezed up and cemented together by several layers of snow, making it resemble one huge solid piece. Although the sun has been very warm all day, the temperature has been down to minus 11°. Distance marched six miles; made good one mile.

' 7th.—We had scarcely advanced a couple of hundred yards with one sledge, " standing pulls " the whole distance, the prospect ahead being heavy hummocks and deep snow-drifts, when it became painfully evident that neither Pearce nor Shirley were able to walk. Under these distressing circumstances there was nothing to be done but to advance with one sledge, unload it, return with it empty, and then bring on the remainder of the gear and invalids. The snow being very deep, the continual walking backwards and forwards is very fatiguing to the men ; they find it easier to drag a sledge through the deep snow than to walk without the support of the drag belt. Distance made good a quarter of a mile. Temperature minus 9°

‘ 8th.—The interiors of our tents in the evening have more the appearance of hospitals than the habitations of strong working-men. In addition to the “ cripples,” four men belonging to the “ Marco Polo ” are suffering from snow-blindness, although in a mild form. At noon started all available hands under Parr, with pick and shovel road-making, as we are desirous of ascertaining if this apparently interminable line of hummocks is of great extent. To solve this is all we can now expect to do. A bright warm day. Aired and dried all tent gear, &c. Walked on with Parr towards the end of the day about a mile to the northward, selecting a route for the sledges. At our farthermost point from the summit of a high hummock we saw, about two or three degrees to the northward of Cape Aldrich, either land or the loom of it. The hummocks around us are of different heights and bulk, varying from small fragments of ice to huge piles over forty feet high.

‘ 9th.—We have at length arrived at the conclusion, although with a great deal of reluctance, that our sick men are really suffering from scurvy, and that in no mild form. Should our surmise be correct, we can scarcely expect to see any of the afflicted ones improve until they can be supplied with fresh meat and vege-

tables.   We are unwilling for the men to suspect that
they are really suffering from this terrible disease, but
at the same time are issuing to those attacked a small
quantity out of the very little limejuice we brought
away with us.   It is given to them in lieu of their
grog, as being a better blood-purifier.   We have only
two bottles on each sledge of this excellent anti-scor-
butic.   It is another beautifully warm sunny day, with
the temperature only a degree or two below zero.
Made a start at half-past twelve by advancing with
one sledge with half its load and two invalids upon it.
This was dragged up to the extreme of yesterday's
road-making, a distance of three-quarters of a mile,
when the tent was pitched, the invalids placed inside,
and the sledge taken back, again loaded, and again
advanced with two more invalids; the men returning
and bringing up the other two sledges, with the remainder of the gear and the fifth invalid, one at a
time.   It was past eight o'clock before the last sledge
arrived, and though we had only made good three-
quarters of a mile, so tortuous was our road, winding
round and about the hummocks, that to accomplish
this distance we marched between six and seven miles
through very deep snow.   After the tents were pitched,
a party of road-makers were advanced to prepare a
road through the hummocks.

' 10th.—There was a slight fall of snow during
the day, when the temperature rose to 15°.   Distance
made good three-quarters of a mile.

' After very serious consideration, I have arrived at
the conclusion, though sorely against my inclination,
that this must be our most northern camp.   With five

out of our little force totally prostrate, and four others exhibiting decided symptoms of the same complaint, it would be folly to persist in pushing on. In addition to which the greater half of our provisions have been expended. To-morrow will be our fortieth day out; only thirty-one days' full allowance of provisions remain, so that prudence and discretion unite against our own desire of advancing, and counsel a return. A complete rest to the invalids of a couple of days may be productive of much good, during which time we may be usefully engaged in making observations in various interesting matters. With this we must be content, having failed so lamentably in attaining a high northern latitude. It is a bitter ending to all our aspirations.

' 11*th*.—As it was desirable to benefit by the heat of the day during the time we were employed making our observations, breakfast was ready at half-past eight. Immediately after, the men were set to work to cut a hole through some young ice that lay between the hummocks bordering our floe. This they accomplished in three hours, the thickness of the ice being sixty-four inches. With a hundred-fathom line, we sounded to ascertain the depth of water, and to our great surprise obtained soundings in seventy-two fathoms, the bottom consisting of clay. Arming the lead, and appending to it various other contrivances for the purpose of collecting a specimen of the nature of the bottom, we succeeded in obtaining a small quantity, which has been carefully preserved in a small bottle for conveyance to the ship. The hardness of the substance prevented a large supply being obtained. A series of temperatures was taken at every ten fathoms from the surface ; the temperature between the surface and a depth of twenty fathoms being 28°·5, and that between thirty fathoms and the bottom in seventy-two fathoms being 28°·8.'

The specific gravity of the surface-water as afterwards ascertained by Dr. Moss was, at a temperature of 60°, 1·0246 and 1·0241 ; standard water at 39° equal unity.

'Tidal action was apparent, but with the rough appliances at our disposal it was impossible to make any accurate observations regarding it, the set being, as near as we could judge, N.W. and S.E. Improvising a dredge, and baiting it with the scrapings of our pannikins, &c., it was lowered down the hole, and on being hauled up after remaining some hours at the bottom, was found to be literally swarming with small crustaceans, apparently of two different kinds. Several specimens of these were collected, and placed in spirits of wine for preservation. Hooks were baited and attempts made to catch fish, but without success. Took a complete double series of magnetic observations for inclination and total force.

' 12th.—Breakfasted at 8.30, immediately after which, leaving the cooks behind at the camp to attend upon the invalids, the remainder of the party carrying the sextant and artificial horizon, and also the sledge banners and colours, started northwards. We had some very severe walking, struggling through snow up to our waists, over or through which the labour of dragging a sledge would be interminable, and occasionally almost disappearing through cracks and fissures, until twenty minutes to noon, when a halt was called. The artificial horizon was then set up, and the flags and banners displayed; these fluttered out bravely before a fresh S.W. wind, which latter, however, was decidedly cold and unpleasant. At noon we obtained a good altitude, and proclaimed our latitude to be 83° 20′ 26″ N., exactly 399½ miles from the North Pole. On this being duly announced three cheers were given, with one more for Captain Nares; then the whole party, in the exuberance of their spirits at having reached their turning point, sang the "Union Jack of Old England," the "Grand Palæocrystic Sledging Chorus," winding up, like loyal subjects, with "God save the Queen." These little demonstrations had the effect of cheering the men, who nevertheless enjoy good spirits. The instruments were then packed, the colours furled, and our steps retraced to the camp. On arrival the flags were hoisted on our tents and sledges and kept flying for the remainder of the day A magnum of whisky that had been sent by the Dean of Dundee, for the express purpose of being consumed in the highest northern latitude, was produced, and a glass of grog served out to all. It is needless to add his kindness was thoroughly appreciated, nor was he forgotten in the toast of ' absent friends.'

' We all enjoyed our supper, for we had the hare shot by Dr. Moss at Depôt Point, equally divided between our two tents, cooked in our allowance of pemmican, making the latter uncommonly good and savoury. After supper a cigar, presented to us by May before leaving the ship, was issued to each man, and the day was brought to a close with songs, even the invalids joining in.   All seemed happy, cheerful, and contented.

'13th.—A fresh breeze from the north-west and much snow-drift.   Our outward-bound tracks nearly obliterated.   The invalids appear no better for their long rest.   Started with two sledges, leaving the tents pitched and the sick inside, and commenced our march to the southward.

'Having advanced the two sledges for some distance, they were unpacked and dragged back to camp empty.   The tents were then struck, and putting two invalids on each of the small sledges, and one in the boat on the large sledge, again advanced by short stages, dragging the lighter ones single-banked, six hands to each, the whole party returning to drag the heavy one.   As this will be our future mode of travelling, no further reference will be made regarding the details of our order of marching, unless an alteration occurs.   Distance made good one mile and-a-quarter.

'14th.—A dull, cloudy day.   Sky and ground, from the equal diffusion of light, appear to be the same; and although dark objects are readily distinguishable at some distance, it is impossible to see many yards ahead : this makes following the old road a task of much difficulty.   A hummock passed yesterday, although composed of one piece of ice, was of two different colours, a deep blue and a pale yellow, the two colours gradually blending one into the other without exhibiting any definite line of demarcation. The yellow colour was doubtless due to the presence of diatomaceæ.   It is a curious fact that for the last week or ten days our appetites have been decreasing in a marvellous manner. For the first three weeks after leaving the ship the majority of us were perfectly ravenous, and could easily at supper-time have devoured an extra pannikin full of pemmican. Now we are seldom able to consume what is served out to us, although little more than half the allowance is cooked. It is with great difficulty the patients can be induced to eat anything, their mouths being too tender to eat the biscuits, although well soaked. Distance made good one mile. Temperature 11°.

' 15th.—A fine day, but misty over the land. A sharp south-easterly breeze, and a temperature at 6° touches us up unpleasantly about. the face. We are still following up our old road, and devoutly trust we shall be able to adhere to it the entire distance—to make a new road will cause much detention. Distance made good one mile and a half.

' 16th.—Our appetites are still on the decline, and to rather an alarming degree. At breakfast to-day, in one tent, scarcely a pannikin full of pemmican was consumed by the whole party. On the other hand we seem to be assailed by an unquenchable thirst, that can only be alleviated at meal-times, as we are unable to spare fuel to make extra water. Distance made good one mile and a half. Temperature 4°.

' 17th.—A beautifully sunny day, with a light breeze from the N.E. The sun was so powerful as to cause the temperature to rise inside our tent after supper to 50°, whilst all our foot-gear, &c., which was left outside when we retired, was perfectly dry when put on before breakfast. After serious thought we have resolved, should any more men be compelled to fall out from the drag ropes, upon abandoning the boat. We look upon it as a *dernier ressort*, but an imperative necessity. If any more men are attacked our only chance of reaching the shore, before our provisions are expended, will be by lightening our sledges as much as possible, and the first thing to be discarded must be the boat. We must take our chance of the ice remaining stationary, and hope that no disruption will take place before we gain the shore. The first part of the day was occupied in dragging the sledges over our rough road through the hummocks, but at length we arrived on our old friend the large floe, over which we made good travelling. The time and trouble devoted to making a road during our outward journey is now amply compensated for.

' "Old Joe," as the men irreverently term Cape Joseph Henry, is looming larger and darker, and Mount Pullen was seen to-day for the first time for some days. Again, strange to say, have we come across the tracks of a hare, being fully twenty-three miles from the land. The traces were almost too indistinct to determine the direction in which the little animal was travelling, but it appeared to be going to the northward, and was, like the one observed on our outward journey, evidently worn out and tired, the footsteps being short. Distance made good two miles and-a-quarter.

' 18*th*.—The sun is very powerful, and thaws and dries everything that may happen to be exposed to it resting on a dark substance. The snow on the floes is not yet in any way affected by its influence.

'Our small modicum of limejuice is nearly all expended, although it has been most carefully husbanded, and only issued to the sick every other day.

'The travelling to-day has been very heavy, the road being rough and the snow deep. On account of the thick weather we had great difficulty in adhering to the old track, and on several occasions the sledges had to be halted until the trail was picked up on the opposite side of the floe amongst the hummocks.

'Ominous signs, predicting a movement of the ice, were visible. A crack in some young ice had perceptibly opened since we passed over it three weeks ago, and layers or flakes of ice from one to three inches in thickness were squeezed up along the crack. Not 200 yards from this rent a large portion of a hummock situated at the extreme end of a floe had lost its equilibrium and toppled over; from the marks left in the snow this must have occurred quite recently. These movements may be attributed to a slight tidal motion, but it is a warning for us to get off the pack as quickly as possible. Distance made good one mile and-a-half.

'19th.—A thick overcast day, with snow falling heavily. Travelling very rough, jolting the invalids considerably. Passed two more cracks in the ice that have opened a great deal since they were crossed on our outward journey. One of these was the opening between two large floes, conclusive evidence that one or other, or both, had been in motion. At 10 P.M. the fog lifted, and the sun shone clear and bright, but shortly after midnight a dense fog rolled down from the northward, in which we were completely enveloped during the remainder of the day. A thick mist or sleet also prevailed that actually wetted us. Distance made good one mile and-three-quarters.

' 20*th*.—Temperature 20°, a thick foggy day making it extremely difficult to keep to the road. We must endeavour to adhere to it at all hazards.

' The hummocks have been deprived of a great deal of their niveous covering since we last passed them, and have lost in a great measure their resemblance to the tops of wedding cakes, and are instead fringed with long icicles, giving them a picturesque and fairy-like appearance. Distance made good one mile and-three-quarters.

' 21*st*.—A foggy overcast day, and snow falling more or less the whole time. So difficult was it to adhere to the old track that on several occasions the sledges had to be halted for a considerable time, whilst the officers pushed on ahead to the opposite end of the floe, and there branching off, one to the eastward, the other to the westward, discovered, by skirting along the line of hummocks fringing the edge of the floe, the old cutting through. This accomplished, they would return to assist in dragging the sledges up. The continual strain to the eyes is also most trying. All the party are more or less suffering from stiffness and aching bones. Distance made good one mile and-three-quarters.

' 22*nd*.—After the tents were pitched last night the temperature rose as high as 33°, and inside the tent was as much as 61°. Another dull, overcast day. Several times did we wander off the track, and then, when found, were compelled to drag the sledges back to get on the trail again. Floundered through some deep snow-drifts, and passed some enormous hummocks.

'The height of one of the latter that we ascended was estimated at over fifty feet—the pocket aneroid determined its height to be a little over that measurement. It appeared to be a floeberg, but was so disguised by its thick covering of snow that we could only form a conjecture. It was on one side nearly precipitous, and was surrounded by a number of small hummocks and broken floe-pieces. The temperature is so high now that the men get terribly heated whilst dragging, but during a halt, even for a short time, they soon get thoroughly chilled. Distance made good one mile.

'23rd.—The weather still continues dull and cloudy, but not quite so thick and overcast as it has been for the last few days. We can just discern a portion of Cape Joseph Henry and Conical Hill looming through the mist. The travelling to-day has been fairly easy, although the snow has been very deep in places. Collected for analysis some specimens of discoloured ice from two separate hummocks, of a yellowish and brown hue respectively. Distance made good one mile and-three-quarters.

'24th.—A bright sunny day enabled us to follow our tracks with ease. The land is plainly visible. We seem to have neared it considerably since we last obtained a good glimpse of it. Several dark patches on the hills give undoubted indications of returning summer, whilst the sides of Joseph Henry are almost destitute of snow. The fore part of the day we were engaged struggling through a long line of hummocks, after emerging from which the travelling became comparatively good, and we made fair progress. Being the Queen's birthday, the colours were displayed at lunch time, the "main brace" spliced, and Her Majesty's health drunk by her most northern, though not the less loyal subjects.

'25th.—The fine weather of yesterday was too good to last. To-day there is a great change. Heavy lowering clouds hang all around—a dull and dismal day with a sharp keen wind from the S.W. Great difficulty in keeping to the track; several times we lost it, and did not succeed in picking it up again without expending much time and trouble. Travelling over an extensive floe, but with deep snow, with numerous hard snow ridges and hillocks, that made the operation of dragging the sledges *up* very laborious, whilst the coming down was just as bad, as the "cripples" had scarcely time to jump on one side before the sledge was on the top of them. Ferbrache appears very bad, but pluckily sticks to the drag ropes; not, poor fellow, that he is of much use there, as he can hardly keep pace with us, much less pull; it serves, however, as a support to him. Rawlings and Simpson are not much better. Out of thirty-four legs in the whole party we can only muster eleven good ones—even some of these are shaky. Distance made good one mile and-a-half.

'26th.—Blowing a strong S.W. gale, accompanied by a heavy fall of snow and a dense snow-drift. Called the cooks and had breakfast, holding ourselves in readiness for a start should weather permit. In this, however, we were grievously disappointed and were again doomed to a day of forced idleness. To pack the sledges and place the invalids on them without their being almost buried in the blinding snow-drift was quite out of the question, and even if there was a chance of advancing it was impossible to see a sledge's length ahead. This delay causes us great anxiety, as every day, every hour, is of importance to us, as we know not when we may, one and all, be attacked and rendered useless for further work.

' 27*th*.—Wind having moderated, we made a start, the weather remaining thick and gloomy. The large quantity of snow that has fallen renders the travelling very heavy, in addition to which the high temperature, causing a partial thaw, has made the snow assume a sludgy consistency, which clings tenaciously to our legs and sledge-runners, making the dragging very laborious. The men are no better for their rest of yesterday, indeed may be said to be worse ; the only two men at present scatheless, with the exception of the officers, being Radmore and Maskell. This diminution of our force was an event which we were quite prepared for, therefore preparations were made for abandoning the boat and all superfluous weights. Our object now must be to reach the shore as speedily as possible.

' Left the boat as conspicuous as possible, adopting the same means as we did on the previous occasion, and depositing a record in a tin cylinder stating the approximate position of the floe and our reasons for deserting the boat. Temperature 22°. Distance made good one mile.

' Our appetites are still on the wane ; scarcely more than half a pannikin of pemmican is consumed by any

one individual at any meal ; some go without altogether,
and these latter in consequence are not allowed to
smoke or to have their grog. As we possess a surplus
of bacon, this is issued, in addition to the pemmican,
to those who wish it.

' 28*th*.—Yesterday, a bird was seen by a few of the
sick men who were remaining by the advanced sledges
whilst the party was returning for the heavy sledge,
which from their description appears to have been a
turnstone. The weather cleared up slightly after
lunch, and the sun made vain efforts to pierce the
clouds and murky atmosphere, and the land was
occasionally seen. Travelling across the heavy floes
and the young ice, over which we journeyed on the
21st ult., the snow-drifts are far deeper and more
frequent now than then ; pools of water were forming between the snow-drifts, and a large quantity of
sludge was encountered, that made the travelling
very disagreeable. These pools of water were all
brackish.

' Shortly before the tents were pitched, much excitement was caused by the appearance of a little snow-
bunting, which fluttered around us for a short time,
uttering its to us rather sweet chirp, and then flew
away to the northward and westward, in the direction
of Cape Joseph Henry. This was an event of no small
interest to our party, as it was the first bird seen by the
majority for a period of nine months ; even the sick
men on the sledges requested they might have their
heads uncovered and lifted, so as to obtain a glimpse
of the little warbler. Distance made good two miles.

' 29*th*.—A glorious day, with the sun shining

brightly, which we appreciate the more as we have been so long deprived of its presence. The temperature, however, is as low as 5°. At lunch time the colours were again displayed and the 'main brace' spliced, to commemorate the first anniversary of our departure from England. Got on to a heavy floe on which we had left our 20-foot ice-boat on the 19th of April, and pitched our tents alongside the boat. Found her exactly as she had been left, but surrounded by an embankment of snow. Distance made good two miles.

' 30th.—Our usual weather has returned—thick fog and snow falling. Before lunch a strong breeze sprang up from the N.W., which quickly freshened into half a gale of wind. This with a dense snow-drift compelled us to halt and pitch our tents on the southern edge of a large floe, having completely lost our track. Walked with Parr for a long distance along the fringe of hummocks skirting the floe, but failed to discover our old cutting through. Distance made good one mile and a-half.

' 31st.—Struck camp, and started at 8 P.M.; Parr and myself having previously walked on to endeavour to find the old route, which we luckily succeeded in doing, being, as we anticipated, more than half-a-mile to the westward of it. Crossed a fringe of hummocks, which had evidently been in motion since we passed them on our outward journey; but what was still more alarming, whilst dragging the sledges over a small patch of young ice the heavy sledge broke through, and we had no little trouble in saving it from a complete immersion, which might have resulted seriously to one of the unfortunate invalids who was securely lashed on the top. As it was, the whole of the rear part of the sledge was immersed in the water. The thickness of this ice was only three or four inches. The wind freshening into a strong gale, and blowing upon us with all its fury, precluded any farther advance, and necessitated a halt at 3.15 A.M., we being then unable to distinguish more than a couple of sledges' length ahead. We were all wet through, and very wretched and uncomfortable, the falling snow and drift thawing on our clothes as quickly as it fell. Distance made good half-a-mile.

'*June* 1*st.*—The wind subsided considerably during the night, although the weather remained thick, and snow and wind squalls were prevalent. Our old track is completely obliterated, and it is only occasionally by seeing evidences of our former journey, such as bits of tobacco, tin pots, &c., that we know we are still adhering to it. Travelling altogether very heavy. Snow in places up to our waists, and very wet between the hummocks, our foot-gear being literally soaking. Distance made good two miles. Temperature 34°.

'2*nd.*—A sad list of sick this morning. Rawlings and Simpson completely done up, and utterly incapable of further work. It is marvellous how they have kept on so long. Lawrence is also attacked in his arms as well as his legs. We are now reduced to only six men, and they anything but healthy or strong, and two officers. Five men are carried on the sledges, and four can just manage to crawl after. Our routine is first to advance the heavy sledge, which is dragged by the whole available party, namely, eight; then return and bring up the other two sledges, single banked, four dragging each.

'The weather has at last proved triumphant, and has robbed us of our road. The track was lost, despite our utmost efforts to adhere to it, shortly before lunch, and we have now to renew the arduous task of road-making. Unless the weather clears sufficiently to enable us again to pick up our track, our intention is to make straight for the land in the direction of the Snow Valley. Camped on a small floe completely surrounded by hummocks, through which we had to cut our way. Distance made good one mile and three-quarters.

' 3rd.—Parr and myself started at 7·45 P.M. to select a route, leaving a party of three road-makers to follow and cut a road in our footsteps, the remaining three to strike the tents and pack the sledges. Our way lay entirely through hummocks with no appearance of a floe of any dimensions. The road being completed, the sledges were advanced until more hummocks were encountered, when the same system was adopted. It was *very* hard work. At 5 A.M. we succeeded in reaching a magnificent floe, on which we camped. Distance made good one mile and a-half.

' 4th.—Shortly after starting we were again enveloped in a dense fog, through which the sun made ineffectual efforts to penetrate. Arriving at the edge of the large floe, we had to cut through a long fringe of hummocks; then winding about amongst snow-drifts and young ice, through deep sludge, emerging on a small floe, on which we halted for lunch. A skua flying lazily about, apparently steering in a north-west direction, or towards Conical Hill, excited a good deal of interest.

'Leaving the road-makers to follow in our track, Parr and myself pushed on for the shore, which was reached in about half-an-hour. We here observed the recent traces of a dog-sledge and human footsteps. Observed the tracks and heard the howling of a wolf, but did not succeed in seeing it. On reaching the depôt we learned to our disappointment that the Captain, May, and Feilden had only left for the ship the previous day. This was very unfortunate. Twenty-four hours earlier and we should have met them. They had obtained three hares, which they kindly *cached* in a crevice formed between two hummocks for our use. Taking our letters, and carrying the hares, we returned to our party; and the road being completed, the sledges were dragged through, and the tents pitched for the night on a small piece of ice about 300 yards from the shore.

'*5th.*—A beautifully bright clear day. To see the sun again in all its glory is indeed a treat; it seems to invigorate us all, and appears even to instil new life and energy into the invalids. Our supper last night consisted of a hare to each tent, which was much relished and will doubtless do good. By eleven we were all once more on *terra firma*, after an absence of over two months.

'A strong south-westerly gale sprang up just before halting for lunch, which did not add to the comfort of our meal; had excessively hard work in dragging the sledges through the deep snow on the incline of the hill; blowing very hard, the squalls exceedingly violent with a blinding snow-drift. Halted and camped abreast of the depôt.

' 6th.—Wind moderated during the night, but not before it had nearly blown our tent down ; one of the bow lines gave way, and a tent pole started, and we were momentarily expecting to have our house down about our ears. Fortunately for us it resisted all efforts.

' During the latter part of the day, to our great surprise, one of our Eskimo dogs was seen threading her way slowly through the hummocks ; on being called she approached somewhat timidly, but ate ravenously of some pemmican that was thrown to her. Poor Flo! she is wretchedly thin and emaciated; she must have escaped from the Captain's dog-team. After a long consultation with Parr it has been resolved that he shall proceed to-morrow morning, if fine, and walk to the ship. Our only chance of saving life is by receiving succour as soon as possible. Although the distance from us to the ship is nearly thirty miles, over floes covered with deep snow, and girt by heavy hummocks, he has nobly volunteered to attempt it, and has confidence in being able to accomplish it. He is the only one of the party strong enough to undertake such a march, and we all have the utmost confidence in his judgment and ability to perform it.

' 7th.—A bright sunny day ; the sun so powerful, although the temperature of the air was two degrees below freezing-point, as to raise the temperature in my tent to 82°, rendering it almost unbearable. Having written to Captain Nares, Parr started off as lightly accoutred as possible. We all wished him God-speed, and will be anxious to hear of his safe arrival. All hands appear very stiff and in pain. Porter is very low, and is undoubtedly in a very precarious state.

' 8*th*.—Poor Porter is no more! He expired at ten minutes past noon. He was sensible to within a few minutes of his death, and his end was calm and quiet. This is a sad calamity, although we were not totally unprepared for it, and I fear the depressing moral effect that this lamentable event will have on those who are very sick, and who consider themselves to be in nearly as precarious a condition.

' With the ensign half-mast, and the Union Jack as a pall, the funeral procession, attended by all but the four very bad cases, started at nine ; and the burial service being read, the remains were consigned to their last icy resting-place in this world. Improvising a rude cross, formed with a boat's oar and a spare sledge-batten, it was placed at the head of the grave, with the following inscription :-

BENEATH THIS CROSS LIE BURIED THE REMAINS

OF

GEO. PORTER, R.M.A.,

WHO DIED ON JUNE 8TH, 1876.

" Thy will be done."

' Of all the melancholy and mournful duties I have ever been called upon to perform, this has been the saddest. A death in a small party like ours, and under the present circumstances, is a most distressing event, and is keenly felt by all. During the service all were more or less affected, and many to tears.

' *9th*.—A wild thick day, with a fresh breeze from the northward. Invalids in a very depressed state, notwithstanding all efforts made to cheer them. All eyes eagerly directed to the southward, the quarter from which we are anxiously expecting succour. We had advanced the heavy sledge one stage, and had just returned to drag up the two smaller ones, when something moving between the hummocks was espied, which from its rapid motion was soon made out to be the dog-sledge. Hoisted colours. The men appeared quite carried away by their feelings, and it was with difficulty they could muster up a cheer as May and Moss arrived and shook us heartily by the hands. Our delight was enhanced on being informed that they were only the advance of a larger party coming out to our relief, headed by the Captain himself, and nearly all the officers. A halt was immediately ordered, cooking utensils lighted, water made, and we were soon all enjoying a good draught of limejuice, with mutton for supper in prospective. Our spirits rose wonderfully, and, as if nature also wished to participate in our joy, the weather began to break, and the sun shone out. Resumed the march, May pushing on with his dog-sledge, and camping about half-a-mile to the southward of us, they not having rested for many hours so eager was he to afford us relief. The travelling was very good, and we got along famously, every one apparently much invigorated, cheerful, and in good spirits.

' 10*th*.—We all, including the sick, consumed and

relished our pannikin full of ox-cheek and mutton that we had for supper last night, and agreed that it was one of the most delicious repasts that we had ever partaken of. After lunch sighted the main party coming towards us. Hoisted colours. 12.45, met the Captain and his party, from all of whom we received a warm and kind greeting. No time was wasted in asking questions, but the march renewed—my party, the lame ducks, dragging one sledge, the relief party dragging the other two, the invalids who had been walking being put on the dog-sledge.

'12th.—May went on with dog-sledge to the ship, taking Shirley and Pearson. The travelling all day has been remarkably good, and we succeed in getting along famously; our only difficulty is in going through deep snow, when the men, their legs being so bad, are compelled to stop and drag them out of the holes into which they sink. Winstone, with the aid of a staff, manages to keep up with us.

'13th.—Legs very stiff, but the idea of soon getting on board the ship acted as a good restorative. Observed the dog-sledge coming over Mushroom Point. Hoisted colours. Sent Winstone, Lawrence, and Harley to the ship on May's sledge. Arrived on Mushroom Point at 8.30. Deposited, in tent pitched there, all provisions. Resumed the march, arriving alongside the ship at half-past one on the morning of Wednesday the 14th of June.

'Out of my original party of fifteen men, three only —namely, Radmore, Joliffe, and Maskell—were capable of dragging the sledge; the remaining eleven having been carried alongside on the relief sledges.'

After his return Commander Markham reported :—

' I feel it impossible for my pen to depict with accuracy, and yet be not accused of exaggeration, the numerous drawbacks that impeded our progress. One point, however, in my opinion is most definitely settled, and that is, the utter impracticability of reaching the North Pole over the floe in this locality ; and in this opinion my able colleague, Lieutenant Parr, entirely concurs. I am convinced that with the very lightest equipped sledges, carrying no boats, and with all the resources of the ship concentrated in the one direction, and also supposing that perfect health might be maintained, the latitude attained by the party I had the honour and pleasure of commanding, would not be exceeded by many miles, certainly not by a degree.'

In this I most fully concur. Markham's journey, coupled with the experience gained by Sir Edward Parry in the summer of 1827, and more recently the memorable retreat of Lieutenant Weyprecht and his companions after having abandoned the ' Tegetthoff' off the coast of Francis Joseph Land, proves that a lengthened journey over the Polar pack-ice with a sledge party equipped with a boat fit for navigable purposes is impracticable at any season of the year. The much-to-be-deplored outbreak of scurvy in no way affects the conclusions to be derived from the journey.

END OF THE FIRST VOLUME.

Spottiswoode & Co., Printers, New-street Square and Parliament Street.